Sustaining
China's
Economic
Growth
After the Global
Financial Crisis

Sustaining
China's
Economic
Growth
After the Global
Financial Crisis

Nicholas R. Lardy

PETERSON INSTITUTE FOR INTERNATIONAL ECONOMICS

Washington, DC
January 2012

Nicholas R. Lardy, called "everybody's guru on China" by the *National Journal*, is the Anthony M. Solomon Senior Fellow at the Peterson Institute for International Economics. He joined the Institute in March 2003 from the Brookings Institution, where he was a senior fellow from 1995 until 2003. He served at the University of Washington, where he was the director of the Henry M. Jackson School of International Studies from 1991 to 1995. From 1997 through the spring of 2000, he was also the Frederick Frank Adjunct Professor of International Trade and Finance at the Yale University School of Management. He is author, coauthor, or editor of *The Future of China's Exchange Rate Policy* (2009), *China's Rise: Challenges and Opportunities* (2008), *Debating China's Exchange Rate Policy* (2008), and *China: The Balance Sheet—What the World Needs to Know Now about the Emerging Superpower* (2006). He is a member of the Council on Foreign Relations and a member of the editorial boards of the *China Quarterly, China Review,* and *Journal of Contemporary China.*

PETER G. PETERSON INSTITUTE FOR INTERNATIONAL ECONOMICS
1750 Massachusetts Avenue, NW
Washington, DC 20036-1903
(202) 328-9000   FAX: (202) 659-3225
www.piie.com

C. Fred Bergsten, *Director*
Edward A. Tureen, *Director of Publications, Marketing, and Web Development*

Typesetting by Diacritech
Printing by Versa Press, Inc
Cover design by Fletcher Design
Cover photo: © Paul Souders—Corbis and Kick Images—Photodisc

Printed in the United States of America
14   13   12   5   4   3   2   1

Library of Congress Cataloging-in-Publication Data

Lardy, Nicholas R.
 Sustaining China's economic growth after the global financial crisis / Nicholas R. Lardy.
   p. cm.
 Includes bibliographical references.
 ISBN 978-0-88132-626-0
 1. China--Economic policy--2000-
 2. China--Economic conditions--2000-
 3. Global Financial Crisis, 2008-2009. I. Title.

 HC427.95.L37 2012
 338.951--dc23
                                    2011043034

Contents

Preface

China has now sustained extraordinarily rapid economic growth for more than three decades, largely by allowing market forces to play a role in increasingly broad swaths of its domestic economy. Even during the recent global financial and economic crisis China's economic growth was remarkably strong. While the global economy suffered its sharpest decline in 60 years, China's expansion in 2009 ticked down only slightly to 9.2 percent. Thus China has emerged as a critical growth engine for the entire world economy.

Despite this impressive performance, Senior Fellow Nicholas Lardy in this book argues that various troubling imbalances have emerged in the Chinese economy over the past decade and that China must adopt a fundamentally new growth model if it is to sustain anywhere near its recent pace of economic growth. These imbalances include a very low share of private consumption expenditure and a super elevated share of investment in GDP, an outsized manufacturing sector and a diminutive service sector, and the buildup of an unprecedentedly large hoard of official holdings of foreign exchange. The book gives special attention to another indicator of economic imbalance—China's increasingly outsized and probably unsustainable rate of investment in residential property.

Lardy argues that mitigating these imbalances will require fundamental market-oriented reforms, particularly in the financial sector, the exchange rate regime, and the pricing of factors of production such as energy, water, and land. He argues that continuing modest, marginal, and incremental reforms in these domains will not be sufficient to propel China onto a new growth path. Lardy analyzes both the technical and political challenges these reforms pose.

The Institute has a long history of studies on the Chinese economy dating back to Lardy's 1994 book *China in the World Economy*. More recently, as China has become even more important to the global economy, the Institute has stepped up its research on China, notably in a three year China Balance Sheet project that led to two volumes: *China: The Balance Sheet—What the World Needs to Know Now about the Emerging Superpower* (2006) and *China's Rise: Challenges and Opportunities* (2008). Most recently the Institute published Arvind Subramanian's *Eclipse: Living in the Shadow of China's Economic Dominance* (2011).

The Peter G. Peterson Institute for International Economics is a private, nonprofit institution for the study and discussion of international economic policy. Its purpose is to analyze important issues in that area and to develop and communicate practical new approaches for dealing with them. The Institute is completely nonpartisan.

The Institute is funded by a highly diversified group of philanthropic foundations, private corporations, and interested individuals. About 35 percent of the Institute's resources in our latest fiscal year were provided by contributors outside the United States. The Folger Fund provided generous support for this study.

The Institute's Board of Directors bears overall responsibilities for the Institute and gives general guidance and approval to its research program, including the identification of topics that are likely to become important over the medium run (one to three years) and that should be addressed by the Institute. The director, working closely with the staff and outside Advisory Committee, is responsible for the development of particular projects and makes the final decision to publish an individual study.

The Institute hopes that its studies and other activities will contribute to building a stronger foundation for international economic policy around the world. We invite readers of these publications to let us know how they think we can best accomplish this objective.

C. Fred Bergsten
Director
November 2011

Acknowledgments

This volume could not have been completed without the support of many individuals. My greatest debt is to Patrick Douglass and Nicholas Borst, research analysts who made it possible for me to keep up with the large flow of primary source material on which the volume draws heavily. I am also indebted to participants in a study group that met to critique a draft of the manuscript in mid-year 2011. This group included Vivek Arora, C. Fred Bergsten, Anders Åslund, Nigel Chalk, William Cline, Robert Dohner, Steven Dunaway, Nicolas Ericsson, Morris Goldstein, Yukon Huang, Albert Keidel, Kenneth Lieberthal, David Loevinger, Daniel Rosen, Nicolas Véron, John Williamson, Christopher Winship, and Zhu Min. Dwight Perkins and an anonymous reviewer critiqued the final manuscript. Others who offered useful written comments at various stages include Joseph Gagnon, Robert Lawrence, and Paul Vandenberg. Jin Mei of the Monetary Policy Department of the People's Bank of China clarified the scope of some of the data reported in the bank's quarterly *Monetary Policy Reports*, one of the most important primary sources on the Chinese economy.

I also benefited from the opportunity to present the findings of the study to audiences at the Peterson Institute for International Economics, the Brookings Institution, Stanford University, the University of Toronto, the International Monetary Fund, at a conference in Beijing organized by the Asian Development Bank and the Chinese Ministry of Finance, and at two meetings of a Track II Economic Dialogue organized by the National Committee on US-China Relations and the Beijing University China Center for Economic Research. Comments and feedback from these sessions led to numerous refinements in the analysis in the book.

A special thanks to C. Fred Bergsten, the director of the Peterson Institute, who has consistently been a strong supporter of the Institute's work on China, including this study. The publications department at the Peterson Institute, led by Ed Tureen, transformed the manuscript into the final printed form in an expeditious manner. I particularly thank Susann Luetjen and Madona Devasahayam, who were responsible, respectively, for production and design coordination and managing the editing.

Introduction

This study seeks to explain China's economic policy during the global financial crisis of 2008–09 and to analyze the challenges China's leadership faces in sustaining growth over the medium term. China's policymakers responded strongly to the global financial crisis. They launched a major economic stimulus program that largely offset the negative effect on the Chinese economy of a sharp slowdown in global trade. While China's growth in 2009 did slow compared with the trend of prior years, the slowdown was quite modest, especially when compared with the absolute shrinkage in global output. A central thesis of this study, however, is that the policy mix that brought China so well through the biggest global financial and economic crisis in several decades will be less successful going forward.

Chapter 1 provides an overview of the policy response to the global financial crisis and a more detailed analysis of the criticisms that have been made of this program by both external and Chinese observers. Among the most important conclusions is that the stimulus program did not advantage state-owned companies at the expense of private firms and, more importantly, did not alter the long-term trend of China's reform, in which private firms have increasingly become the most important driver of economic growth. Of particular note, the chapter shows that, contrary to the often repeated assertion, bank loans in 2009–10 did not flow primarily to state-owned companies and that the access of both private firms and household businesses to bank credit improved considerably.

While the stimulus program was successful in sustaining China's economic growth during the global crisis, it was not intended to address the longer-term structural problems that led China's premier, Wen Jiabao, to characterize China's growth as early as 2007 as "unsteady, imbalanced, uncoordinated, and unsustainable" (Wen Jiabao 2007). Chapter 2 lays out the nature of the economic imbalances that emerged after the early 2000s, notably China's heavy reliance on investment and exports to generate growth; the decline in household disposable income as a share of GDP; the relatively low and still declining share of consumption in GDP; the reemergence of a relatively outsized manufacturing sector and a correspondingly underdeveloped services sector; and a sharp increase in the national savings-investment imbalance, reflected in the emergence of an unusually large external surplus.

Chapter 3 examines the policy options that are available to the government to address these various imbalances and assesses the progress to date and prospects in each of the policy domains. Several broad conclusions emerge. First, among options available to Chinese policymakers to achieve their rebalancing objectives, further fundamental reform of the financial system is central. Over the past decade several indicators—negative real interest rates on household savings, an increasingly elevated required reserve ratio (the share of deposits that commercial banks must place at the central bank), the emergence of a significant informal credit market, a sharp decline in the share of government bonds held by the public—all suggest that China's financial system has become more repressed. The negative real interest rate on savings that emerged since 2003 has suppressed the growth of household income below the level it would have achieved had the government not abandoned its policy of interest rate liberalization after 2004. Negative real deposit rates, in turn, appear to have led to an increase in the household saving rate and simultaneously led households to allocate a rising share of these savings to real estate, where real returns have become much more favorable over time relative to bank deposits. Resuming the policy of gradual interest rate liberalization, which was largely abandoned in 2004, is a prerequisite to rebalancing and sustaining China's rapid economic growth.

Chapter 3 also explores the relationship between negative real deposit rates and other dimensions of financial repression that emerged after 2003, on the one hand, and the government's policy of keeping the exchange rate of the renminbi undervalued, on the other hand. The central bank has kept the currency undervalued by intervening massively in the foreign exchange market, ultimately buying up more than $3 trillion in foreign exchange. To prevent the resulting expansion of the domestic money supply from leading to high inflation the central bank has engaged in large-scale and sustained sterilization operations. It accomplished this by raising the required reserve ratio to an extremely high level and issuing large quantities of central bank bills to China's commercial banks. The chapter explains how the central bank has controlled interest rates in order to hold down the costs of these sterilization operations and why a more flexible exchange rate is an important prerequisite for liberalizing interest rates.

In addition to allowing the market to play a greater role in determining the value of the renminbi and liberalizing interest rates, the government should simultaneously continue to build a stronger social safety net to facilitate a reduction in the household saving rate and undertake long-promised fundamental reforms of factor prices, not only for capital but also for water, electricity, and fuels. Chapter 3 also examines the possibility that the widely noted increase in real wages in the past few years could simultaneously raise both the share of wages in GDP, thus boosting consumption as a source of growth, and production costs relative to China's trading partners, thus reducing China's external surplus. While real wages have been rising rapidly for many years, the growth of labor productivity in the tradable goods sector has been just as rapid. Thus relative to its trading partners China's unit labor costs apparently are not increasing, so that endogenous rebalancing through rising real wages is not yet underway.

Chapter 4 addresses the international implications of a rebalancing of China's growth. China and the United States were the principal sources of the large global economic imbalances that emerged in the decade leading up to the financial crisis. The interaction of these imbalances with weak financial regulation and credit market distortions in many advanced economies, along with the loose monetary policy stance of the US Federal Reserve, led to the global financial crisis. China has been a key participant in the Group of Twenty process that has led to the adoption of a set of indicative guidelines to address persistently large external imbalances in order to achieve strong and sustainable global economic growth. Thus there now appears to be an alignment between China's stated national and international economic policy objectives.

Despite this alignment of national and international objectives, it is far from clear that China will embark on the concerted and sustained effort needed to remove the underlying distortions that stand in the way of the economic rebalancing necessary to sustain economic growth in the current global environment. These distortions include financial repression, an under-valued exchange rate, and subsidized factors of production. Chapter 5 explores how the beneficiaries of imbalanced growth—including export and import competing industries (which have enjoyed elevated profits at the expense of firms in the services sector), coastal provinces (which have enjoyed super-charged economic growth at the expense of inland regions less able to tap into the growth generated by trade expansion), the real estate and construction industries (which have benefited from interest rate policies that have made residential property a preferred asset class), and China's commercial banks (which enjoy lofty profits that come with high spreads between deposit and lending rates generated by the central bank's interest rate policy)—have acquired a disproportionate influence over economic policy and to date have been able to block most needed policy reforms. China's National People's Congress in the spring of 2011 reflected a renewed emphasis on the policies necessary for rebalancing, and most of these policies were enshrined as well in the 12th Five-Year Plan (2011–15), which was made public shortly after the Congress adjourned. Whether or not this renewed emphasis on policies intended to rebalance China's economy will be enough to overcome the existing domestic political constraints to further economic reform has yet to be seen.

China's Response to the Global Crisis

China's policy response to the global financial and economic crisis was early, large, and well designed. Although Chinese financial institutions had little exposure to the toxic financial assets that brought down many large Western investment banks and other financial firms, China's leadership recognized that the country's high dependence on exports meant that it was acutely vulnerable to a global economic recession. The Chinese government did not subscribe to the view sometimes described as "decoupling," the idea that emerging Asian countries, simply by increasing intraregional trade, could by and large weather the global financial storm that originated in the United States and other advanced industrial economies. They understood that China inevitably would suffer from the backwash of a sharp economic slowdown in its largest export markets—the United States and Europe.

In anticipation of a global slowdown, the central bank initiated a policy of monetary easing in September 2008. The State Council, China's cabinet, followed up a few weeks later by rolling out a RMB4 trillion ($586 billion) stimulus program that immediately ramped up expenditures on affordable housing, rural and other infrastructure (highways, railways, and airports), public health and education, the environment, and technical innovation. The program started immediately with the goal of spending RMB100 billion in the fourth quarter of 2008, with the balance to be spent over the following two calendar years. In contrast, the American Recovery and Reinvestment Act of 2009 was not passed by Congress and signed into law by President Barack Obama until mid-February 2009. Moreover, in addition to its delayed rollout, the US stimulus package compared with China's suffered in two respects. First, relative to the size of the respective economies the US stimulus was much smaller.[1] Second, while the Chinese program consisted overwhelmingly of increased expenditures, about a third of the US stimulus consisted of tax cuts (Council of Economic Advisors 2010, 53).[2] But much of the increased income received by US households as a result of these tax cuts was used to pay down debt rather than to finance additional consumption expenditures. While this was rational from the point of view of heavily indebted individual households, paying down debt did nothing to increase aggregate demand. These differences in the timing, size, and design of the two stimulus programs contributed to the markedly different economic outcomes in the two countries in 2009—a sharp absolute decline in real output in the United States but only a modest growth slowdown in China.

China's leadership grew increasingly concerned in the summer and fall of 2008 that slowing exports would adversely affect economic growth, as China's growth had already begun to slow significantly, well before the onset of the global financial crisis. In 2007 the authorities, fearing that domestic economic growth had become unsustainably rapid, took a number of tightening measures. Beginning in January the central bank repeatedly raised the required reserve ratio, the share of deposits that banks must place with the central bank. That reduced the funds that banks had available to lend to customers. To further reduce the flow of credit to the economy the central bank, starting in March, on five occasions in 2007 also raised the benchmark interest rates that guide banks' lending rates. Toward the end of the year these market-oriented steps were reinforced by the reintroduction of quantitative limits on bank lending.[3] As a result of these policy initiatives, after the first quarter of 2007 China's economic growth began to gradually slow.

Several of the monetary tightening measures the authorities introduced in the latter part of 2007 focused on the property sector, which had undergone a substantial boom and at the time was frequently characterized by external observers as a bubble. In September the authorities increased the required down payment for purchasers of multiple properties to 40 percent, while leaving the ratio at either 20 or 30 percent for mortgages on owner-occupied property (People's Bank of China and China Banking Regulatory Commission 2007).[4] The central bank at the same time introduced penalty

---

1. The US stimulus package was $787 billion, a third larger than China's, but the size of the US economy is two and a half times that of China's.

2. China's stimulus had no pure tax cuts at all. As explained later in this chapter, it included a tax expenditure component. This took the form of tax cuts on certain durable goods. But to gain the benefit of the reduced tax a Chinese citizen had to purchase the item on which the tax had been reduced. Thus the tax expenditure part of China's stimulus program led directly to increased expenditures.

3. Mao Lijun and Wang Bo, "Lending Caps to Reduce Liquidity," *China Daily*, January 21, 2010, 10.

4. The minimum down payment of 20 percent of the purchase price applied to residential units of 90 square meters or less; the 30 percent requirement applied to units over 90 square meters in size.

interest rates for property investors by raising the interest rate on mortgages for non-owner-occupied property to a 10 percent premium over the central bank benchmark lending rate, while leaving the interest rate on mortgages on owner-occupied property at a 15 percent discount relative to the benchmark lending rate (China Banking Society 2008, 470). On a five-year mortgage, for example, taking into account both the increase in the five-year benchmark lending rate and the new penalty rate applicable to property investors, the interest rate for a mortgage on an owner-occupied property increased in 2007 by a fifth (from 5.50 to 6.58 percent), while for property investors the mortgage interest rate rose by a little more than half (from 5.50 to 8.51 percent). Finally, the authorities lengthened to five years the period of time an owner must hold a property in order to avoid paying a 5.5 percent sales tax on property transactions.[5] These policy steps were clearly designed to reduce the demand for housing by real estate investors and speculators.

By 2008 the policy of monetary tightening, with a focus on the housing sector, proved quite successful in moderating the property boom. Starting late in the final quarter of 2007 the pace of property sales slowed sharply, and by 2008 monthly sales were consistently below their 2007 levels. With slowing sales the pace of property price appreciation moderated substantially, falling from double-digit year-over-year growth rates in late 2007 and early 2008 to the low single digits by the late summer and early fall of 2008. Beginning in December 2008 property prices began to fall modestly in absolute terms on a year-over-year basis. This trend continued for six months, cumulatively reducing prices by about 5 percent. Growth in new housing starts also slowed sharply in the first half of 2008 and turned negative in the second half of the year, i.e., floor space started in the second half was substantially less in absolute terms than in the same month in 2007.[6] Correspondingly, the pace of economic growth, which had peaked in the first quarter of 2007 at 17 percent, also moderated, falling to 4.3 percent in the third quarter of the year (People's Bank of China Statistical Investigation Office 2010).[7]

Beijing initially welcomed the slowing of domestic economic growth, especially the moderation of the housing boom (discussed further below). But starting in September 2008, as the global financial crisis intensified, the authorities reversed economic course by launching a policy of monetary easing in order to offset the additional drag on China's growth caused by the sharp slowdown in global trade. There were several components to the policy of monetary easing, summarized in box 1.1. First, the central bank cancelled the lending quotas that had previously restricted the ability of banks to fully meet the demand for loans from their customers.[8] Second, to ensure that banks

---

5. Previously the minimum holding period to avoid the tax was two years.

6. Monthly data on property sales, prices, and starts from ISI Emerging Markets, CEIC Database.

7. These are quarter-over-quarter seasonally adjusted growth rates.

8. Mao Lijun and Wang Bo, "Lending Caps to Reduce Liquidity," *China Daily*, January 21, 2010, 10.

Box 1.1 Chronology of major policy changes, 2007–11

Date	Policy change
January 2007	■ People's Bank of China (PBC) increases required reserve ratio due to fears of an overheated economy
March 2007	■ First of five increases in benchmark interest rates in 2007
September 2007	■ Down payment for investment properties increased to 40 percent
	■ Interest rate penalty for mortgages on investment properties raised to 10 percent premium over benchmark lending rate
	■ Property ownership tax-exemption period lengthened to five years
Late 2007	■ Quantitative limits put on bank lending
September 2008	■ PBC begins monetary easing as part of stimulus effort
	■ State Council unveils RMB4 trillion stimulus plan
	■ Mortgage loan discount from benchmark interest rate increased
	■ Minimum down payment for all mortgages cut to 20 percent
January 2009	■ Property ownership tax-exemption period shortened to two years
Mid-2009	■ PBC strengthens window guidance and other policies to slow bank lending
	■ China Banking Regulatory Commission (CBRC) strengthens requirements for bank capital adequacy ratio and disallows the inclusion of subordinated debt
December 2009	■ 40 percent down payment for mortgages on investment properties reinstated
January 2010	■ CBRC announces tightening measures to slow growth of lending, including mandatory loan quotas for some banks
	■ First of six increases of the required reserve ratio in 2010

(box continues next page)

Box 1.1 Chronology of major policy changes, 2007–11 *(continued)*

Date	Policy change
April 2010	■ State Council raises down payment for investment properties to 50 percent, reintroduces penalty interest rates for mortgages on investment property, limits property purchases by foreign investors, and suspends mortgage lending to nonresidents
Late 2010–early 2011	■ PBC shifts to a tighter monetary policy stance, increases the benchmark rate and reserve requirement
January 2011	■ Down payment for mortgages on investment properties increased to 60 percent
	■ Property tax pilot program begins in Shanghai and Chongqing
	■ First of six increases of the required reserve ratio in the first half of 2011
February 2011	■ First of four increases in benchmark interest rates in the first half of 2011

would have a sufficient supply of funds to meet this demand, the government repeatedly reduced the share of deposits that banks had to place with the central bank. Banks were not forced to engage in this expanded lending, as has often been asserted. Xiao Gang, chairman of the Bank of China, acknowledged that once annual lending limits were lifted it was in the economic self-interest of banks to expand their lending.[9] The interest rate that the banks could charge on loans in the waning months of 2008 was several times the interest they earned on funds previously placed either with the central bank or in the interbank market.[10] Thus, the government's first step in monetary easing was to increase the supply of loanable funds.

---

9. Andrew Peaple, "Reassessing China's Lending Binge," *Wall Street Journal*, August 27, 2010, available at http://online.wsj.com (accessed on September 12, 2011).

10. In December 2008, for example, the central bank paid banks an interest rate of 1.62 percent on reserves placed at the central bank, and the interest rate banks could earn by placing funds in the interbank market ranged from 1.0058 percent for one-month maturities to 2.3579 percent for one-year maturities. In contrast, in the same month the average interest rate banks charged on a one-year loan was 6.64 percent (People's Bank of China Monetary Policy Analysis Small Group 2009a, 6, 11, 21). Given the interest rates that the central bank set on deposits made at commercial banks, the banks almost certainly lost money on funds they placed at the central bank or in

The authorities simultaneously took steps to increase the real demand for loans. First, they repeatedly lowered the benchmark interest rates that guide the rates that banks can charge on loans. Between mid-September and year-end 2008 the authorities cut benchmark lending rates on five occasions. Those cuts took the benchmark rate on a five-year loan, for example, from 7.74 to 5.76 percent. Second, they made deeper cuts in the rates for mortgage loans. Prior to the fall of 2008, the rate that applied to mortgage loans that banks made to individuals for the purchase of owner-occupied property was 0.85 times the benchmark rate. Beginning in September the government reduced this multiple to 0.7. The combined effect of a reduction in the benchmark five-year loan rate and the adjustment in the mortgage rate factor meant a two-fifths reduction in the interest rate a potential home buyer would pay on a mortgage with a term of five or more years, from 6.66 to 4.16 percent. This meant that the monthly payment on a 20-year mortgage was reduced by 18.6 percent (People's Bank of China Monetary Policy Analysis Small Group 2009a, 46). The minimum down payment for all mortgages was set at 20 percent, a significant reduction both for larger units and for property investors, and the compulsory penalty interest rates that had applied to property investors starting in September 2007 were eliminated. A few months later, in January 2009, the authorities reduced back to two years the period of time investors must hold a property in order to avoid a sales tax when a property is sold.[11]

The result of these policy initiatives was a massive increase in bank lending, particularly in the first half of 2009, when domestic currency loans outstanding increased by RMB7.4 trillion, three times greater than the increase in the first half of 2008. Loan growth moderated substantially in the second half, but for the year as a whole bank loans outstanding in domestic currency increased by RMB9.59 trillion, about twice the RMB4.91 trillion increase in bank lending in domestic currency in 2008 (People's Bank of China Monetary Policy Analysis Small Group 2010a, 3). Mortgage lending made up a large component of the expansion of loans in 2009. Individual mortgage loans outstanding increased by RMB1.4 trillion, about six times the increase of 2008 (People's Bank of China Monetary Policy Analysis Small Group 2010a, 48). To put this number in perspective, at the end of 2009 one-third of all mortgage loans outstanding to households had been extended by banks during 2009.

Shortly after the authorities launched their policy of monetary easing in September 2008, they announced a RMB4 trillion stimulus program, largely devoted to investment expenditures. This program began immediately in the

---

the interbank market during a time when banks potentially could have had significant positive earnings on additional lending. From November 27, 2008, through December 22, 2008, for example, the rate banks paid on one-year deposits was 2.52 percent, substantially more than banks could earn if they either had to deposit these funds with the central bank or were constrained to lend these funds in the interbank market.

11. "China Imposes Tougher Home Sales Tax to Control Bubble," People's Daily Online, December 10, 2010, available at http://english.people.com.cn (accessed on September 12, 2011).

fourth quarter of 2008 and extended through 2010. In practice the stimulus program was closely linked to monetary easing, since the plan from the outset was that the vast majority of the funding for the stimulus program would be financed by increased bank lending made possible by monetary easing. The authorities announced that only RMB1.18 trillion of the RMB4 trillion stimulus package would be financed from the central government budget and called both for additional fiscal spending by local governments on the identified investment priorities and for increased outlays by firms. But, given the paucity of fiscal resources available to provincial and subprovincial governments and the declining cash flows in most of the corporate sector as a result of slowing economic growth, it was apparent from the outset that increased bank lending would be the major source of funding for the stimulus program.

The results of China's stimulus program were impressive, making China the first globally significant economy to begin to recover from the global economic recession. Measured on a quarter-over-quarter basis the economy bottomed out in the fourth quarter of 2008, when economic growth slowed to only 4.3 percent. As the stimulus package began to take hold, China's growth accelerated significantly, to 9.5 and 11.4 percent, respectively, in the first and second quarters of 2009 (People's Bank of China Statistical Investigation Office 2010). In January 2010 the statistical authority's preliminary estimate of year-over-year GDP growth in 2009 was 8.7 percent, well above the pace that most external observers had expected a year earlier (National Bureau of Statistics of China 2010a). In July 2010 this preliminary figure was revised upward to 9.1 percent (National Bureau of Statistics of China 2010d). The final figure, announced in early 2011, put economic growth in 2009 at 9.2 percent (National Bureau of Statistics of China 2011a). Growth strengthened to 10.4 percent in 2010 and then, according to the preliminary estimate released in July 2011, moderated to 9.6 percent in the first half of 2011 (National Bureau of Statistics of China 2011d, 2011e).

China's growth in 2009–11 was impressive compared with the absolute downturns in economic output in the United States, Europe, Japan, and many other developed economies in 2009 and with the very modest recoveries these countries experienced in 2010–11. China was the fastest growing emerging-market economy both during and immediately after the global financial and economic crisis.

Critiques of the Stimulus Program

Despite this strong growth performance, critics, both in China and abroad, charged that the stimulus program was badly flawed and that the rate of growth achieved in 2009–10 was not sustainable. One critique was that China's growth during and following the crisis was especially imbalanced, relying on an unsustainable burst of investment financed largely by an unprecedented increase in bank lending.[12] According to the critics, the massive increase in loans had several adverse consequences. First, it inevitably entailed the risk of rising inflation, a risk that materialized in the closing months of 2010 and in 2011, when inflation for several months exceeded 5 percent on a year-over-year basis, the highest rate since mid-2008. Pessimists argued that to curtail inflation the authorities would be forced to slam on the monetary brakes, leading to a sharp slowdown in economic growth—the hard landing scenario. Second, the credit boom potentially created bubbles in the property and equity markets based on mortgage lending to households and the leakage of funds lent to corporations for construction and other forms of investment. Third, according to critics who took a seemingly opposite view, the massive investment program financed with the expanded supply of credit would inevitably lead to excess industrial capacity and thus, with a slight lag, result in downward pressure on prices and profits of manufacturing firms (European Chamber 2009). That, in turn, would impair the ability of these firms to amortize their bank debt and thus lead to a large increase in nonperforming loans. This potentially would require the state to recapitalize the banks once again, with adverse consequences for the government's fiscal position (Walter and Howie 2011, 26).

Skeptics also charged that the stimulus program would ultimately exacerbate China's dependence on exports and investment and hamper the growth of consumption, especially household consumption. McKinsey, for example, judged that "the stimulus package does little to tilt the balance in favor of private consumption. In the short term, it will do just the reverse" (McKinsey & Company 2009, 49). In short, while many critics acknowledged that the stimulus program did prop up economic growth, they argued that this was temporary and that the stimulus program exacerbated China's underlying structural problems and ultimately would lead to a substantial slowing of economic growth (Pettis 2009, 2010).

Finally, critics argued that the stimulus program substantially enhanced the role of the state at the expense of the private sector, fundamentally setting back China's long-term reform trajectory.[13] One analyst characterized 2009–10 as one of the most statist periods in the entire reform era (Huang Yasheng 2011). This line of argument has several strands. One is that the expanded volume of bank loans went disproportionately to state-owned companies, particularly manufacturers (Bremer 2010, 143–44). This left nonstate companies, particularly private firms, starved for credit and resulted in state companies contributing a disproportionate share of China's economic growth during the crisis. A second strand in the argument is that direct state ownership of productive assets rose when state-owned firms took over nonstate firms or when the state

12. Stephen Roach, "An Unbalanced World Is Again Compounding Its Imbalances," *Financial Times*, October 7, 2009, 23.

13. David Piling, "The State's Dead Hand Returns to Haunt China," *Financial Times*, October 15, 2009, 11.

nationalized formerly private firms.[14] The combination of these two factors, say the critics, meant that state companies expanded their economic footprint at the expense of the private sector. A third strand in the argument that the global financial and economic crisis has diminished the role of the market and expanded the role of the state focuses on the enhanced role of industrial and technology policy (Naughton 2011). These actions go far beyond the widely noted and criticized policies to promote indigenous innovation, notably the identification by the State Council of seven emerging strategic industries that will receive special state support (State Council 2010).

While China's economy is marked by substantial imbalances that will be discussed in detail in chapter 2, many of these criticisms of China's stimulus program seem exaggerated. The 9.2 percent growth that was achieved in 2009 was the slowest since 1992. At a minimum the critics do not recognize that the alternative to China's massive stimulus program was a much more marked slow-down in economic growth. Moreover, much of the criticism directed at China's stimulus ignores or understates the substantial advantages China accrued as a result of coming through the crisis with strong economic growth momentum and fails to appreciate the steps that the authorities have taken in anticipa-tion of the negative side effects of the stimulus policy. The criticism directed toward China also fails to recognize the advantages stemming from China's long-standing very conservative fiscal and financial regulatory policies. Most obviously, since China's financial regulatory agencies had steadfastly refused to permit the creation of complex derivative products in the domestic market and severely limited financial institutions' exposure to foreign sources of these products, Chinese financial institutions had little exposure to toxic financial assets. Thus the government did not have to take on additional debt in order to inject funds into failing financial institutions during the crisis. Outstanding government debt thus remained quite modest, around 20 percent of GDP. The value of China's fiscal and financial conservatism is heightened by the lessons of the global financial and economic crisis.

Excessive Growth of Bank Lending?

The charge of excessive growth of bank lending fails to take adequately into account two important factors—initial conditions in terms of leverage and the steps being taken by monetary authorities in China as early as mid-2009 to slow the growth of bank lending. Total public and private debt in China at year-end 2007, on the eve of the global financial crisis, was about RMB41 trillion, or 160 percent of GDP.[15] In contrast, in the United States at the same time, public

---

14. "Nationalization Rides Again," *Economist*, November 14, 2009, 68–69.

15. Chinese data on household and corporate bank debt from People's Bank of China (2008). Data on bonds outstanding from the government, corporations, and financial institutions from ISI Emerging Markets, CEIC Database.

and private debt combined totaled $48 trillion, or 350 percent of GDP.[16] The contrast was most extreme in the financial sector, where Chinese institutions had debt of less than 15 percent of GDP, while financial institutions in the United States had debt equivalent to almost 120 percent of GDP. Thus, when credit markets froze up in advanced industrial economies at the onset of the crisis, US financial institutions were extremely exposed, leading to the failure of several large institutions and a massive curtailment of credit in the US economy. Chinese financial institutions were unaffected by the abrupt credit stop in advanced industrial countries and thus were in a strong position to increase the supply of credit to sustain growth. There was also a marked difference in leverage in the household sector: At year-end 2007 total household debt in China was only 20 percent of GDP, while in the United States it was fully 100 percent of GDP. Similarly, government debt in the United States as a share of GDP was twice the share in China.[17] Only in the nonfinancial corporate sector did leverage in China exceed that in the United States, and the differential was modest. Thus both the households and the government in China were much more able to assume additional debt. In short, China's growth in 2009–10 was to a considerable extent due to the ability of the financial system to provide additional credit and the ability of households and the government—and to a lesser extent corporates—to assume additional debt. As will be analyzed in more detail in chapter 3, as the growth of bank lending exploded in 2009–10, the share of lending flowing to households rose sharply, from 14 percent in 2008 to 36 percent in 2010. In contrast, the shrinkage of the US economy in the first half of 2009 and the subpar recovery since reflects the household deleveraging process that is likely to continue for some time (McKinsey Global Institute 2010).

The second important factor to consider in evaluating the critique that lending grew excessively during the crisis is that the People's Bank of China increased its window guidance to banks and took other initiatives to slow the growth of lending starting in mid-2009. As a result, new loans extended in the second half of the year were less than a third of the new lending volume in the first half. Although lending spiked upward in January 2010, the China Banking Regulatory Commission (CBRC) the same month announced tougher measures to moderate the pace of lending over the balance of 2010. The CBRC reinstated mandatory lending quotas on individual banks and imposed tougher regulations to prevent banks from lending out most of their lending quota in the first quarter or two of the year.[18] They also raised the required reserve ratio

---

16. Data for the United States are from Flow of Funds of the United States, table D.3, Credit Market Debt Outstanding by Sector, available at www.federalreserve.gov (accessed on September 13, 2011).

17. This is a comparison of US Treasury debt with government bonds issued by the Chinese Ministry of Finance.

18. The government set the aggregate quota for the increase in bank loans outstanding in 2010 at RMB7.5 trillion. Moreover, the CBRC announced that each bank should advance in each month no more than 12 percent of its annual quota and in each quarter no more than 30 percent of its annual quota. This would limit the expansion of loans outstanding to RMB900 billion per month,

by 50 basis points in January, in February, and again in March 2010. This had the effect of cutting banks' excess reserves and signaled the transition away from the "appropriately loose" (*shidu kuansong*) monetary policy initiated in November 2008 to the appropriately loose monetary policy implemented with "better targeting and more flexibility based on changing conditions" in 2010. The central bank followed up by hiking benchmark lending rates and further increasing the required reserve ratio in late 2010 and the first half of 2011, key steps inaugurating a "tight" (*wenjian*) monetary policy.[19]

The CBRC also took a series of other steps to curtail the expansion of bank credit. In 2008 it had put pressure on banks to increase their minimum bank capital adequacy ratio by 2 percentage points (from 8 to 10 percent) and in late summer 2009, when the commission sought to slow the lending growth, it apparently raised this ratio further, to 12 percent, for selected city commercial banks.[20] In August 2009 the commission circulated a draft regulation stating that banks would no longer be able to count subordinated debt and hybrid capital as part of their tier-two capital.[21] During the lending boom of 2009 banks had kept their capital adequacy ratios from falling sharply by selling large amounts of subordinated debt.[22] But over half of the subordinated bonds sold by banks were purchased by other banks. The CBRC recognized that these large cross-holdings of subordinated bank debt did not add any capital to the banking system as a whole, revealing that high capital adequacy ratios reported

---

although the authorities acknowledged that this limit would be exceeded in January since the new regulations were not announced until the second half of January, when new lending had already exceeded RMB1 trillion. Mao Lijun and Wang Bo, "Lending Caps to Reduce Liquidity," *China Daily*, January 21, 2010, 10.

19. The language on implementing monetary policy with better targeting and more flexibility in response to evolving conditions was first used in People's Bank of China Monetary Policy Analysis Small Group (2010b, 8–9). The language "tight monetary policy" was first used in People's Bank of China Monetary Policy Analysis Small Group (2011b, 9).

20. "Beijing Urges China's City Banks to Bolster Capital Reserves," Market Watch, August 5, 2009, available at http://marketwatch.com (accessed on September 12, 2011). It does not appear that the CBRC formally raised the legal 8 percent minimum capital adequacy ratio in 2009 for all financial institutions, but the bank regulator may have required individual banks to achieve the higher ratio. The regulator denied that it was imposing the 12 percent capital adequacy requirement for city commercial banks. Most likely it was imposing this requirement selectively, focusing on those banks that had increased their lending most rapidly in 2009.

21. "China Lenders Asked to Rein In Record Loans," People's Daily Online, August 21, 2009, available at http://english.people.com (accessed on September 12, 2011). Banks had been able to count their holdings of subordinate bank debt as part of their tier-two capital starting in 2004.

22. Banks issued a growing volume of subordinated debt in 2009, RMB236.7 billion in the first half alone. "China Lenders Asked to Rein In Record Loans," People's Daily Online, August 21, 2009, available at http://english.people.com.cn (accessed on September 12, 2011). For the year as a whole, banks issued subordinated debt valued at RMB266.9 billion. "The Financial Market Situation in 2009," People's Bank of China, February 2, 2010, available at www.pbc.gov.cn (accessed on September 12, 2011). Thus once the new CBRC draft regulation was circulated in August, bank issuance of subordinated debt halted.

by individual banks overstated the soundness of the banking system.[23] Thus the draft regulation restricting the use of subordinated debt was adopted in what the CBRC chairman described as a "historic decision" (Liu Mingkang 2010).

Raising the capital adequacy ratio and disallowing subordinated debt as a source of capital meant that banks had to either raise more equity capital or slow down their lending and other activities that require capital backing. In practice they did both. In 2010 the actions of the CBRC compelled China's commercial banks to raise RMB264.4 billion in new capital via rights issues and the sale of convertible bonds.[24] This policy continued in 2011. By mid-year 14 banks had announced plans to raise additional capital.[25]

As noted above, these measures to moderate the growth of bank lending were not sufficient to prevent the emergence of higher inflation starting in late 2010. Several caveats, however, should be kept in mind before attributing higher inflation uniquely to the credit expansion of the stimulus program. First, while headline inflation in China picked up, core inflation was still quite modest. Most of China's higher consumer price inflation was caused by rising food prices, which were increasing at an annual rate of more than 10 percent; nonfood price inflation was less than half the headline number.[26] Thus China's inflation in part reflects rising global agricultural prices rather than more generalized price inflation caused by excessive domestic monetary expansion.[27] Second, in early 2011 China's price inflation was quite modest in comparison with other emerging markets.[28] Third, in response to the central bank's additional tightening measures, by mid-year 2011 the growth of broad money had converged back to about 15 percent, a pace that prior to the global financial and economic crisis had been consistent with strong economic growth combined with moderate price inflation.[29]

---

23. Fang Huilei, Zhang Man, Chen Huiying, and Feng Zhe, "Regulator to Curb Banks' Cross-holdings of Subordinated Debt: New Draft Rules on Subordinated Bonds Will Lower Banks' Capital Adequacy Ratios and Reduce the Systemic Risk of Cross-Holding," *Caijing*, August 24, available at http://english.caijing.com.cn (accessed on September 19, 2011).

24. Feng Zhe, "Bank of China Raises 100 Bln Yuan in 2010," Caixin Online, December 14, 2010, available at http://english.caing.com (accessed on September 12, 2011).

25. Wen Xiu, "Under the Gun for Capital," Caixin Online, June 28, 2011, available at http://english.caing.com (accessed on June 28, 2011).

26. In April 2011, headline consumer price index inflation was 5.3 percent. Food price inflation was 11.5 percent and nonfood inflation was 2.7 percent. National Bureau of Statistics of China, "Report on Important National Economic Statistical Indicators for April," May 11, 2011, available at www.stats.gov.cn (accessed on May 11, 2011).

27. The IMF food price index reached a new high in early 2011 after rising more than 40 percent since mid-2010 (IMF 2011b, 37).

28. Measured by core inflation momentum China ranked 27th among a group of 38 emerging markets in early 2011 (Anderson 2011b).

29. Year-over-year growth of M2 by May 2011 had slowed to 15.1 percent, down from 21.0 percent in May 2010, and 25.7 percent in May 2009.

The critique charged that the stimulus was inherently inflationary. But to head off excessive price inflation, the authorities, in a manner reminiscent of 2007, began in late 2009 to focus special attention on moderating price inflation in the property market. Property prices had resumed their upward climb in June 2009, and by December 2009 the pace of price increase rose to about 8 percent on a year-over-year basis. In that month the government reinstated the 40 percent minimum down payment requirement for mortgages made to property investors and lengthened to five years the period that investors would have to hold a property in order to avoid sales tax when a property is sold.[30] Both of these measures cut the potential profits of property investors and speculators. Regulatory pressure to control lending and reduce financial risk led at least one major bank, the Bank of China, to announce in early February 2010 that it would no longer make any mortgage loans at an interest rate reflecting a 30 percent discount to the relevant benchmark lending rate but would reinstate the 15 percent discount that had prevailed before the authorities had widened the discount in September 2008. These moves cut the pace of property sales in late 2009 and early 2010.

Property prices, however, continued to rise and broke into double-digit territory in February and March 2010. The increase in March was the highest monthly increase recorded since the 70-city property price index was introduced in 1998. Thus in April 2010 the State Council promulgated further tightening measures. It raised the down payment required to qualify for a mortgage on a non-owner-occupied property to a record 50 percent, reintroduced a penalty interest rate of 1.1 times the benchmark for mortgages on non-owner-occupied property, and restored the minimum 30 percent down payment for first-time buyers for properties 90 square meters or more in size.[31] In addition, in 2010 the State Council gave banks the authority to refuse to extend mortgages on any terms to individuals who already own two properties, limited purchases of housing by foreign residents, and suspended all mortgage lending to individuals who are not resident in the city where the property is located.[32] The last restriction appears designed to curb property speculation by nonresidents in the most desirable cities, such as Shanghai and Beijing, as well as resort-type locations such as Sanya City on Hainan Island.

The combination of the measures announced in December 2009 and in April 2010 led to a moderation in housing prices beginning in May 2010. December 2010 marked the eighth consecutive month of price moderation,

---

30. "China Imposes Tougher Home Sales Tax to Control Bubble," People's Daily Online, December 10, 2009, available at http://english.people.com.cn (accessed on September 12, 2011).

31. "China Vows to Curb Property Bubble," People's Daily Online, April 20, available at http://english.people.com.cn (accessed on September 12, 2011).

32. Foreign residents have been subject to two new restrictions since November 2010. First, they are not allowed to purchase more than one residence under any circumstances. Second, they are required to prove that they have worked in the country for at least one year before purchasing a residence.

with a year-over-year increase in the price of residential property of 7.6 percent, half of the 15.4 percent peak rate in April 2010.[33]

Unsatisfied with the pace of price moderation, the government took two additional steps in early 2011 to take additional froth out of the housing market. In late January the down payment required for a mortgage for a non-owner-occupied house was boosted to an unprecedented 60 percent. The following day the State Council approved a pilot program to tax residential property. While this initiative was begun in only two cities, Shanghai and Chongqing, in China regional pilot programs are often expanded to the whole country within a year or two. Thus the government, in effect, put property investors on notice that their carrying costs on speculative real estate transactions would likely increase. The details of the property tax varied between the two cities, but in both cases the target was clearly investors, who typically invest in high-end property, rather than first-time property buyers. The property tax systems of the two cities share several characteristics.[34] First, the annual property tax applies to all purchasers of second homes. Second, tax policy discriminates against nonresidents.[35] Third, in both cities the rates are higher for more expensive property.[36]

Cumulatively these measures led to further moderation in the growth of property prices in the first half of 2011.[37] However, the absolute level of prices of residential property, particularly in tier-one cities, remains quite high, and a major property price correction is still possible. But it is important to recognize that even a major property price correction in China probably would not have the same systemic implications for the financial system that it had for the United States and several other major industrial countries where housing prices fell sharply. The reason is simple—there is much less leverage in China's residential property market than there is, for example, in markets in the United States and the United Kingdom. This difference is clearly reflected in two metrics: the ratio of household debt to disposable income and the loan-to-value ratio of mortgages used to purchase residential property.

---

33. ISI Emerging Markets, CEIC Database.

34. "A Tale of 2 Cities for Property Tax Reform," *China Daily*, January 18, 2011, available at http:// english.people.com.cn (accessed on January 28, 2011).

35. In Shanghai property taxes will be levied even on first-time purchases if they are by nonresidents.

36. For example, in Shanghai the tax is 0.6 percent, but if the value of the property is less than two times that of the average housing price, the rate is reduced to 0.4 percent. Chongqing has rates of 0.5, 1.0, and 1.2 percent, depending on the value of the property.

37. The National Bureau of Statistics discontinued publishing its 70-city index of residential property prices after December 2010. But it continued to publish the data for the 70 cities separately. The unweighted monthly average of the prices in the 70 cities shows a continuous moderation of prices, from 3.6 percent in January 2011 to 2.2 percent by June 2011. This unweighted average appears to substantially understate the rate of price increase compared with the index that the National Bureau of Statistics previously published, but it is probably directionally accurate.

The boom years in the United States and some other advanced industrial economies in the mid-2000s were fueled by a decline in the household saving rate and an increase in personal indebtedness that allowed consumption to rise substantially more rapidly than household income, thus supercharging economic growth. By the onset of the crisis, household indebtedness relative to household disposable income (after-tax income) had risen to about 130 percent in the United States and 150 percent in the United Kingdom, with much of this debt taking the form of mortgages on residential property. In the United States in 2005 and 2006, an increasing share of these mortgages was underwritten on very lax terms known as subprime. As long as housing prices continued to rise the increase in household leverage was manageable. However, when housing prices began to decline in many local markets, investors, who had paid little or nothing down, simply walked away from their properties and defaulted on their mortgages. As a result the value of securities backed by subprime loans plummeted in value, leaving major financial institutions in the United States and Europe with gaping holes in their balance sheets that ultimately had to be plugged by a combination of write-downs in equity and massive infusions of government capital.

In contrast, as already noted, Chinese households were substantially less leveraged in the run-up to the global financial crisis. At year-end 2007, loans of all types outstanding to households—including mortgages, auto loans, credit card debt, loans to family businesses, and seasonal working capital loans to farmers for the purchase of seeds and fertilizer—stood at RMB5.1 trillion, just 32 percent of household disposable income (People's Bank of China 2008; National Bureau of Statistics of China 2010f, 80–81).

Not only were Chinese households in the aggregate much less leveraged than their counterparts in several major advanced industrial countries, their exposure to debt for the purchase of property was relatively small. In part this reflects the relatively high down payment ratios that the CBRC requires as a precondition to qualify for a mortgage on a residential property. Moreover, the Chinese regulator has never approved the introduction of home equity lines of credit, which inevitably result in increased leverage as the lines are drawn upon. In part low leverage of Chinese households reflects the not uncommon practice in China of buying property entirely with cash. Of households' total borrowing at year-end 2007, mortgage debt accounted for RMB2.8 trillion, barely over half of all household debt. In contrast, in the United States in the same year mortgage debt and home equity lines of credit in use combined accounted for about three-quarters of total household debt. Thus mortgage debt at year-end 2007 was the equivalent of 18 percent of household disposable income in China, while it was 100 percent in the United States.

The second metric reflecting the extent of leverage in the property market is the loan-to-value ratio, which is simply the ratio of the size of the mortgage relative to the purchase price of the property. For example, with a 20 percent down payment and the balance of a property purchase financed by a mortgage, the loan-to-value ratio is 80 percent. We can estimate the annual loan-to-value ratio for the entire residential property sector in China by comparing the annual increase in the amount of individual home mortgage loans with the value of housing purchased in the same year. In 2007, when the residential housing market boomed, the value of housing sales reached RMB2.55 trillion, while mortgages outstanding rose by RMB515 billion. Thus in net terms one-fifth of the value of house purchases was financed, while almost four-fifths was paid in cash, so the loan-to-value ratio was 20 percent. In 2008, as analyzed earlier, the authorities took steps to cool the housing market so total housing sales fell by about a fifth, to only RMB2.1 trillion, and mortgages outstanding rose by a much more modest RMB215 billion. Thus the loan-to-value ratio fell from one-fifth in 2007 to only one-tenth in 2008. In 2009, when the housing market boomed again, total purchases rose 80 percent, to RMB3.8 trillion, while the increase in individual mortgage debt jumped to a record RMB1.4 trillion (People's Bank of China Monetary Policy Analysis Small Group 2010a, 48). Thus on a net basis, compared with 2008, the loan-to-value ratio in 2009 almost quadrupled, to a little over one-third. The implication of these numbers and comparable data for earlier years is clear. At a minimum a homeowner in China has an equity stake equal to 20 percent of the purchase price, and the average equity stake at year-end 2009 was almost 70 percent.[38] Thus the average loan-to-value ratio on mortgage borrowing in China at year-end 2009 was less than 40 percent, very low compared with some advanced industrial economies, where in the years leading up to the financial and economic crisis a large share of new mortgage loans was made with loan-to-value ratios of 100 percent.

The point is simple; a housing price correction in a market with a relatively small amount of leverage has financial implications that are likely to be different from a price correction in a much more highly leveraged market. In the former case defaults are likely to be few in number, since price declines would have to exceed 20 percent before any owners reached negative equity. In the latter case, as in the United States, subprime loans frequently required no money down, making the loan-to-value ratio on these transactions 100 percent. Thus even an initially modest price correction put many owners with subprime mortgages into negative equity positions on their properties. As these subprime borrowers defaulted on their mortgages and went through foreclosure, the banks put these properties back into the market, further increasing the supply of houses and reinforcing the initial downward property price correction. This pushed even more borrowers into a negative equity position. As a result, defaults on subprime loans rose sharply, negatively affecting the value of securities backed by subprime loans and eventually even impacting somewhat higher-quality tranches of mortgages, such as Alt-A. This brought down several major US financial institutions that either held these securities or had issued guarantees on the value of these securities.

---

38. The weighted average of one minus the ratio of the increase in mortgages outstanding relative to the value of housing purchased in the same year for the years 1999 through 2009 is 0.68.

Creation of Excess Industrial Capacity?

What about the assertion that the investment boom in 2009 and 2010 created excess industrial capacity that will lead to downward pressure on prices and thus on profits of manufacturing firms, perhaps resulting in defaults on the loans that financed the expansion of capacity? This argument too seems not well founded. In a high-growth, high-investment economy such as China's, there are inevitably some products for which there is at least some temporary excess capacity. The issue, however, is whether this excess capacity is so large, widespread, and enduring that it could contribute to price deflation, putting downward pressure on profits of a large number of manufacturing firms operating across many product lines. That would not only impair the ability of individual firms to repay their loans but also potentially lead to large-scale losses across the banking system.

Any evaluation of excess capacity in China must take into account several factors. First, Chinese firms have historically tended to hold on to outdated equipment, perhaps with a view that if demand for their product surged the firm could bring this old, higher-cost production capacity back on line. Therefore Chinese data on capacity utilization may overstate the extent of excess capacity compared with that of other countries. Second, there is a substantial difference in excess capacity—of, say, 20 percent—in different contexts, such as a mature economy growing at 2 to 3 percent per year versus China, where growth has averaged about 10 percent for three decades. In the mature economy the cost of financing excess capacity for the seven or eight years it might take for demand to catch up with potential supply would be substantial and would probably put enormous financial pressure on the firms with excess capacity. However, in high-growth China, 20 percent excess capacity might be absorbed in only a year or two.

Steel is commonly identified as an industry that has tended toward excess capacity in China. A European Chamber of Commerce report estimated that China's excess production capacity in steel at year-end 2008 was between 100 million and 200 million metric tons, which translates into excess capacity of 15 to 30 percent (European Chamber 2009, 20). This estimated overcapacity alone is more than the steel output of the two next largest global steel producers after China—Korea and Japan.

But this analysis fails to adequately consider the pace of growth of apparent steel consumption in China, which has been over 15 percent annually between 2000 and 2008.[39] China's apparent steel consumption in 2009 and 2010 soared by 157 million metric tons and 85 million metric tons, respectively (National

---

39. Apparent steel consumption is steel production minus net exports. This long-term series is compiled by World Steel Dynamics. True steel consumption would also take into account changes in steel inventories. But such data are not available. In any case, while changes in inventories could potentially have a large effect on year-to-year rates of growth of true steel consumption, changes in inventories are much less likely to affect growth rates of steel consumption over longer periods of time.

Bureau of Statistics of China 2010c, 2011c). In short, what appeared to outside observers to be massive excess capacity at year-end 2008 was more than fully absorbed by 2010.

Finally, it is important to note that the investment boom of 2009–10 that was fueled by China's stimulus program was not focused on expanding production capacity in China's traditional industries, such as steel. One important indicator of this is the sectoral allocation of medium- and long-term bank loans. These are loans of more than one year that are used to finance fixed investment, as opposed to loans of a year or less, which typically are used to finance working capital. In 2009 medium- and long-term bank loans outstanding expanded by RMB4.9 trillion and accounted for almost half of the total increase in renminbi lending by the banking system that year. Of these loans financing fixed investment, only 10.2 percent, or RMB502.5 billion, were extended to manufacturing firms. Fifty percent went to infrastructure projects, 13.1 percent to leasing and business services, and 10.2 percent to property development (People's Bank of China Monetary Policy Analysis Small Group 2010a, 3). A similar pattern emerged in the first three quarters of 2010. The share of medium- and long-term loans going to manufacturing was only 12.7 percent, to infrastructure projects 43.7 percent, and to property 18.8 percent (People's Bank of China Monetary Policy Analysis Small Group 2010b, 2; 2010c, 3).

It is also revealing to examine the overall investment in the steel industry, whether financed by medium- and long-term loans, by issuance of debt, or by cash flow of the firms in the sector. Investment in the steel industry in both 2009 and 2010 was substantial, RMB400 billion and RMB450 billion, respectively. But the growth of investment in the industry was minimal in 2009, only 3 percent, and a modest 10 percent in 2010, compared with an increase of investment for the economy as a whole of 30 and 25 percent, respectively, in 2009 and 2010 (National Bureau of Statistics 2010b, 2011b). Again, this reflects the priorities of the stimulus program—more for infrastructure and less for traditional industries such as steel. Thus at a time of minimal growth in investment in steel, investment in the rail network, for example, rose by a stunning 67.5 percent in 2009 and a further 13 percent the next year to reach RMB750 billion in 2010 (National Bureau of Statistics of China 2010b, 2011b).[40]

Neglect of Consumption?

China's stimulus program did rely heavily on expanding investment demand in order to offset the drag on growth caused by a moderating trade surplus. Evaluating whether or not this policy has set back China's efforts to achieve

---

40. These are increases in what the Chinese statistical authorities call "fixed asset investment," a measure that overstates the growth of capital formation. While the data on fixed asset investment are biased upward, the relative rate of expansion of fixed asset investment in steel compared with the economy as a whole is likely to be a good indicator of the modest growth of capital formation in the steel industry in 2009.

more balanced growth by encouraging private consumption is complex. Consumption growth in 2009 was actually quite robust; indeed, 2009 was the first year in a decade that consumption growth almost matched GDP growth. Thus the long-term decline in the consumption share of GDP, discussed further in chapter 2, slowed substantially in 2009.

In a year in which GDP expansion was the slowest in almost a decade, how could consumption growth in 2009 have been so strong in relative terms? How could this happen at a time when employment in export-oriented industries was collapsing, with a survey conducted by the Ministry of Agriculture reporting the loss of 20 million jobs in export manufacturing centers along the southeast coast, notably in Guangdong Province?[41]

The relatively strong growth of consumption in 2009 is explained by several factors. First, the boom in investment, particularly in construction activities, appears to have generated additional employment sufficient to offset a very large portion of the job losses in the export sector. For the year as a whole the Chinese economy created 11.02 million jobs in urban areas, very nearly matching the 11.13 million urban jobs created in 2008 (Wen Jiabao 2009, 2010). Second, while the growth of employment slowed slightly, wages continued to rise. In nominal terms wages in the formal sector rose 12 percent, a few percentage points below the average of the previous five years (National Bureau of Statistics of China 2010f, 131).[42] In real terms the increase was almost 13 percent. Third, the government continued its programs of increasing payments to those drawing pensions and raising transfer payments to China's lowest-income residents. Monthly pension payments for enterprise retirees increased by RMB120, or 10 percent, in January 2009, substantially more than the 5.9 percent increase in consumer prices in 2008.[43] This raised the total payments to retirees by about RMB75 billion.[44] The Ministry of Civil Affairs raised transfer payments to about 70 million of China's lowest-income citizens by a third, for an increase of RMB20 billion in 2009 (Ministry of Civil Affairs 2010).[45]

The combined effect of increasing employment, wages, pension income, and transfer payments contributed to a 9.8 percent increase in the disposable

---

41. "20 Million Migrants Lost Jobs: Survey," *China Daily*, February 2, 2010, available at www. chinadaily.com.cn (accessed on September 12, 2011); "20 Million Migrant Workers in China Can't Find Jobs," *New York Times*, February 2, 2009, available at www.nytimes.com (accessed on September 12, 2011).

42. See chapter 3 for a discussion of wages of migrant workers, private-sector workers, and the self-employed, the segments of the labor force that are outside what I am calling the formal sector.

43. This was the fifth consecutive year in which retirees from enterprises received increases in their monthly pensions. "China to Raise Pensions from 2010," People's Daily Online, December 23, 2009, available at http://english.people.com.cn (accessed on September 12, 2011).

44. There were an average of 51 million enterprise retirees in 2009.

45. For further discussion of the income transfer program for low-income residents see chapter 3.

income of urban residents and an increase of 8.5 percent in the net income of rural residents in 2009 (National Bureau of Statistics of China 2010c).[46] Given that urban incomes are about three times those in rural areas, the average household disposable income increased about 9.5 percent. This was slightly ahead of the growth of GDP and provided a potentially strong foundation for increasing consumption as a share of GDP.

Fourth, the government, recognizing it could not rely entirely on increased investment to offset the drag on growth from shrinking exports, adopted as part of its stimulus program several specific incentive measures to encourage consumption. Three of the incentives were designed to stimulate car sales. One of these incentives, implemented in 2009, cut by half the 10 percent tax on vehicles with small-displacement engines, purchased mainly in rural areas.[47] The program was extended in 2010, but the tax rate was moved up to 7.5 percent. Another incentive, implemented in March 2009, introduced a 10 percent discount on new cars, minivans, and light trucks purchased by rural residents.[48] A third incentive, begun in June 2009, initiated a program of special trade-in allowances for older rural and farm vehicles that did not meet China's emissions standards.[49] This program was budgeted at RMB5 billion, providing individuals with subsidies of between RMB3,000 and RMB6,000 for their trade-ins. This program was extended in June 2010 and the subsidies were boosted to between RMB5,000 and RMB20,000.

In addition to these programs to stimulate vehicle sales, in 2009 the government also initiated a home appliance subsidy program in four cities and five provinces. This scheme provided a 10 percent discount to buyers of new televisions, refrigerators, washing machines, air conditioners, and computers, conditional only on recycling the appliances they were replacing. In June 2010 the government expanded the program to 28 cities and provinces and extended the program to the end of the year. In total, central government subsidies benefiting rural areas under these programs in 2009 were RMB45 billion (Wen Jiabao 2010).[50]

Given the relatively high price elasticity of demand for consumer durables in rural China, these subsidies probably boosted 2009 rural consumption by a few percentage points over the level of 2008.[51] A few percentage points may

---

46. The National Bureau of Statistics does not regularly release data on the disposable income of rural residents. Net income is a close approximation.

47. Eligible vehicles had engines with a displacement of 1.6 liters or less.

48. The program also included a 13 percent discount on motorcycles.

49. The eligible trade-in vehicles were old three-wheeled and four-wheeled farming vehicles with engines displacing 1.3 liters or less.

50. The bulk of this subsidy number appears to come from the tax expenditures associated with the reduction in the tax rate on vehicles with engines with a displacement of 1.6 liters or less.

51. RMB45 billion is equal to 1.6 percent of the RMB2,883.4 billion making up rural household consumption in 2009 (National Bureau of Statistics of China 2010f, 56). But given the high price

sound small; it is not. As will be laid out in detail in chapter 2, between 2002 and 2008 the gap between the average annual growth of GDP and the average annual growth of private consumption expenditure was only 4 percentage points. Therefore if government programs similar to the ones just analyzed had been in place for a number of years, the consumption share of GDP might not have fallen so dramatically after 2002.

Fifth, substantial increases in household borrowing, induced by government lending policies, almost certainly bolstered consumption in 2009–10. Households increased their borrowing by RMB2.5 trillion and RMB2.9 trillion in 2009 and 2010, respectively, an average annual increase of almost four times the RMB700 billion increase in 2008.[52] Household borrowing of RMB2.8 trillion in 2009–10 was used to finance the purchase of housing (People's Bank of China Monetary Policy Analysis Small Group 2010a, 48; People's Bank of China 2011b). The remainder, RMB2.6 trillion, might be considered an upward bound estimate of the amount of increased household borrowing that potentially was available to finance increased consumption expenditures.[53] This is a substantial amount, 3.5 percent of total GDP in the two-year period.

In sum, the strong growth of personal income, price incentives, and a marked increase in leverage on the part of China's households in 2009 made it possible for private consumption expenditure to register a decline of only one-tenth of 1 percent of GDP, the smallest decline in nine years. And, including government consumption expenditure, total final consumption expenditure played a larger role in generating economic growth in 2009 than in any year in the previous decade.

However, preliminary data for 2010 are not nearly as positive. Household consumption as a share of GDP declined by a relatively large 1.2 percentage points of GDP to fall to a new all-time low of only 33.8 percent, and final consumption demand (private and government combined) accounted for the smallest share of GDP growth since 2003.[54] Thus the evidence does suggest that the critique discussed above—that the stimulus program generated growth largely through increased investment and left little or no role for consumption—is exaggerated for 2009 but valid for 2010. Chapter 3 will

---

elasticity for consumer durables in rural areas, the stimulus to consumption significantly exceeded the value of the subsidies.

52. The increase in lending to households is a comprehensive measure that includes mortgages, credit card debt, auto loans, seasonal working capital loans to farmers to finance seed and fertilizer purchases, and loans to proprietorships and other unincorporated businesses. When farmers and proprietors have better access to working capital from banks, they can devote more of the income from their farms and small businesses to personal consumption.

53. It is an upward bound because lending to households includes lending to unincorporated household businesses. Some of this lending presumably was used to finance fixed investment or inventories rather than consumption.

54. ISI Emerging Markets, CEIC Database.

explore a variety of policy reforms that might be undertaken to reverse the long-term decline in the consumption share of GDP.

Fiscal Sustainability?

An additional critique of China's stimulus worth examining here is that it led to a massive increase in implicit government debt that ultimately could lead to a banking crisis that would threaten the health of government finances. Fitch, a prominent ratings agency, predicts that there is a 60 percent probability that China will experience a banking crisis by 2013 as a consequence of the deterioration in credit quality associated with the excessive credit creation of the stimulus program.[55] China's explicitly acknowledged government debt remains relatively low, only about one-fifth of GDP. Since the stimulus was financed primarily by bank credit, rather than deficit spending financed by the sale of government bonds, explicit government debt (i.e., bonds outstanding issued by the Ministry of Finance) as a share of GDP actually declined slightly in 2009–10. But much of the medium- and long-term bank lending for infrastructure investment went to local government-linked agencies, called local investment companies.[56] Although local governments legally are not allowed to borrow or run budget deficits, lending to these local investment companies is legal and has been a successful mechanism for financing local infrastructure for more than a decade (Kroeber 2010).[57]

Critics, however, argue that starting in 2009 the scale of borrowing by these platform companies increased so rapidly that they are unlikely to be able to repay these loans and that the obligation to repay could ultimately fall on the central government. This view is not unreasonable. While in many instances local governments have provided guarantees for loans to their local investment companies, local governments are not likely to be able to repay all of this debt, particularly if local fiscal revenue from the leasing and sale of property were to decline. If this occurs, ultimately the central government might have to assume the burden of repaying much of the borrowing by local platform companies. Thus total government debt, including not only outstanding Ministry of Finance bonds but also this implicit local government debt, is much higher than the one-fifth of GDP figure commonly cited for government debt.

---

55. "Fitch's Bold Call on China Banking-System Risk," China Real Time Report, March 9, 2011, available at blogs.wsj.com/Chinarealtime (accessed on March 14, 2011).

56. These are usually referred to as *difang zhengfu rongzi pingtai* (local government financing platforms) or *chengtou gongsi* (municipal investment companies) in Chinese-language sources and in secondary English-language sources as local government investment companies (commonly abbreviated as LICs), local government financing platforms, or conduit companies.

57. Legally local governments are not allowed to issue debt, except under special circumstances. For example, as part of the economic stimulus package in 2009 China's Ministry of Finance issued RMB200 billion in debt on behalf of local governments.

How large might this debt potentially be? A broad range of estimates has been made. Perhaps the most widely cited estimate was made by Victor Shih, a Northwestern University political science professor. He placed this debt at year-end 2009 at RMB11.4 trillion, almost twice the official figure of RMB6.5 trillion for outstanding Ministry of Finance bonds.[58]

However, this estimate is likely to be on the high side. To start with, consider medium- and long-term bank lending that the central bank specifically identifies as going to infrastructure projects. These loans amounted to RMB1.1 trillion and RMB2.5 trillion in 2008 and 2009, respectively (People's Bank of China Monetary Policy Analysis Small Group 2009a, 4; 2010a, 3). If we assume that all of these infrastructure loans went to local investment companies and that none of the principal on loans of this type made in the five years 2005–09 was repaid, the bank debt of these infrastructure companies at year-end 2009 would have been RMB5.666 trillion.[59] These firms also issue bonds, a reported RMB121.2 billion in 2009, an amount slightly more than the cumulative debt issued by these firms in the prior four years.[60] Adding bank borrowing and bond issuance brings the total debt of local investment companies to approximately RMB5.9 trillion at year-end 2009.

Chinese press reports quoting Ba Shusong, the deputy director of the Institute of Finance of the Development Research Center, a leading government think tank, placed the debt of local government investment companies at mid-year 2009 at more than RMB5 trillion, up from about RMB1 trillion at the beginning of 2008.[61] Adding medium- and long-term infrastructure lending by banks in the second half of 2009 and bond issuance by these firms in the second half to the mid-year figure of more than RMB5 trillion would bring the total debt to RMB6 trillion, very close to the bottom-up estimate just laid out.[62]

A fourth approach is to accept the official data. Liu Mingkang, the head of the CBRC, in a March 2010 speech placed outstanding local investment

---

58. Victor Shih, "China's 8,000 Credit Risks," *Wall Street Journal Asia,* February 9, 2010, available at http://online.wsj.com (accessed on February 12, 2010).

59. Medium- and long-term infrastructure lending in 2005, 2006, and 2007 was RMB617.50 billion, RMB650.48 billion, and RMB 798.36 billion, respectively.

60. Andrew Batson, "China's Localities Feel Pinch of Tighter Credit," *Wall Street Journal,* February 25, 2010, available at http://online.wsj.com (accessed on February 25, 2010). The issuance of bonds in the first 11 months of 2009 almost equaled bond issuance by these companies in the previous four years (Xu Lin 2010, 28).

61. Wang Bo, "'Systematic Risks' Warning," *China Daily,* November 9, 2009, 7.

62. In the second half of 2009 banks extended RMB900 billion of medium- and long-term loans for infrastructure and local investment companies issued RMB55.2 billion in bonds (Xu Lin 2010).

company bank borrowing at year-end 2009 at RMB7.38 trillion.[63] Adding in the value of the bonds issued by these companies would bring their total debt to about RMB7.8 trillion.[64] A more comprehensive survey undertaken by the National Audit Office in 2011 placed total debt of local governments, including borrowing by their local investment companies, at RMB10.75 trillion at year-end 2010. About 70 percent of these funds were allocated to local infrastructure projects (National Audit Office of the People's Republic of China 2011).

Local government debt at year-end 2010 as measured by the National Audit Office was equal to about 25 percent of China's GDP and was about a third larger than the outstanding government debt issued by the Ministry of Finance. The RMB7.38 trillion of bank borrowing by local investment companies in 2009 was equal to almost a fifth of renminbi loans outstanding from the banking system at year-end 2009. In short, by almost any standard both the total debt and the bank borrowing of local government platform companies are quite large.

Judging the ability of the platform companies and other public service providers to service their debt in the future is difficult. Some charged that many of the infrastructure projects funded by the stimulus program are white elephants and would fall short of the goal of creating employment and jump-starting private consumption.[65] This view was fostered by wide-spread reports that in the fall of 2008, shortly after the central government announced the RMB4 trillion stimulus program, thousands of provincial and municipal government officials descended on Beijing seeking central government approval and funding for projects that together totaled more than RMB10 trillion.[66]

While local investment companies undoubtedly did fund some white elephants, most public infrastructure projects initiated in 2009–10 will eventually generate large positive economic returns. Some projects were based on detailed long-term plans that were developed years in advance of the global financial and economic crisis. The dramatic expansion of rail development starting in 2009, for example, was based on the detailed Mid- to Long-Range

63. Jin Shuiming, "Liu Mingkang: Local Financial Platform Bank Loans Outstanding at Year-End 09 are RMB7.38 Trillion," *Securities Daily*, May 25, 2010, available at http://finance.qq.com (accessed on September 13, 2011).

64. This is substantially below Victor Shih's estimate of RMB11 trillion; see "China's 8,000 Credit Risks," *Wall Street Journal Asia*, February 9, 2010, available at http://online.wsj.com (accessed on February 12, 2010). It is above a figure of RMB5 trillion given by People's Daily, an agency of the Chinese Communist Party. "China on High Alert for Large-Scale Bad Loans," People's Daily Online, February 25, 2010, available at http://english.people.com.cn (accessed on February 26, 2010).

65. Victor Shih, "Beijing's 'Legless' Stimulus," *Wall Street Journal Asia*, April 3, 2009, available at http://online.wsj.com (accessed on September 12, 2011).

66. Andrew Batson, "China's Stimulus Race Sparks Fears of Excess," *Wall Street Journal*, November 24, 2008, available at http://online.wsj.com (accessed on September 12, 2011).

Network Plan for rail development approved by the State Council in 2003. This plan, which covers rail development through 2020, calls for a separation of passenger and freight on capacity-constrained trunk routes and the development of high-speed intercity regional passenger networks in densely populated areas. It is designed to address China's endemic rail transport capacity shortages. The World Bank characterizes it as "perhaps the biggest single planned program of passenger rail investment there has ever been in one country" (Amos, Bullock, and Sondhi 2010, 7–8).

Spending on rail development accelerated as the Mid- to Long-Range Network Plan was implemented, with total investment in 2003–07 reaching RMB522 billion. But, as the economic stimulus program was rolled out in the fall of 2008, the Ministry of Railroads brought forward eight specific rail projects from the plan that originally were scheduled for construction in later years. The planned investment in these accelerated projects, which will take more than a year to complete, totaled RMB405 billion, including outlays of about RMB25 billion for the acquisition of land for the 1,318 kilometer Beijing-Shanghai dedicated high-speed passenger line, which opened in mid-year 2011. Thus, while originally the ministry had planned to expand the high-speed rail network by 12,000 kilometers in 2009, under the accelerated plan this number was bumped up to 16,000 kilometers. As a result investment in rail construction, which had totaled RMB155 billion in 2006 and RMB177.2 billion in 2007, jumped to RMB335 billion in 2008. Outlays on rail construction in 2009 soared further, to RMB623 billion, with about 60 percent of the funding going to the development of the high-speed rail network. In 2010 rail construction was budgeted at RMB823.5 billion, or $120 billion.[67] In contrast, President Obama's economic stimulus program allocated $8 billion to develop high-speed rail in the United States in 2010 and promised an additional $1 billion annually in federal funds for several additional years.[68]

The stimulus program also accelerated the development of China's electrical grid, notably the expansion of the network of ultra-high-voltage

---

67. For funding details see Bullock, Sondhi, and Amos (2009, 79–84); Amos, Bullock, and Sondhi (2010, 8); Xin Dingding, "Locomotion," *China Daily Business Weekly*, November 17–23, 2008, 3; "High-Speed Rail Spearheads China's Efforts to Boost Economy," People's Daily Online, March 3, 2010, available at http://english.people.com.cn (accessed on March 3, 2010); and "High-Speed Railway Accounts for Over Half of China's Railway Investment," People's Daily Online, April 27, 2010, available at http://english.people.com.cn (accessed on April 27, 2010). Fixed asset investment in rail, which also includes the costs of acquiring rolling stock and land, was even higher than the numbers in the text—RMB682.3 billion in 2009 and RMB407 billion in 2008, according to the National Bureau of Statistics (2010e, 58). The Ministry of Railroads put fixed asset investment in 2009 slightly higher, at RMB701.3 billion, according to the article in People's Daily Online of April 27, 2010, just cited.

68. The gap between the levels of funding for high-speed rail in China and in the United States is even greater than these numbers suggest since construction and rolling stock capital costs are significantly lower in China than in the United States (Amos, Bullock, and Sondhi 2010, 2). Moreover, some of the funds for high-speed rail in the United States were not spent and were cut from the fiscal 2011 budget as part of the deficit reduction program passed by Congress in early 2011.

(UHV) transmission lines. UHV lines, which include lines with a voltage of 1,000 kilovolts or above of alternating current and 800 kilovolts or above of direct current, allow the efficient transmission of large amounts of power over long distances. China was the first country to deploy UHV transmission lines, giving it the ability to carry much more power efficiently over longer distances than is possible, for example, in the United States. This substantial increase in cross-regional power transmission capacity over time will allow China to overcome bottlenecks in its electrical grid system and thus use its large power-generating capacity more efficiently as well. State Grid Corporation, which is China's largest electrical distributor, plans on investing an additional RMB500 billion in the 12th Five-Year Plan (2011–15) to extend its UHV transmission network to 40,000 kilometers by the end of 2015.[69]

While accelerated rail development and the development of the UHV electrical transmission network were clearly based on well-developed plans designed to address unmet demand for transportation services and to increase cross-provincial electrical power transmission capacity, respectively, the question remains as to whether local infrastructure projects also will satisfy unmet needs. What about the municipal infrastructure projects, such as roads, airports, subways, water supply, and wastewater treatment systems, undertaken by local quasi-governmental agencies?

One legitimate concern is that some services provided by quasi-governmental agencies are priced substantially below the level that would allow full cost recovery, i.e., they do not generate revenue sufficient to pay operating as well as capital costs. Because increases in tariffs over the last decade or more have lagged rising costs, most municipal water companies in China have lost money every year since the mid-1990s.[70] Similarly, the fares on subway systems in China, as in virtually every other country in the world, are so low that fare box revenue usually does not even cover operating costs. According to the head of China's Civil Aviation Administration, landing fees and other related revenues don't cover operating costs at most of China's airports, making them money losers.[71] Fares on the high-speed intercity passenger trains China is building will not generate revenue sufficient to cover both operating and capital costs. Thus underpricing of some services provided by quasi-governmental agencies will impair the ability of these agencies to repay the loans taken out in order to meet the growing demand for these services. To the extent that platform companies invest in activities that do not generate revenue, their ability to repay is even more impaired.

---

69. "State Grid to Invest RMB500 Billion Yuan in China," People's Daily Online, January 6, 2011, available at http://english.people.com.cn (accessed on January 6, 2011); US Department of Energy, "Secretary Chu Remarks at the National Press Club," November 29, 2010, available at www.energy.gov/news (accessed on February 7, 2011).

70. "High Price for Water Reform?" People's Daily Online, October 29, 2009, available at http://english.people.com.cn (accessed on September 12, 2011).

71. Li Jiaxiang, quoted in *Dragon Week*, GavekalDragonomics, February 28, 2011.

While the financial returns to some of the investments undertaken by platform companies and other public service providers may be modest, several additional factors need to be taken into account in any evaluation of the magnitude of the burden of debt created by the rapid build out of China's infrastructure in 2009–10. First, and most important, it is likely that over the medium and long term the real economic returns to the economy as a whole on many of these infrastructure investments will be high. China is in the midst of the largest rural-to-urban migration in global history, and thus the demand for services in urban areas has been rising and will continue to rise steadily. The real economic returns to infrastructure investment in China therefore are likely to be high. This is a general phenomenon in emerging markets, where infrastructure investment typically generates higher returns than other forms of physical capital (Calderon, Moral-Benito, and Serven 2009). Indeed, the rapid development of infrastructure slightly ahead of demand has been a hallmark of China's economic growth, particularly in the last decade. Unlike India, where insufficient infrastructure investment has been a brake on economic growth, rapid infrastructure development in China has facilitated and stimulated its superior growth performance (Naughton 2010, 449–50).

Second, the financial viability of some infrastructure investment projects should not be evaluated on a stand-alone basis. Some critics, for example, have challenged the economic viability of China's high-speed rail program on the grounds that while the fares are high relative to personal income in China, they are not high enough to cover the operating and capital costs of the high-speed rail network. But, China's high-speed rail system seeks to compete with airlines on major intercity routes, such as Guangzhou-Wuhan and Beijing-Shanghai, where relatively well-to-do passengers are paying high airfares. Moreover, according to an analysis by the World Bank, the main economic and financial benefit of building a dedicated high-speed passenger rail network on new alignments is that it frees up capacity on existing rail lines that can then be used to haul more freight (Bullock, Sondhi, and Amos 2009, 74; Amos, Bullock and Sondhi 2010, 8, 15). The Bank estimates that over time the capital costs of most of China's planned high-speed rail network can be largely recouped from the additional revenues that the previously existing rail system can garner from hauling more freight; the fares for high-speed rail service need to cover only the operating costs of the system.[72] This cross-subsidy from freight to passenger traffic is feasible since the Chinese rail system is under the uniform administration of the Ministry of Railroads and its various regional operating subsidiaries (Freeman 2010).

Third, while some local investment companies may have weak cash flow, on average they are not insolvent. At year-end 2009 the assets of these companies amounted to RMB8 trillion, slightly more than their outstanding

---

72. The Bank does express some skepticism that this will be true for high-speed lines planned to extend into China's far western regions, where the population density is far lower than in the Guangzhou–Wuhan and Beijing–Shanghai corridors, where the initial lines have been built.

debt.[73] Thus lending to these companies is not likely to have the same adverse financial and fiscal consequences as did large-scale bank lending to chronic money-losing state-owned companies in the mid-1990s. Many of these state-owned borrowers at that time had liabilities far exceeding their assets, so that when they were ultimately closed and liquidated the banks recovered little or nothing (Lardy 1998, 43, 142–43). Ultimately the government had to inject about RMB3.4 trillion into the banking system to facilitate its restructuring (Ma Guonan 2006, 22).

In short, eventually, municipalities and other local governments will probably have to assume responsibility for repaying some of the borrowing that their local investment companies are unable to repay. But the services these companies provide are likely to contribute to sustaining China's economic growth and thus, over time, will help generate increased government tax revenues as well. Moreover, absent a major property price correction, local governments are likely to continue to enjoy substantial income from the leasing of land, revenue that is not reflected in local government budgets but that has become an increasingly important source of revenue in recent years. Finally, the pilot property tax programs initiated in Shanghai and Chongqing in early 2011 are likely to become national programs, and over time the share of property owners subject to the tax likely will increase. This will provide additional revenues to local governments to repay loans that local investment companies cannot repay.

In the longer term, China needs to adopt different policies to finance infrastructure projects. The current system of financing long-term infrastructure development with short-term bank loans and bonds is far from optimal. China needs to develop a sizeable longer-term bond market to provide a source of funding for infrastructure projects that have economic payoffs that materialize over many years or even decades. Half of the local government debt of RMB10.7 trillion outstanding at year-end 2010 comes due in 2011–13. Only 30 percent of the total is scheduled for repayment in 2016 or later (National Audit Office of the People's Republic of China 2011). Thus the average maturity of local government debt is relatively short. Similarly, at mid-year 2011 the average remaining maturity of the RMB585.5 billion in outstanding bonds issued by the Ministry of Railroads is less than two and a half years.[74] But the

---

73. "China on High Alert for Large-Scale Bad Loans," People's Daily Online, February 25, 2010, available at http://english.people.com.cn (accessed on September 12, 2011).

74. One source reports total bonds outstanding at year-end 2010 of the Ministry of Railroads were RMB585.5 billion and total scheduled payments of principal and interest in 2011 were RMB144.8 billion. "Bond Market Gives the Ministry of Railways a Hard Look," Caixin Online, August 1, 2011, available at http://english.caing.com (accessed on August 1, 2011). The China Daily reports that the ministry paid bond interest of RMB19.3 billion in 2010. Yu Hongyan, "Banks May Raise Lending Interest Rates to Railway Ministry," China Daily, July 29, 2011, available at www.china-daily.com.cn (accessed on July 29, 2011). Based on the growth of the stock of bonds outstanding between 2010 and 2011, I estimate that interest payments in 2011 will be about RMB22 billion, meaning repayments of principal will be an estimated RMB123 billion. At that pace the ministry's

ministry's rail expansion program has very high initial costs and will generate increased revenues over a period of decades. The growth of revenue in the early years of the development of high-speed rail will be slow for two reasons. First, the large increases in freight throughput will depend on the completion of the four north-south and four east-west high-speed passenger corridors, which will allow the development of longer freight corridors. Second, over time, as passenger demand develops, the intervals between trains on the high-speed network will be reduced, thus increasing revenues.

In addition to developing longer-term financial instruments, the Chinese government might consider subsidizing the cost of debt financing for infrastructure, just as the United States does by providing favorable federal tax treatment on interest paid on municipal bonds issued by state and local governments.

Rise of the State and the Demise of Reform?

What about the charge that the stimulus program substantially enhanced the role of the state and thus fundamentally undermined China's long-term economic reform trajectory, in which the private, market-driven economy has increasingly supplanted state-owned companies and the state more generally? In this view China previously "thrived by allowing once-suppressed private entrepreneurs to prosper," but now "it is often China's state-run companies that are on the march."[75] Assessing this charge, captured in the Chinese phrase *guojin, mintui* (advance of the state, retreat of the private) is complex. On the one hand the government launched no important reform measures to enhance the role of the market during the stimulus program. Indeed, since President Hu Jintao and Premier Wen Jiabao assumed office in 2003, the pace of fundamental, market-enhancing, economic reform has slowed and, as this study will show, in some cases has been reversed. On the other hand, as will be argued below, the momentum generated by earlier market-oriented reforms continues to play out in very important ways.

This interpretation tends to be borne out by a variety of important metrics showing that the stimulus program did not fundamentally change the nature of resource allocation in China's economy by enhancing the role of the state at the expense of the market. First, the pattern of bank lending to businesses in 2009–10 does not support the contention that loans during the stimulus program went primarily to state-owned firms, squeezing out private firms. To analyze this issue we have to rely on an analysis of lending by size of firm since data on bank lending to various categories of firm ownership is not available. Previously published data usually gave the breakdown of loans to large firms

outstanding bonds will be repaid in 4.8 years, meaning the average remaining maturity of the bonds is 2.4 years.

75. Michael Wines, "China Fortifies State Businesses to Fuel Growth," *New York Times*, August 29, 2010, available at www.nytimes.com (accessed on September 12, 2011).

and to medium-sized and small firms combined. Fortunately data now show lending to small and medium-sized firms separately.[76] Because two-thirds of small firms are private, with the balance being mostly firms of mixed ownership, such as collective or cooperative, lending to small firms is a good proxy for lending to private firms (Liu Xiangfeng 2007). At the other extreme, two-fifths of large firms are state-owned, and fewer than 10 percent are private (National Bureau of Statistics of China 2009d, 1). Thus data on lending to large firms are a reasonable proxy for lending to state-owned companies.[77] Finally we have data on lending to the self-employed or what are sometimes called household businesses.[78] This lending should be regarded as going to private firms although in the Chinese statistical system household businesses are not classified as firms.

As shown in figure 1.1, in percentage terms the growth of borrowing by household businesses in 2009 and 2010 outstripped the pace of borrowing by all firms, regardless of size. In 2009 and 2010 borrowing by family businesses and farmers expanded by RMB660 billion and RMB1,100 billion, respectively. Business loans outstanding to individuals cumulatively over the two-year period grew by 90 percent, compared with a 60 percent expansion in total credit extended to businesses by the banking system. Moreover, at the end of 2010 one-third of individual business loans outstanding were for a term greater

---

76. The focus here is on data for the small firms only rather than the more frequently encountered data covering the universe of small and medium-sized firms (SMEs). The reason is that medium-sized firms in China can be rather large. In the industrial sector, for example, medium-sized firms may employ as many as 3,000 workers, have assets as large as RMB400 million, and have sales as great as RMB300 million. Small industrial firms employ fewer than 300 workers, have assets under RMB40 million, or sales less than RMB30 million. "Interim Regulations on SME Categorizing Criteria," May 16, 2007, available at www.sme.gov.cn (accessed on September 12, 2011).

77. In this study, except where explicitly stated to the contrary, "state-owned companies" refers to the universe of both traditional state-owned companies and those formerly state-owned firms that have converted into joint-stock companies, i.e., shareholding companies, in which the state remains the dominant shareholder. The former are governed by the People's Republic of China Law on Industrial Enterprises Owned Wholly by the People, which dates from 1988. The latter group of firms is governed by the Company Law, which came into effect on July 1, 1994. This group is designated as *guoyou konggu qiye*. Chinese authorities invariably translate this as "state-holding companies." I prefer to translate this term as "state-controlled shareholding companies." State-controlled shareholding companies began to emerge in the second half of the 1990s as traditional large state-owned companies converted to ownership by shares and then listed on domestic and international stock exchanges.

78. "Self-employed individuals" is the usual Chinese translation for *geti* or *geti hu*. I also use the terms "family business" or "individual business" to identify these units. They are unincorporated, and thus are not included in the category private firms. Historically these family businesses have been limited to fewer than eight workers. However, in March 2011 the State Council, China's cabinet, approved legislation eliminating limits on the number of workers these businesses may hire. "China's Cabinet Approves Individual Business Legislation," People's Daily Online, March 31, 2011, available at www.english.people.com.cn (accessed on March 31, 2011).

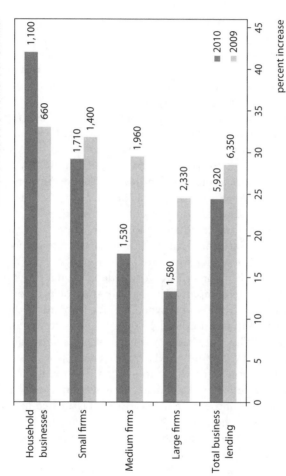

Figure 1.1   Bank lending to businesses by type of borrower, 2009–10

numbers at bars are in billions of renminbi

percent increase

- 2010
- 2009

Household businesses — 1,100 / 660

Small firms — 1,710 / 1,400

Medium firms — 1,530 / 1,960

Large firms — 1,580 / 2,330

Total business lending — 5,920 / 6,350

Note: Data are for state-owned commerical banks, China Development Bank, policy banks, joint-stock commercial banks, city commercial banks, postal savings bank, city credit cooperatives, and foreign banks.

Sources: China Banking Regulatory Commission (2010, 44–45; 2011, 49); People's Bank of China (2010b, 2011b).

than one year. Thus the self-employed and farmers are able to rely on bank borrowing not only for working capital but also to finance some of their fixed investment.

Small firms in both 2009 and 2010 were able to increase their borrowing much more rapidly than both medium-sized and large companies. In 2009 and 2010 bank lending to small-scale enterprises expanded by RMB1.4 trillion and RMB1.7 trillion, respectively. Indeed, in 2010 the pace of growth of lending to small firms was more than twice as rapid as the growth of lending to large firms, and the absolute amount of new lending to small firms exceeded that going to large firms.

In short, both individual businesses, which are entirely private, and small firms, which are predominantly private, were able to access a large share of the expanded supply of bank credit, which was one of the most prominent features of China's stimulus program starting in late 2008. The expansion of credit to household businesses was particularly notable. In 2008, the last precrisis year, household businesses were able to expand their borrowing by only half the pace of growth of total loans, so their additional borrowings were a very modest RMB192.5 billion. As noted, this pattern reversed in 2009–10. The charges that China's "banks exist to provide funding for the government and its state-owned enterprises" (Wolfe and Aarsnes 2011) and that "Chinese banks overwhelmingly lend to SOEs [state-owned enterprises] and always have" (Walter and Howie 2011, 43) are outdated and wholly inaccurate. Similarly an estimate that "90 percent of the stimulus funds have gone to state-owned enterprises" (Huang Yasheng 2011, 4) is not supported by the evidence.

The second strand of the critique that the stimulus program privileged state-owned over private companies is that the state-owned companies, flush with funds borrowed from state-owned banks, expanded their economic footprint during the financial crisis by buying up private-sector competitors (Bremer 2010, 144). The state did nationalize some small-scale, private coal mines in 2009 and in a well-publicized case forced the privately owned Rizhao Steel Company to merge with the state-owned Shandong Steel (Naughton 2009).[79] But these were isolated incidents that were not designed to expand the economic footprint of the state. The campaign launched in 2009 in Shanxi Province to consolidate the coal industry by nationalizing small, private coal mines and turning them over to large state-owned operators was motivated by the desire of the national government to reduce mining fatalities in China, which have been horrifically high. Private coal mining in China has been quite profitable, in part because owners of small-scale private mines are much more prone to cut corners on safety, and thus these mines account for a disproportionate share of mining accidents and deaths.[80] Previous attempts by the

---

79. See also "The Pendulum Swings against the Pit," *Economist*, October 17, 2009, 54.

80. Leslie Hook, "China Digs Deep to Reshape its Coal Mining Industry," *Financial Times*, April 29, 2011, 21.

government to enforce safety regulations in numerous, small-scale private mines met with limited success (Wright 2007). The Rizhao Steel case was complex, as Naughton's (2009) analysis shows, but was not part of a broader trend of expanding the role of state-owned steel companies. Indeed, private steel firms, which already accounted for about 40 percent of crude steel output in 2008, flourished in 2009–10 as national investment soared, boosting the demand for steel products.

Aggregate data on the expansion of industrial production by ownership also support the view that the nationalization of private companies did not extend to sectors other than coal. If takeovers of private firms by state-owned firms were widespread, one would expect to see an uptick in the share of output produced by state firms. But 2009–10 was marked by a substantial continuity in the long-term decline in the role of state-owned firms in China's economy, particularly in the industrial sector, which accounts for fully two-fifths of China's GDP. In 1978 the share of industrial output produced by state-owned firms was 81 percent; 30 years later, as the global financial crisis began to unfold, it was 28 percent (National Bureau of Statistics of China 1987, 257; 2009b, 487, 498).[81] Contrary to the assertion of Naughton (2011, 324) that "the shrinkage of the state sector has now stopped," the shrinkage trend continued unabated during the global financial and economic crisis. National industrial value added rose by 11.0 and 15.7 percent in 2009 and 2010, respectively.[82] This industrial growth is disaggregated by ownership in figure 1.2. The output of state-owned firms rose only 6.9 and 13.7 percent in 2009 and 2010, respectively. Given their below-average growth performance, the share of industrial output contributed by state-owned firms continued to decline in 2009–10, extending the pattern evident for three decades prior to the onset of the global financial crisis.

What can we learn by examining the performance of industrial firms with other types of ownership, shown in figure 1.2? In 2009 the weakest economic growth performance, at 6.2 percent, was turned in by foreign-owned companies.

---

81. In 2008 traditional state-owned companies accounted for 9 percent of industrial output, and state-controlled shareholding companies for 19 percent. The long-term decline from 81 to 28 percent in the share of output produced by state-owned companies probably understates the decline. This is because the 28 percent share in 2008 is based on a total industrial output number that excludes the output of nonstate firms with sales under RMB5 million per year. In 2004, the only year for which I have been able to find the data, these smaller firms accounted for 16 percent of industrial output value (see note immediately below). If these smaller, nonstate firms accounted for the same share of industrial output in 2008 as in 2004, then the two types of state-owned companies combined accounted for only 24 percent of industrial output in 2008.

82. These data are for the universe of industrial firms that includes all state-owned firms and firms with other forms of ownership if their sales exceed RMB5 million per year. Chinese authorities refer to this universe as "all state-owned enterprises and non-state-owned enterprises above designated size." These firms account for the overwhelming majority of industrial output. For example, in 2004 state-owned enterprises and non-state-owned industrial enterprises above a designated size accounted for 84 percent of the gross value of industrial output (National Bureau of Statistics of China 2005, 488; 2006b, 505).

Figure 1.2   Growth of industrial value-added by ownership, 2009–10

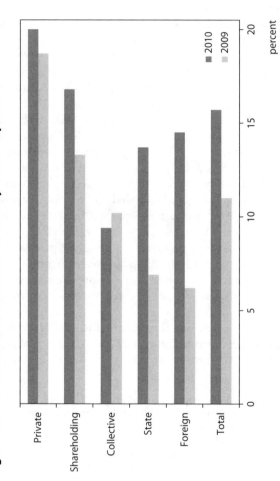

Notes: "State" includes shareholding firms in which the state is the controlling shareholder. "Foreign" includes firms with funding from Taiwan, Hong Kong, Macao, and other countries.

Sources: National Bureau of Statistics of China (2010c, 2011c).

But these firms are disproportionately export oriented, producing half of China's total exports. Given the sharp decline in China's exports in 2009, it is natural that the growth of these firms slowed substantially relative to firms with other types of ownership. When China's exports soared by more than 30 percent in 2010 and the value of exports exceeded the previous record of 2008, the growth of foreign-funded firms rebounded sharply, to 14.5 percent, and outpaced the rate of expansion of state firms. Private firms in both years were at the top of the performance league by ownership, expanding by 18.7 and 20 percent in 2009 and 2010, respectively. Firms with various hybrid types of ownership—collective, cooperative shareholding, and shareholding— also outperformed state-owned firms, though by smaller margins than private firms (National Bureau of Statistics of China 2010e, 133; 2011c).

State-owned firms continued to underperform and private firms to overperform in another domain—exports. As recently as 1995 state-owned companies accounted for fully two-thirds of China's exports. By 2008 their share had fallen to 18 percent, and that share continued to fall during the crisis, reaching 14 percent in 2010. Initially, foreign-funded firms took up most of the slack left by the declining export prowess of state-owned firms. But their share peaked in 2005 and from 2005 through the end of 2010 the share of exports produced by private firms doubled, to 30 percent. Private firms for the first time ever in 2009–10 became the most important source of China's growth of exports.[83]

Finally, we can examine the growth of assets of state-owned firms compared with private firms. In the two years prior to the crisis, private firms' assets grew by an average of 37 percent, twice the 18 percent average rate for state-owned firms. During the stimulus program the pace of growth of assets of private firms relative to state-owned firms fell to about 1.5:1.[84] So only in this one domain of the four examined is there any evidence that state-owned firms benefited during the stimulus program compared with private firms. Two caveats should be noted. First, this outcome almost certainly reflected the substantial ramping up of infrastructure investment during the stimulus program, almost all of which is state-owned, rather than an erosion of the ability of private manufacturing and services firms to expand their investment. Second, the stimulus program did not absolutely advantage the ability of state-owned firms to expand their assets; it is more accurate to say that the stimulus program only diminished somewhat the ability of private firms to expand their assets more rapidly than state-owned firms.

China's economic stimulus program was far from perfect. But the political system did generate a rapid and reasonably coherent response that was successful in bringing China through the biggest global economic crisis in

---

83. ISI Emerging Markets, CEIC Database.

84. Assets of private firms grew by an average of 19.8 percent in 2009–10, while state-owned firms expanded their assets by 12.9 percent. ISI Emerging Markets, CEIC Database.

several decades with relatively strong growth momentum. The banks largely financed the program with a huge increase in lending. This entailed risk of increased inflation, which materialized beginning near the end of the second year of the stimulus. But the People's Bank of China continued the gradual tightening measures begun in mid-2009, and by mid-2011 the rate of growth of broad money was down to a pace consistent with strong growth and moderate inflation. While the authorities were successful in controlling the buildup of financial leverage associated with the acceleration of the housing boom during 2009–10, they did not avoid excessive investment in housing; this may constitute a significant macroeconomic risk to China's future growth, an issue that is examined in some detail in chapter 3. The stimulus did not lead to significant excess capacity in manufacturing as there is no evidence of any price deflation for industrial goods in 2010–11. Private consumption expenditure held up unexpectedly well in 2009 but resumed its underperformance in 2010, giving some support to critics on that issue. While there are legitimate concerns about the magnitude of local investment company debt, most of this debt financed infrastructure investment that is likely to have positive long-run economic returns. Successful financing of this debt and future infrastructure projects requires further reforms, notably the development of a long-term bond market and perhaps some explicit mechanism to subsidize the interest cost on debt related to infrastructure development.

Finally, the stimulus program did not lead to a wholesale advance of the state at the expense of either private firms or individual businesses. Even at the height of the crisis, state-owned firms did not increase their share of bank lending, indeed their share shrank, and the share of industrial value added and exports produced by state-owned firms continued to shrink at roughly the same pace as they did prior to the global financial crisis. Purely private firms, on the other hand, became the most important contributor to the growth of both manufacturing output and exports. Similarly, there was a large increase in the share of bank lending going to households, both to support the expansion of their individual businesses and to finance mortgages on residential property. While some describe China as the poster boy for a model of state capitalism that is successfully challenging the Western free-market model, the stimulus program has not reversed the long-term trend of a declining role for state-owned companies, whether measured by their share of total bank lending, their share of industrial output, or their share of exports.[85] Needless to say state-owned companies in telecommunications, finance, petroleum, and a few other sectors maintained their monopoly or quasi-monopoly positions during the global financial and economic crisis. But the domination of state-owned firms in these sectors has been a constant feature of China's economic landscape for more than three decades. Focusing excessively on the continuing important

---

85. Geoff Dyer, "China's 'Market-Leninism' Has Yet to Face Biggest Test," special report, *Financial Times*, September 14, 2010.

role of these firms can lead one to overlook significant developments in other sectors of the Chinese economy.

It is too early to judge whether or not the stepped-up level of state industrial policy that emerged in 2009–10 will have a decisive impact on the evolution of China's economic growth. As Naughton (2011, 318-19) notes, the origins of China's "indigenous innovation" policy clearly date to the promulgation of the Medium and Long-Term Developmental Program for Science and Technology Development (2006–10) in 2005, long before the global financial and economic crisis. It remains to be seen how this initiative, including some of the supplementary policies rolled out during 2009–10, will ultimately affect the balance between state and market.

2

Imbalances and Their Implications for China's Economy

China's early, large, and well-designed stimulus program meant that China came through the global financial and economic crisis in an unusually strong economic and financial position. While global output shrank by more than 2 percent in 2009 and then recovered at a subpar 3.9 percent pace in 2010, China powered ahead with growth of 9.2 and 10.4 percent in 2009 and 2010, respectively (IMF 2011b, 2; National Bureau of Statistics of China 2010f, 40; 2011e).[1] Similarly, while global trade fell by 23.5 percent in 2009 (the sharpest decline in 70 years) and then recovered by an estimated 13.5 percent in 2010, China's trade fell only by 14 percent in 2009 and then roared back with a 35 percent expansion in 2010.[2] That meant global trade in 2010 was well below the previous peak level of 2008, while China's trade in the same year was well above its 2008 level. Finally, global foreign direct investment (FDI) flows fell sharply in the downturn in 2009 and were stagnant at that depressed level in 2010. China's inbound FDI also fell sharply in 2009 but soared by almost two-thirds in 2010, reaching $185 billion, an all-time high. China's outbound FDI did contract by almost 20 percent in 2009, but it rose by 37 percent to reach a record high of $60 billion in 2010 (State Administration of Foreign

---

1. Global growth rates are measured at market exchange rates. China's GDP growth of 10.4 percent in 2010 is an upward revision of the initially reported 10.3 percent.

2. Figures for global and Chinese trade are in volume terms, i.e., current prices, and are from World Trade Organization press releases of March 26, 2010, and September 20, 2010, available at www. wto.org (accessed on February 1, 2011) and China General Customs Administration data releases of January 10, 2010, and January 10, 2011, available at www.customs.gov.cn (both accessed on September 12, 2011).

Exchange International Balance of Payments Analysis Small Group 2011).[3] Despite China's impressive economic performance, the central thesis of this study is that sustaining a high rate of economic growth in China over the medium and longer run will require a fundamentally new growth model.

China's premier, Wen Jiabao, apparently shares the belief that significant reform is needed to sustain China's economic development. In what appeared to be an unscripted response to a question at his press conference following the annual meeting of the National People's Congress in March 2007, Premier Wen said that "China's economic growth is unsteady, imbalanced, uncoordinated, and unsustainable." This was a remarkable characterization of an economy that had just recorded its fastest annual growth in 11 years and, since 1978, had expanded at an average annual rate of almost 10 percent, faster than any other economy in the world. Premier Wen subsequently has used the same or similar language to describe China's economy on a number of occasions, and Hu Jintao used similar language in his July 1, 2011, address on the occasion of the 90th anniversary of the founding of the Chinese Communist Party.[4] This chapter analyzes the factors that may have led to the premier's characterization of the economy in this way; the following chapter examines the policies the government has pursued to correct the various imbalances in order to make China's economic growth more sustainable.

There are four different but complementary approaches to examining the structure of an economy and evaluating the degree to which it might be considered "imbalanced." The first, called the expenditure approach, looks at the sources of growth, i.e., the sources of demand. What is the mix of demand among consumption (by households and the government), investment, and net exports? How has this changed over time? The second, called the production approach, examines the economy from the supply side, i.e., the structure of output. What are the relative contributions of agriculture, industry, and services to total output? The third, called the income approach, looks at the shares of income accruing to workers, enterprises, and the government. The fourth method, called the savings-investment approach, looks at the balance between national savings and national investment. When national savings exceed national investment, a country necessarily has an external surplus. Conversely, when savings fall short of investment, a country has an external deficit. The specific source or sources of the national external imbalance can be identified by disaggregating national savings and national investment into the contributions of households, the corporate sector, and the government.[5]

---

3. An annex to the cited report contains China's revised balance of payments data for the years 2005–09. These revised data are used throughout this study.

4. Hu Jintao, speech at the 90th Anniversary of the Founding of the Chinese Communist Party, July 21, 2011, available at www.gov.cn (accessed on August 23, 2011).

5. Chinese data also break down the corporate sector into financial firms and nonfinancial firms. Since the contribution of nonfinancial firms to China's GDP is more than 10 times the

As I will show, considered by each of these four approaches, the Chinese economy became increasingly imbalanced after 2002 or 2003.

The material in this chapter is dry and technical yet important. In economic policy, as in medicine, the prescription is of little value if the diagnosis of the underlying problem is wrong. This saying is especially apt in the case of China because revised economic data require a substantial change in the diagnosis of the nature and causes of the country's economic imbalances. For example, on the basis of data published through the summer of 2010, it appeared that the main reason for the dramatic fall in the consumption share of GDP was that the growth of wages lagged far behind the growth of labor productivity, with the result that the wage share of income had fallen sharply while the share of national income accruing to corporates had soared (Luo and Zhang 2009, 157; Pettis 2011, 3–4). However, new data published in September 2010 show that the wage share of national income has fallen, but only slightly, and that the share of national income accruing to corporates was virtually unchanged.[6]

The Expenditure Approach

In any economy, output growth is the sum of the change in the three basic components of GDP: consumption (both private and government), investment, and net exports of goods and services. Analyzing the relative importance of these three components helps us understand the sources of growth in an economy.

Expanding investment has been a major and increasingly important driver of growth in China. Figure 2.1 shows investment averaged 36 percent of GDP in the first decade or so of economic reform, a share that is high relative to developing countries generally but comparable to China's East Asian neighbors when their investment shares of GDP were at their highest (Lardy 2006). China's average investment rate rose somewhat in the 1990s compared with the 1980s but is still roughly in line with historic high levels seen in newly industrializing economies. But since 2003 investment has consistently exceeded 40 percent of GDP, a level well above even that of China's East Asian neighbors during their periods of highest investment (National Bureau of Statistics of China 2010f, 55). Rising investment has been fueled by a rise in the national saving rate, which reached an unprecedented level of more than 50 percent of GDP in 2006–10.[7] Investment in 2003–10 accounted for an average of 54 percent of China's economic growth, an exceptionally high share by international standards (National Bureau of Statistics of China 2010f, 57).

---

contribution of financial firms, disaggregating the corporate sector into the two components does not provide any additional insights and is not undertaken in this study.

6. See section entitled "Shares in National Income" in appendix A.

7. By definition, the national saving rate is equal to investment as a share of GDP plus the current account as a percent of GDP. In China, these were 42 and 9 percent of GDP, respectively, in 2006.

Figure 2.1   Investment as a share of China's GDP, 1978–2010

percent

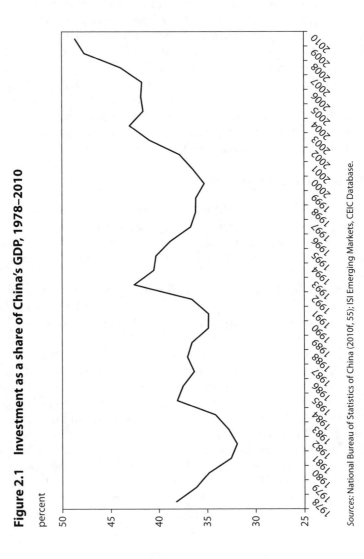

Sources: National Bureau of Statistics of China (2010f, 55); ISI Emerging Markets, CEIC Database.

The growth of both household and government consumption has been rapid in absolute terms throughout the reform period. But in most years, household consumption growth has lagged the underlying growth of the economy, a lag that has become particularly noticeable since about 2002. As shown in figure 2.2, household consumption averaged slightly more than half of GDP in the 1980s. This share fell to an average of 46 percent in the 1990s. Then starting in 2003, household consumption as a share of GDP fell sharply, accounting for only 35 percent of GDP in both 2008 and 2009 (National Bureau of Statistics of China 2010f, 55–56). Preliminary data show a further decline to 34 percent occurred in 2010.[8]

As shown in figure 2.3, there appears to be no strong long-term trend in government consumption as a share of GDP, which has averaged around 14 percent throughout the reform period. But government consumption has declined in recent years, from a peak of 16 percent of GDP in 2001 to less than 13 percent by 2009 (National Bureau of Statistics of China 2010f, 55–56). Preliminary data show an uptick of a few tenths of a percentage point in 2010.[9]

As a result of these trends in household and government consumption, the relative importance of total consumption as a source of growth diminished substantially during the past two decades, particularly when compared with that of investment. In the first half of the 1980s, consumption growth accounted for almost four-fifths of China's economic expansion, whereas from 2003 through 2010 this share averaged barely two-fifths (National Bureau of Statistics of China 2010f, 57).

Beginning in 2005 and continuing through 2008 the growth of net exports of goods and services also became, for the first time in almost a decade, a major source of economic growth. As shown in figure 2.4, compared with $40 billion, or 2.5 percent of GDP, in 2004, net exports of goods and services in 2005 more than doubled to exceed $100 billion, or 5.5 percent of GDP. They more than doubled again in the ensuing two years, reaching $235 billion by 2007, or 8.8 percent of GDP. As a consequence, the contribution of net exports to economic growth increased dramatically, from an average of less than 5 percent (0.35 percentage points of GDP growth) in the four years 2001 through 2004 to an average of almost 20 percent (1.98 percentage points of GDP growth) in 2005–08 (National Bureau of Statistics of China 2010f, 57).

These metrics suggest that China's economy became highly imbalanced starting about 2003. The share of investment in GDP and investment's contribution to economic growth have been quite elevated since 2003. Similarly, China's external surplus during 2005–08 was extremely large, and net exports made an unusually high contribution to China's growth during those years. But the global recession, which led to the sharpest downturn in global trade in

---

8. ISI Emerging Markets, CEIC Database.

9. ISI Emerging Markets, CEIC Database.

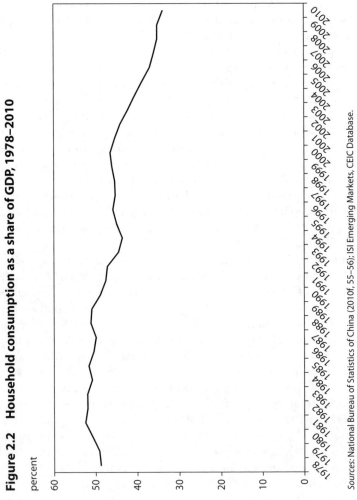

Figure 2.2   Household consumption as a share of GDP, 1978–2010

percent

Sources: National Bureau of Statistics of China (2010f, 55–56); ISI Emerging Markets, CEIC Database.

Figure 2.3　Government consumption as a share of GDP, 1978–2010

percent

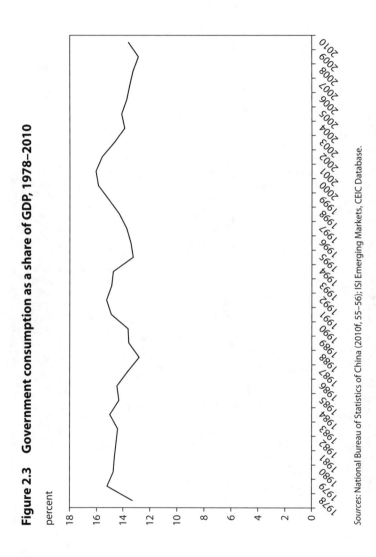

Sources: National Bureau of Statistics of China (2010f, 55–56); ISI Emerging Markets, CEIC Database.

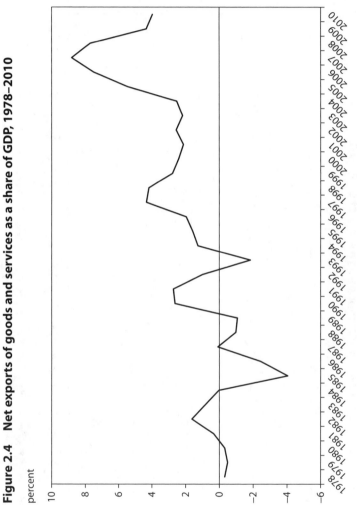

Figure 2.4   Net exports of goods and services as a share of GDP, 1978–2010

percent

Sources: National Bureau of Statistics of China (2010f, 55); ISI Emerging Markets, CEIC Database.

60 years, brought an end to the outsized contribution of net exports to China's growth in 2009.

But the clearest indicator of imbalance in China's economy that emerges from the expenditure approach is the extremely low share of private consumption in GDP. The 34 to 35 percent share of 2008–10 is far and away the lowest share of any major economy in the world. The United States, where household consumption accounted for 70 percent of GDP just prior to the onset of the global financial crisis, was an outlier in the other direction.[10] More typical consumption shares in developed and emerging-market economies are reflected in the 63 percent consumption share in the United Kingdom and the 56 percent share in India, both in 2007.[11]

In the United States the lowest share of private consumption in GDP in the modern era was 50 percent in 1943-44, during World War II.[12] But that was an extremely unusual time in economic terms. Most of the capacity of US firms to produce automobiles, trucks, and other consumer durables had been converted to wartime production of aircraft, tanks, and other military equipment, severely limiting the availability of consumer durables. Most nondurable goods, such as gasoline, food, and clothing, were rationed starting in 1942. Thus the supply of consumer goods, both durables and nondurables, was extremely limited. On the demand side, households, encouraged by patriotic campaigns, purchased large numbers of war bonds, reducing the income available to them for consumption spending. By the end of the war Americans had purchased $186 billion in ten-year war bonds that paid well below market rates of interest. Thus the war bond program both increased household savings as a share of disposable income and reduced household income growth below the trajectory it otherwise would have achieved. After reaching an average of 25 percent of disposable income in 1942-44, the household saving rate fell back into the middle single digits within a few years after the conclusion of the war, roughly where it had been prior to the onset of the Depression.

Implications of China's Expenditure Imbalances

Before analyzing the implications of these imbalances it is important to note an important caveat. Official data on GDP by expenditure published by the National Bureau of Statistics probably underestimate housing services by a few

---

10. US data are available at US Department of Commerce, Bureau of Economic Analysis, National Income and Product Accounts Tables, www.bea.gov (accessed on September 12, 2011).

11. UK data are from UK Statistics Authority, National Statistics, "UK Output, Income and Expenditure—Q4 2007," available at www.statistics.gov.uk (accessed on September 12, 2011). Indian data are from Press Information Bureau, Government of India, "Press Note: Quick Estimates of National Income, Consumption Expenditure, Saving, and Capital Formation, 2006-07," January 31, 2008, available at http://mospi.nic.in (accessed on September 12, 2011).

12. Bureau of Economic Analysis, Table 2.1, Personal Income and Its Disposition, available at www.bea.gov/national/nipaweb/SelectTable (accessed on January 20, 2010).

percentage points of GDP.[13] Since housing services is a component of private household consumption, the underestimation implies that official data also underestimate the consumption share of GDP. But, even after any reasonable upward adjustment, the consumption share of GDP in China would still be very low in comparative terms.[14]

The main implication of the expenditure perspective is that China's imbalanced growth has led to suppressed levels of household expenditure and correspondingly lower levels of household welfare. Between 2002 and 2008 GDP measured in nominal prices grew at an annual rate of 17.3 percent per year. During the same period household consumption, also measured in current prices, grew at an annual rate of 13.2 percent (National Bureau of Statistics of China 2010f, 55–56). If household consumption had grown as rapidly after 2002 as GDP, household consumption by 2008 would have been one-quarter higher than was actually achieved.[15] So the main implication from the expenditure perspective is that imbalanced growth has suppressed Chinese household consumption by a fifth compared with what would have been achieved via a more balanced growth strategy.[16]

The Production Approach

The imbalanced character of China's economic growth is also evident in the structure of production. The evolution of the shares of agriculture, industry, and services in China's GDP is shown in figure 2.5. When economic reform began in China in 1978 the share of agriculture in total output was about 30 percent. Through the mid-1980s agricultural output surged as the rural communal production structure was dismantled and political constraints on marketing and other distortions of the Cultural Revolution era were lifted (Lardy 1978). As a result the growth of agriculture no longer lagged that of other sectors, and its share in GDP remained at just under a third. But, as the easy output gains in agricultural growth were exhausted by mid-decade,

---

13. See appendix A for a more detailed analysis.

14. If housing services are underestimated, that means both GDP and consumption are underestimated. So if the magnitude of housing services in 2009 was revised upward by 3 percentage points of GDP, the consumption share of GDP would be revised upward by only about 2 percentage points, from 35.1 to 37.0 percent (37.0 = (35.1 + 3)/103). It would take an upward revision of housing services by 30 percentage points of GDP to make the household consumption share of GDP equal to 50 percent, the share last recorded in 1989. This demonstrates that the undercount of housing services can't possibly be more than a minor contributor to China's extraordinarily low share of private consumption in GDP.

15. As can be seen in figure 2.2 the decline in the consumption share of GDP between 2002 and 2008 was almost linear. Thus it is the case that under the alternative scenario consumption in every year during that period would have been one-quarter higher than was actually achieved.

16. The implicit assumption is that the growth of GDP would not have been slower under a more balanced growth strategy.

Figure 2.5   Agriculture, industry, and services as a share of GDP, 1978–2010

percent

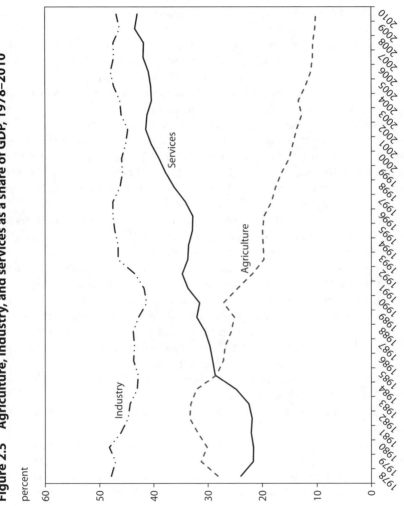

Sources: National Bureau of Statistics of China (2010f, 39); ISI Emerging Markets, CEIC Database.

agricultural expansion lagged and the share of agriculture in GDP began a gradual decline, reducing its share to just 10 percent by 2010 (National Bureau of Statistics of China 2011c). This path of decline in the share of agriculture in China's economy is typical as a developing economy reaches higher and higher levels of per capita GDP.

However, the evolution of the shares of industry and services in China has not been so typical.[17] China's industrial sector is larger than would be expected in a country at China's level of economic development, while its services sector is unusually small. The relatively high share of industry reflects the emphasis on manufacturing development that characterized the era of economic planning from the 1950s until the beginning of the reform period. Thus on the eve of reform in 1978 the industry share of GDP was 48 percent. Services, as in other planned, socialist economies, were undervalued, and their share of GDP on the eve of reform was quite depressed at just under one-quarter.

As market forces became more important in the 1980s and the 1990s, the share of services in the economy grew while the share of industry shrank. The services share of GDP reached a peak of 41.5 percent by 2002; industry's share gained in the first half of the 1990s and then ebbed for the balance of the decade and the first two years of the 2000s. The share of agriculture, as already noted, began a long-term steady decline after the mid-1980s.

However, in the 2000s the growth pattern changed in certain critical respects. Most importantly the services share of GDP, after steadily advancing for two decades, essentially stagnated. Its 43.0 percent share in 2010 was only 1.5 percentage points above that in 2002. Thus in the 2000s China was a conspicuous exception to the commonly observed pattern among low- and middle-income economies, in which a rising share of services in total output coincides with sustained growth. A second change was that the manufacturing share of GDP rose after 2002 reaching a peak of 48 percent in 2006, the same highly elevated level prevailing in 1978 on the eve of reform. By 2010 its share had declined by only a fraction to 47 percent.

Given these developments in the 2000s it is not surprising to find that China is an outlier in three respects compared with other countries at similar levels of per capita income. First, China's share of services in GDP is quite low. The average share of services in GDP in 2008 in other emerging markets at comparable levels of per capita GDP was 54 percent, compared with 41.8 percent for China.[18] Second, the share of employment in services in China is "significantly below the level suggested by international experiences, after taking into account China's state of development and other fundamentals" (Guo and

---

17. The Chinese data on industry in this chapter, except in note 19, are inclusive of manufacturing, mining, utilities, and construction.

18. The comparison is with the average share of services in GDP in all middle-income countries as measured by purchasing power parity per capita income. Data on shares of GDP in countries at comparable levels of development are from World Bank, *World Development Indicators*, available at http://databank.worldbank.org (accessed on May 8, 2011).

N'Diaye 2011, 112). Third, the share of GDP originating in manufacturing is half again as high as other countries at comparable levels of development.[19]

Implications of Production Imbalances

The key implication is that there must be some underlying distortion or distortions causing China's pattern of production to diverge so substantially from expectations. Two potential distortions might explain the unusual pattern of change in the structure of output in China after 2002. First, as will be discussed further in chapter 3, China's exchange rate became increasingly undervalued after February 2002. From the mid-1990s to mid-2005 the Chinese currency was pegged to the US dollar. In the first half of this period, through 2001, the dollar appreciated on a trade-weighted basis and thus the renminbi also appreciated in effective terms, by about 3.5 percent per year. During these years there was no trend in China's current account surplus, which averaged a relatively modest surplus of about 2 percent of GDP.

This combination—continuous appreciation of the renminbi and an external surplus that is both relatively small and shows no upward or downward trend—provides substantial support for the view that China has experienced substantially greater productivity growth in the production of tradable goods than in the production of nontradable goods, i.e., the Balassa-Samuelson effect. Conventionally calculated real exchange rates utilize broad price indices to adjust for relative changes in prices in different countries. But when the Balassa-Samuelson effect is present in the country for which the real exchange rate is being measured, these relative price adjustments will be somewhat misleading. For example, assume broadly measured price inflation in China is 2 percent while prices in its trading partners are rising by an average of 5 percent. To make the illustration simple, assume that the nominal value of the renminbi is stable vis-à-vis the currencies of all of China's trading partners. Then the inflation differential would imply that Chinese goods are becoming 3 percent per year cheaper relative to foreign goods, i.e., on a real basis the Chinese currency is depreciating by 3 percent per year. But if China's headline inflation rate of 2 percent is the result of 3 percent inflation for nontradables, such as services, while, because of high productivity growth in manufacturing, the prices of tradables are falling by 1 percent per year, then Chinese goods in international markets are becoming 6 percent per year cheaper relative to foreign goods. Thus the conventionally calculated real exchange rate based on broad price indices, which would show the renminbi in real terms depreciating

---

19. In China manufacturing accounted for 33 percent of GDP. The average for all middle-income countries as measured by purchasing power parity was 21.2 percent. This definition of manufacturing differs from the concept of industry reflected in figure 2.5 and used elsewhere in this chapter. It excludes construction as well as mining and utilities. Data for the average of countries at comparable levels of development are from World Bank, *World Development Indicators*, available at http://databank.worldbank.org (accessed on June 10, 2011).

at 3 percent per year, would substantially understate the pace at which Chinese goods were becoming more competitive in global markets.

The conclusion is that the rate of appreciation of the real, trade-weighted exchange rate of the renminbi of about 3.5 percent roughly offsets the extent to which China's differential productivity growth in the production of tradable goods exceeded that of its trading partners. Absent this real trade-weighted appreciation of the renminbi, Chinese goods would have become increasingly competitive in global markets and China's external surplus would have exhibited a significant rise. Thus, as will be argued in chapter 3, the real effective exchange rate of the renminbi from the mid-1990s through 2001 should be regarded as an equilibrium exchange rate.

But after February 2002 the US dollar began a long period of sustained depreciation on a real, trade-weighted basis. Because China maintained its fixed exchange rate to the dollar, the renminbi also depreciated on a real, trade-weighted basis and its current account began to rise steadily, reaching an unprecedented (for a large economy) peak surplus of 10.1 percent of GDP in 2007. An undervalued currency boosts the profits both of firms that produce exports and of firms that produce goods that compete with imports in the domestic market. Exporters receive more units of domestic currency for each dollar's worth of products sold in international markets so that, ceteris paribus, producers of export goods will have more funds left over, i.e., profits, after paying for their labor and other inputs. Thus an undervalued currency increases the profits associated with producing for the export market. Similarly, when a country's currency is undervalued, would-be importers of goods from abroad will have to pay more in terms of domestic currency for each dollar's worth of imports. This means undervaluation gives scope for domestic producers of goods that compete with imports to raise their prices, again increasing their profits. For this reason it is said that an undervalued currency tends to increase the profits in the tradable goods sector (i.e., firms producing exports and domestic goods that compete with imports).

This theoretical possibility seems to be strongly borne out in China's official data on industrial profits. China's industrial sector accounts for 95 percent of China's exports and 70 percent of domestic goods that compete with imports (National Bureau of Statistics of China 2010e, 67). Profits in manufacturing soared from RMB470 billion, or 4.2 percent of GDP, in 2002 to RMB3.45 trillion, or 10.1 percent of GDP, in 2009 (National Bureau of Statistics of China 2005, 493–94; 2009b, 38, 507).[20]

Because China is predominantly a market economy, in which profit-oriented firms respond strongly to economic incentives, the undervaluation of the renminbi and the resulting increase in the profitability of producing manufactures (generally tradable goods) contributed to an increase in the share of

---

20. These data are for industrial enterprises with annual sales over RMB5 million. Profits of industrial firms also rose from 1998 through 2001 but most of these gains are attributable to restructuring of state-owned firms, including the closure of many loss-making companies.

investment flowing into manufacturing and a decline in the share flowing to services (generally nontradable goods). As analyzed in chapter 5, between 2003 and 2010 the former share rose by 8 percentage points of GDP and the latter share declined by 6 percentage points of GDP.

In short, while it is natural to think of a country's exchange rate as a very important variable influencing trade flows, it is important to recognize that this is true only because the exchange rate is one of the most important prices influencing resource allocation in the domestic market. Through its effect on prices, an undervalued exchange rate artificially raises profitability in the tradable goods sector, which for China overwhelmingly means manufactured goods, and reduces profits in the nontradable goods sector, i.e., services.

Domestic factor prices are a second distortion contributing to the relative stagnation of the services sector and the continued highly elevated share of the manufacturing sector in China's economy. China has had an asymmetric market liberalization process in which the prices of almost all goods now are set by supply and demand in the market but the state has retained control of the pricing of a few key factors of production, such as capital, land, energy, and environmental charges. As will be discussed in chapter 3, since these factor inputs are used disproportionately in manufacturing and are generally underpriced, the state effectively bestows subsidies toward the production of tradable goods (Huang and Tao 2010). Thus the state's price policy further tilts investment toward manufacturing and away from services, contributing to the unusual production structure emerging in China in the 2000s.

Another key implication of the imbalanced production structure that emerged in China after 2002 was slowing growth of employment. The services sector is generally more labor intensive, whereas manufacturing is generally less labor intensive. As analyzed in chapter 3, as the services sector share of GDP stagnated after 2002, the growth of employment slowed. This effect is perhaps a contributor to one of the imbalances that emerges in the income approach, discussed in the next section.

The Income Approach

The third approach to measuring economic imbalances is to examine the shares of national income accruing to households, corporations, and the government. Two types of data derived from China's national income accounts shed light on this division.

The first is data on employee compensation, the operating surplus of enterprises, depreciation of fixed assets, and net taxes on production. Employee compensation is the share of output accruing to labor; the operating surplus and depreciation combined make up the share of output accruing to corporations; and net taxes are the share of output accruing to the government. These data, which are available for 1993–2009, show that labor compensation was a fairly constant 50 percent of national income in the 1990s but subsequently fell slightly, to 47 percent, by 2009.[21] The share of national income accruing to the government in the form of net taxes rose from 12 percent in 1993 to 15 percent in 2009, while the share accruing to corporations fell very slightly, from 39 percent in 1993 to 38 percent in 2009.[22]

It is important to note that this summary is based on a revision in the treatment of the income of the self-employed, discussed in detail in appendix A to this book. Prior to the revision the data showed that there had been a decline in the labor share of income of 10 percentage points of GDP and a 7 percentage point increase in the share accruing to the corporate sector (Ma and Yi 2010, 16–17). The revisions did not significantly affect the share of income accruing to the government.

Similar trends in the share of output accruing to labor, corporations, and the government are reflected in the flow of funds data, which also are derived from the national income accounts but which use a somewhat different income classification scheme. These data are available for the years 1992 through 2008 and, as summarized in table 2.1, show labor compensation declining by 5 percentage points. But the flow of funds also provides other information that allows one to trace the adjustments necessary to get from labor compensation to disposable income, which is simply labor compensation plus property income and net transfers less taxes levied on households. An important starting point to understanding the evolution of household consumption as a share of GDP is disposable income. As reflected in figure 2.6, household disposable income, which stood at 67 percent of GDP in 1992, had fallen to only 58 percent of GDP by 2008, with most of the decline taking place in the 2000s rather than in the 1990s.

Disaggregating the components of disposable income allows us to explain why its share of national income fell so dramatically. A little more than half of the decline can be explained by the fall in the wage share of GDP, as reflected in the flow of funds accounts. About a fifth of the decline is due to a fall in property income (overwhelmingly interest income) as a share of GDP. And another fifth is due to decline in net transfer payments to households as a share of GDP.[23]

Implications of the Income Imbalance

The main implication of the imbalances revealed by the income approach is that the decline in consumption as a share of GDP revealed in the expenditure approach to imbalances is primarily due to falling household disposable income

---

21. Employee compensation includes wages and benefits, including employers' contributions to social insurance funds, and the operating surplus of self-employed individuals.

22. Net taxes are taxes on production less subsidies on production. The share of national income accruing to corporations includes both the operating surpluses of firms and depreciation of fixed assets.

23. A minuscule 2 percent of the decline was due to a slight increase in taxes levied on households.

Table 2.1 Flow of funds summary, 1992–2008 (percent of GDP)

Year	Labor compensation	Production taxes paid by households	Household property income	Net government transfers to households	Household disposable income	Household consumption	Household savings
1992	61.8	1.5	4.3	2.4	66.9	47.2	19.8
2008	56.8	1.7	2.4	0.5	57.9	35.1	22.8
Change	−5.0	0.2	−1.9	−1.9	−9.0	−12.0	3.0

Memo items:

Share of decline in the consumption share due to:
(a) Decline in disposable income: 75 percent
(b) Rise in household savings: 25 percent

Share of decline in disposable income due to:
(a) Fall in labor compensation: 56 percent
(b) Rising taxes: 2 percent
(c) Declining property income: 21 percent
(d) Declining government transfers: 21 percent

Sources: National Bureau of Statistics of China (2010f, 74–83); ISI Emerging Markets, CEIC Database.

Figure 2.6 Household disposable income as a share of GDP, 1992–2008

percent

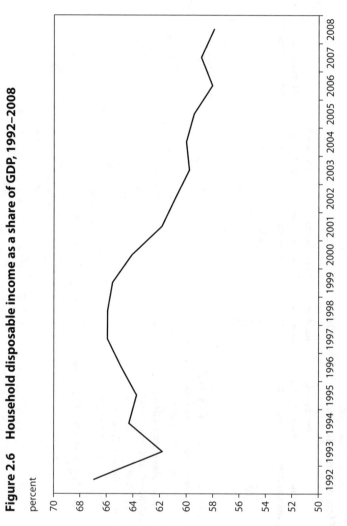

Sources: National Bureau of Statistics of China (2010f, 74–83); ISI Emerging Markets, CEIC Database.

as a share of GDP rather than rising household savings from disposable income. The former factor accounts for about three-quarters of the fall in the consumption share of GDP, the latter factor for only about one-quarter of the fall.

A second implication is that it will be important to understand why interest income fell so sharply over a period when the stock of household savings relative to GDP was increasing. This issue is taken up in chapter 3.

Similarly, the data also imply that to understand the decline in consumption as a share of GDP, we need to understand why net transfer payments to households have fallen by about 2 percentage points of GDP. Particularly in light of the emphasis of President Hu Jintao and Premier Wen Jiabao on creating a "more harmonious society" characterized by reduced economic insecurity, it is worth noting that a substantial portion of the decline in net transfer payments occurred since they came into office.[24]

The Savings-Investment Approach

Analytically the best approach to explaining China's external imbalance is to look at the difference between national savings and investment. When national savings exceed (are less than) national investment a country will be running a current account surplus (deficit). Again the flow of funds provides the data that allow us to look at the evolution of both savings and investment for the three sectors of the economy—the government, corporations, and households. The averages of these data for 1998–2002 and 2007–08 are shown in table 2.2. During the first period China experienced what might be regarded as balanced growth: The exchange rate, measured on a real, effective basis, appreciated steadily and China's average external imbalance was modest (see figure 3.5 in chapter 3); central bank intervention in the foreign exchange market was modest, as reflected in a relatively slow growth of official reserves (see figure 3.4); investment as a share of GDP was high but not superelevated; household consumption as a share of GDP was stable; government consumption as a share of GDP was rising; and the services share of GDP was expanding. In the second period China's growth was quite imbalanced, reflecting developments starting in 2003: The real, trade-weighted value of the currency first depreciated sharply and then (beginning in mid-2005) appreciated gradually, but for the period as a whole (from early 2002 through the end of 2008) it was essentially unchanged, and the external imbalance rose to a record high; central bank intervention in the foreign exchange market was massive and official foreign exchange reserves rose to levels unprecedented for any country; investment rose to superelevated levels while consumption fell to depressed levels; and the share of the services sector stagnated.

---

24. Hu Jintao appears to have first used the phrase "harmonious society" in the fall of 2004. Hu Jintao, speech at the Meeting Celebrating the 55th Anniversary of the Founding of the Chinese People's Political Consultative Conference, September 22, 2004, available at www.people.com.cn (accessed on September 12, 2011).

Table 2.2   Savings and investment balance by component, 1998–2002 and 2007–08 (percent of GDP)

Component	1998–2002	2007–08	Change
Gross capital formation	36.6	42.9	6.3
Households	8.0	8.7	0.7
Enterprises	25.5	29.6	4.1
Government	3.1	4.6	1.5
Gross domestic saving	38.1	52.8	14.7
Households	18.5	22.9	4.4
Enterprises	15.9	21.3	5.3
Government	3.7	8.6	4.9
Savings-investment balance	1.5	9.9	8.4
Households	10.5	14.2	3.7
Enterprises	−9.6	−8.3	1.2
Government	0.6	4.0	3.4

Source: ISI Emerging Markets, CEIC Database.

The data in table 2.2 show that by 2007–08 China's national saving rate reached the extraordinarily high average level of 53 percent of GDP, an increase of almost 15 percentage points compared with the average level of national savings during 1998–2002. Though already high by international standards in the period 1998–2002, investment rose by more than 6 percentage points by 2007–08. So the increase in the surplus of savings over investment rose by 8 percentage points. Thus China's current account surplus with the rest of the world rose by 8.4 percentage points of GDP, reaching an average of 9.9 percent of GDP in 2007–08.[25]

Equally important, table 2.2 allows us to examine more closely the sources of the increase in the national savings-investment imbalance between 1998–2002 and 2007–08. Household savings increased by more than 4 percentage points of GDP, while household investment rose by less than a point. So the household savings-investment imbalance increased by 3.7 percentage points of GDP and accounted for over two-fifths of the increase in the national savings-investment imbalance between the two periods. Corporate-sector savings rose sharply but investment rose almost as much. In the base period the corporate sector invested much more than it saved, so these changes meant the negative corporate savings-investment imbalance became slightly smaller between the two periods. Thus the corporate-sector savings-investment imbalance increased by only 1.2 percent of GDP and accounted for only about a seventh of the increase in the national savings-investment imbalance. Government savings increased sharply between the two periods, while investment rose much less. Thus the government savings-investment imbalance increased by 3.4 percent of GDP

---

25. The officially reported current account surplus in 2007 and 2008 is 10.1 and 9.1 percent of GDP, respectively. Their average, 9.6 percent, is not exactly equal to the calculated Chinese surplus shown in table 2.2 because of various statistical discrepancies.

and accounted for two-fifths of the increased national imbalance between the two periods.

Implications of the Savings-Investment Approach

Several points emerge from the above analysis. First, China's extremely large savings-investment imbalance and external surplus in 2007–08 cannot be attributed primarily to the emergence of a large imbalance in a single sector of the economy. Rather every sector added to the savings-investment imbalance.

Second, this approach leads to conclusions that are quite different from analysis that focuses only on the changes in the saving rate in various sectors over time, ignoring what has happened to investment within the sectors. For example, the corporate sector is correctly identified in many studies as the major contributor to the long-term rise in China's national saving rate (Anderson 2006; Ma and Yi 2010, 11). But this is not the same as saying that the corporate sector is the major contributor to the large national savings-investment imbalance that emerged by 2007–08. Corporate savings did rise but, as shown in table 2.2, corporate investment also rose sharply, so the share of the increase in the national savings-investment imbalance originating in the corporate sector was very modest.

Third, it is somewhat surprising to find that, between the two periods, the government was almost as important a contributor to the rise in the national savings-investment imbalance as the household sector. Stephen Green (2009a, 2009b, 2009c) was the first to draw attention to the remarkable increase in government savings and the government's growing savings-investment imbalance. He points out that reported government budgetary revenues have grown more rapidly than GDP since the mid-1990s. And on-budget revenues understate the flow of resources to the government. Most importantly, the Chinese government budget revenue excludes income from land leases and sales, which amounted to RMB454 billion, or 1.7 percent of GDP, in 2007 but, as will be pointed out in chapter 4, exploded to reach RMB2.9 trillion, or 7.3 percent of GDP, in 2010 (National Bureau of Statistics of China 2010f, 80–81; Ministry of Finance 2011). Government budgetary revenues also exclude social insurance receipts, income from the national lottery, and many other sources.[26] All of these revenues, however, are included in the flow of funds data that underlie the data in table 2.2. These data show government revenues of all types rose by 3 percentage points of GDP between 1998–2002 and 2007–08.

On the other hand, government consumption expenditures declined by 2 percentage points of GDP over the same period. The difference between total revenues, including off-budget revenues, and government consumption is government savings, which rose by 5 percentage points of GDP. Increased

---

26. These receipts were to have been brought into the state budget in 2010, but the presentations by the minister of finance to the National People's Congress show these funds are being administered in separate channels from the budget.

government investment absorbed only a part of this rise in government savings, thus the emergence of a large savings-investment surplus on the part of the government. In part this surplus shows up in the form of the government's ever growing treasury deposits in the banking system. By the end of 2010 these deposits had reached RMB2.5 trillion, or 6.4 percent of GDP. The size of these deposits is initially somewhat surprising, since the government's official budget usually records a modest deficit financed by the issuance of treasury bonds.

But the treasury account includes the surplus social insurance funds administered by the Ministry of Human Resources and Social Security. These amounted to RMB2.3 trillion at year-end 2010 and thus accounted for 90 percent of year-end fiscal deposits (National Bureau of Statistics of China 2010f, 909).[27] This buildup of surplus social security funds largely reflects the government's effort to build up the social safety net, particularly the provision of pensions.[28] As will be analyzed in chapter 3, the number of workers covered by basic pension insurance has grown dramatically over the last decade.[29] On the other hand, the number of retirees drawing pensions has grown more slowly, since the number of retirees eligible for pensions today is a function of the more limited coverage of the basic pension insurance scheme in previous decades. Between 2002 and 2008 the number of workers covered by and thus paying into China's basic pension insurance scheme increased by 55 million, while the number of retirees drawing pensions rose by only 17 million (National Bureau of Statistics of China 2010f, 910). Thus the growth of employee and employer contributions to the national social security fund has tended to exceed the increase in payouts to retirees.[30]

However, most assessments of China's retirement program conclude that to date the buildup of the social insurance surplus is grossly inadequate to fund future retirements, particularly when the working-age population declines by 80 million between 2025 and 2035 (Jackson, Nakashima, and Howe 2009, 2).

---

27. Other pension assets are in the National Pension Fund, which is administered separately by the National Social Security Fund Council. By year-end 2010 the assets of the National Pension Fund were RMB856 billion. Only about 2 percent of these assets were held in the form of bank deposits. These funds too probably are also included in the fiscal deposits of the banking system. See National Social Security Fund Council (2011a).

28. The surplus in the basic pension insurance program accounts for two-thirds of the total surplus in China's social insurance funds.

29. In addition to the basic pension program there are separate pension schemes for the military, for civil servants working for government departments and agencies, and for state-run institutions such as schools, hospitals, and so forth. In 2007 12 million civil servants were drawing pensions, one-fourth the number drawing pensions from the basic pension scheme (Frazier 2010, 2).

30. But the difference was not as great as the increases in the number of workers covered and the number of retirees would suggest because the system remains largely pay as you go, meaning that most contributions are used to pay pensions of those already retired rather than used to build up surpluses to pay future retirees.

The central government has been allocating fiscal funds to support insolvent provincial-level pension schemes since the late 1990s and also has provided funds to the National Social Security Fund, established in 2002 as a fund of last resort (Frazier 2010, 59, 64). By 2010 fiscal contributions to the National Social Security Fund Council, which administers the National Social Security Fund, and to the Ministry of Human Resources and Social Security, which oversees the pension schemes at the local level, reached RMB63.4 billion and RMB156 billion, respectively (National Social Security Fund Council 2011b, Ministry of Finance 2011). The basic conclusion is that the government is certain to be a net saver going forward if for no other reason than to maintain the solvency of the social insurance funds.

All four approaches to examining the structure of the Chinese economy, as it emerged after 2003, confirm the judgment of Premier Wen that the economy is highly imbalanced and that growth is not sustainable on the current economic model. The expenditure approach shows that investment has been superelevated since 2003 while the share of consumption has fallen to unusually low levels. The production approach shows that the services share of output stagnated after 2002 and is now substantially below the level of other emerging markets at comparable levels of development, while the manufacturing sector, which is the source of almost all of China's exports and a very large share of the goods that compete with imports, accounts for an unusually large share of GDP. The income approach shows that household disposable income declined by almost 10 percentage points of GDP between 1992 and 2008 and explains about three-quarters of the decline in the consumption share of GDP. The other quarter is explained by the rise in the household rate of saving from disposable income. The analysis also shows that only half of the decline in disposable income as a share of GDP can be accounted for by a decline in the wage share of GDP; the combined decline in interest income and in net transfer payments from the government to households were equally important.

The four different approaches to examining the structure of China's economy provide the framework for examining policies to reduce economic imbalances, the subject of chapter 3.

3

Policies for Rebalancing Economic Growth

As early as December 2004, China's top political leadership embraced the goal of rebalancing the sources of domestic economic growth. They envision over time transitioning to a growth path that relies more on expanding domestic consumption and less on burgeoning investment and a growing trade surplus (Lardy 2006). Expanding private consumption and providing more social services via government-financed programs is consistent with President Hu Jintao's emphasis on creating a "harmonious society" and a "new socialist countryside." It is also consistent with the leadership's goal of reducing the pace of growth of energy consumption (associated strongly with investment spending), thus curtailing emissions of greenhouse gases and sulfur dioxide.

The aftermath of the global financial and economic crisis has underlined the centrality of the economic rebalancing agenda first adopted in 2004. Although the recession in the United States officially ended in June 2009, the pace of recovery has been quite weak relative to most earlier, postwar recessions. The most cogent explanation is that recovery from a recession induced by a financial crisis is more protracted, as unwinding of the debts accumulated in the boom leading to the crisis means that demand recovers only slowly (Reinhart and Rogoff 2009, McKinsey Global Institute 2010). Europe's recovery has been similarly weak and the prospects in the near term for returning to the precrisis pace of growth quite dim, in view of the need for many euro area countries to significantly reduce government fiscal deficits in order to bring down the magnitude of their sovereign debt to sustainable levels. In this global environment the possibility that China's exports over the next few years can grow at anything like the pace of the previous decade is quite limited.

Successful rebalancing of the sources of economic growth, away from investment and exports and toward consumption, would also lead to changes in the structure of production. Since investment goods, such as machinery and equipment, are produced in the industrial sector, a smaller role for investment in generating economic growth would imply that, over time, the share of GDP originating in the manufacturing sector would be reduced compared with the "business as usual" investment-driven growth model. Similarly, since almost all of China's exports are manufactured goods, less reliance on the expansion of net exports would also imply over time that the share of GDP originating in the manufacturing sector would be reduced compared with the existing export-driven growth model.[1] Since services account for about a third of personal consumption outlays, an increasing role for consumption in generating economic growth implies that the share of GDP originating in the services sector would increase over time as compared with an investment- and export-driven growth path.[2]

Finally, rebalancing would have important implications for the shares of national income accruing to households, corporations, and the government. Based on the analysis of China's flow of funds data in chapter 2, raising household consumption as a share of GDP depends primarily on increasing the share of national income accruing to households. Greater provision of social services by the government depends primarily on increasing the share of national income accruing to the government. Obviously, these changes will require a reduction in the share of national income in the hands of corporations.

Given the complex origins of the economic imbalances analyzed in chapter 2, this chapter advocates a comprehensive policy approach to transitioning to a new growth model in which domestic consumption demand becomes an increasingly important source of economic growth. The authorities should not rely exclusively on one or two policy instruments but rather on multiple policies in order to increase the prospects of reducing economic imbalances and achieving more sustainable growth on a timely basis. This chapter focuses initially on four potential policy domains—fiscal, financial, exchange rate, and price policy; it sketches out the mechanisms through which the sources of economic growth in China might be rebalanced and analyzes the extent to which authorities have actually pursued these potential policies in recent years. The final part of the chapter analyzes whether various underlying endogenous, structural changes that are occurring in the economy and what might be called "policy light" approaches might also contribute importantly to the economic rebalancing objective.

Fiscal Policy

Fiscal policy options to promote economic rebalancing include cutting personal taxes, increasing government consumption expenditures (i.e., outlays

---

1. Manufactured goods accounted for 95 percent of China's exports in 2009 (National Bureau of Statistics of China 2010e, 67).

2. The estimate of the services share in household consumption expenditures is based on urban and rural household surveys conducted annually by the National Bureau of Statistics of China.

for health, education, welfare, and pensions), and increasing dividends paid by state-owned companies to their owner, the state. Cutting personal taxes would directly raise household disposable income and thus, for any given household saving rate, increase consumption expenditure as well. Increasing government consumption expenditures would both increase consumption demand directly and, by reducing household precautionary demand for savings, lead indirectly to an increase in private consumption expenditure. Increased taxes on the corporate sector, whether through an increase in the dividends this sector pays or through other means, would reduce corporate savings and, for any given level of corporate investment, reduce the national savings-investment imbalance—and thus reduce China's external surplus. Simultaneously, increased corporate tax payments would provide additional budgetary revenues to finance larger government outlays on social programs.

The potential contribution of expanded government outlays on social services to reducing imbalances is most easily demonstrated by examining the changing role of individual out-of-pocket expenses as a share in total health care outlays. In the early years of reform the government and state-owned enterprises covered most health care costs; only about a fifth was absorbed by households on an out-of-pocket basis. By the early 1990s the personal contribution to total health care outlays rose to about a third, as state-owned enterprises struggled to maintain profitability and the government contribution also fell. After the aggressive restructuring, downsizing, and bankruptcy of many state-owned corporations in the mid-1990s, the personal share of health care outlays grew rapidly, reaching a peak of 59 to 60 percent in 2000–2001 (National Bureau of Statistics of China 2010f, 875). Similarly, China's household survey data show that the share of health and education expenditures in household spending rose sharply, from 2 percent in 1995 to 14 percent by 2005 (Chamon and Prasad 2008, 5). Part of the increase in household savings as a share of disposable income in the last decade probably reflected the desire of families to build up savings to cover these expenses. Thus according to some estimates, reducing the share of health care expenditures financed on an out-of-pocket basis would substantially reduce urban household savings (Barnett and Brooks 2011).

In the fiscal arena the government has adopted a number of tax and expenditure policies to support increased private consumption expenditures. The authorities reduced the agricultural tax significantly in both 2004 and 2005 and eliminated it entirely by 2007.[3] The State Council doubled the monthly income exempt from the personal income tax levied on wages from RMB800

---

3. The revenue category "agricultural and related taxes" actually includes six specific taxes: agricultural tax, livestock tax, farmland occupancy tax, tax on special agricultural products, deed tax, and tobacco leaf tax. The reforms of 2004–06 eliminated the agricultural tax, the livestock tax, and the tax on special agricultural products. Contrary to widespread assertions in secondary sources that all agricultural taxes have been eliminated, the government continues to collect the other three taxes.

to RMB1,600 in 2006, raised the exemption to RMB2,000 in 2008, and raised it again, to RMB3,500, in 2011. The authorities cut by three-quarters the tax on interest income earned by households on savings deposits, from 20 to 5 percent, in August 2007 and then abolished it entirely in October 2008. Through 2008 these cuts combined raised household disposable income by about 1 percent of GDP per year above the level it would otherwise have attained, contributing modestly to higher levels of household consumption than would otherwise have been achieved (Bergsten et al. 2008, 121). The increase in the exemption to RMB3,500 in 2011 further reduced the tax burden on wage earners by an additional RMB160 billion, less than one-half of 1 percent of estimated 2011 GDP.[4]

These tax reductions are very modest because the potential to adjust direct taxes, such as the agricultural tax and the personal income tax, to promote economic rebalancing is quite limited. China's Ministry of Finance (MOF) relies very heavily on indirect taxes, such as the value-added tax, rather than direct taxes, to finance government expenditures. The entire proceeds from the personal income tax in 2008 were RMB372 billion, only 1 percent of GDP (National Bureau of Statistics of China 2010f, 287). Given the rising income threshold at which the tax kicks in, in 2008 and 2010 only 26 and 28 percent, respectively, of wage earners paid personal income tax.[5] After the income tax threshold was raised to RMB3,500 per month in 2011, only 7.7 percent of wage earners were required to pay the tax. Effectively this latest reform exempts the second- and third-highest deciles of wage earners from paying the personal income tax. Because the saving rate of these high-income individuals is quite high, the increase in the threshold for the income tax to RMB3,500 per month likely will not contribute much to increasing consumption, and it has the added cost that it undermines the government's use of the income tax to redistribute income and thus reduce inequality.

On the other hand, there is substantial potential to reduce individual contributions to social insurance funds.[6] At present, contribution rates to retirement and other insurance programs by individuals in the formal sector are relatively high and cover almost all wage earners in the formal sector. By contrast the income tax falls only on a relatively small number of the highest wage earners. The result is that in recent years the combined contributions of individuals and firms to these funds have been three to four times the amount that wage earners pay in income taxes (National Bureau of Statistics of China 2010f, 74–83). Individual contributions to these funds could be reduced and

---

4. Wang Xing, "Income Tax Threshold in Surprise Increase," *China Daily*, July 1–3, 2011, 2.

5. "China Cuts Taxes for Low Earners Amid High Inflation," *Wall Street Journal*, June 30, 2011, available at www.wsj.com (accessed on July 6, 2011).

6. There are five insurance schemes funded by a combination of employee and employer contributions: basic retirement, medical insurance, unemployment insurance, workers' compensation insurance, and maternity insurance.

the funds replaced with increased dividends paid by large state-owned firms. This would directly increase individual disposable income without jeopardizing the funding of China's retirement system and other social insurance programs.

Adjustments to taxes paid by corporations offer another policy option for rebalancing the sources of growth. The profits of nonfinancial state-owned companies, particularly those in sectors where entry of private firms is restricted and results in abnormally high profits, have soared over the past decade. The profits of state-owned companies were RMB21 billion, or 0.3 percent of GDP, in 1998 but by 2010 had soared to RMB1,987 billion, or 5 percent of GDP (World Bank 2009).[7] A disproportionately large share of these profits accrues to the central state-owned enterprises that are managed by the State-Owned Assets Supervision and Administration Commission (SASAC).[8] These companies pay corporate income taxes but in many cases have paid little in dividends, even as their profits and after-tax income have soared.[9]

After several years of debate, the State Council approved a dividend policy for state-owned firms in 2007. It set dividend rates at 10, 5, and 0 percent on the after-tax profits earned in 2006, with the rate depending on firm profitability. Highly profitable state-owned companies in the petroleum, electric power, and telecommunications sector were slated to pay the 10 percent rate; firms in less profitable sectors such as steel, transportation, electronics, trade, and construction industries were pegged at the 5 percent rate; and a few firms, primarily in the military industry, were to be exempt from the tax for an initial three-year period. The targeted firms were central state-owned enterprises under the jurisdiction of SASAC. The government began to collect dividends in 2007.

---

7. See also "Profits of State-Owned Enterprises Last Year Reached Almost RMB2 Trillion; This Important Indicator of Economic Efficiency Reaches a New High," State-Owned Assets Supervision and Administration Commission, January 18, 2011, available at www.sasac.gov.cn (accessed on May 2, 2011).

8. The firms controlled by SASAC in 2008 generated profits of RMB638 billion out of total profits of state-owned firms of RMB1,184 billion. These figures are for nonfinancial corporations, i.e., they exclude banks, securities firms, insurance companies, etc., many of which are state owned, and they include the profits of both traditional state-owned companies and state-controlled shareholding corporations. Not all centrally owned enterprises are controlled by SASAC. In 2008 profits of central government enterprises not managed by SASAC were RMB187.75 billion. "Profits of State-Owned Companies Rise Continuously for Five Months," State-Owned Assets Supervision and Administration Commission, January 23, 2009, available at www.sasac.gov.cn (accessed on April 15, 2011).

9. A few of the state-controlled shareholding firms managed by SASAC are not 100 percent owned by SASAC. These firms have paid dividends, as determined by their shareholders' general assembly, and the state has received dividends from these firms based on the number of shares owned. For example, in 2007 SASAC managed 159 central state-owned companies, of which 8 were not included in the dividend program because they were not 100 percent owned by SASAC and their dividend payments were established following the provisions of the Company Law (World Bank 2009, 5).

However, three factors have undermined the potential of the dividend policy to contribute to economic rebalancing. First, because the number of firms required to pay dividends was so small and the dividend rates so low, dividends paid in the first three years were very modest. In the first year there was a phase-in allowing firms to pay dividends at only half the established rates. As a result state-owned firms paid dividends of only RMB14 billion in 2007, a trivial 0.05 percent of GDP. Dividends paid by state-owned companies rose to RMB44.4 billion and RMB98.9 billion in 2008 and 2009, respectively. But the latter number represents only 10 percent of the profits of the few firms subject to the tax.[10] This is very low compared with the United States, where industrial firms typically pay dividends ranging from two-fifths to just over half of their earnings (World Bank 2005, 5).

Second, the introduction of the dividend tax coincided with a reduction in the general corporate income tax rate. Domestic firms had long complained that they faced a tax burden of 33 percent, while wholly foreign-owned firms and joint ventures enjoyed a preferential rate of only 15 percent. In 2007, after years of debate, the government decided to unify the rate paid by firms of all types of ownership at 25 percent. This reform reduced the corporate taxes paid by indigenous firms by RMB134 billion, an amount almost eight times the dividend tax imposed on some state-owned firms that year. The net result is that retained earnings of the corporate sector continued to expand in 2007. So the cumulative effect of tax reform in 2007 was to increase corporate retained earnings and thus corporate savings and investment, the opposite of what is needed to rebalance the sources of economic growth.

Third, the dividends paid by state-owned firms are under the control of SASAC and are not available to the MOF to fund increased social programs or similar initiatives that would help to rebalance the sources of economic growth. Rather the funds are administered outside of the state budgetary process through a newly created, separate State Capital Management Budget. In 2008, the first year this new budget was in effect, its total revenue was RMB58.35 billion, which included RMB13.99 billion collected in 2007 and RMB44.36 billion collected in 2008. The vast majority of the expenditures in the 2008 State Capital Management Budget were to finance capital expenditures or to cover operating losses in state-owned companies controlled by SASAC (World Bank 2009). In short, SASAC used the dividend income to strengthen the firms it managed, in effect moving funds from one firm to another within the family of firms within its jurisdiction.

This situation may improve slightly in 2011. The three-tier dividend policy has been maintained, but the dividend rates have been boosted in each category by 5 percentage points. And the number of state-owned firms subject

---

10. "China to Collect More Earnings from SOEs," People's Daily Online, May 15, 2010, available at http://english.people.com.cn (accessed on May 17, 2010).

Table 3.1   Government social expenditures, 2002–10
(billions of renminbi)

Year	Education	Health	Social security and employment	Total
2002	300.6	66.3	268.9	635.8
2003	335.2	83.1	271.2	689.5
2004	385.4	93.6	318.6	797.6
2005	452.8	113.3	378.7	944.7
2006	546.4	142.1	439.4	1,128.0
2007	712.2	199.0	544.7	1,455.9
2008	901.0	275.7	680.4	1,857.2
2009	1,043.8	399.4	760.7	2,203.8
2010	1,245.0	474.5	908.1	2,627.6

Source: Xinhua News Agency, "The Course of Improvements in the People's Livelihood from the Perspective of Public Finance Expenditure over the (Past) Five Years," March 7, 2008, http://news.xinhuanet.com (accessed on August 15, 2011); ISI Emerging Markets, CEIC Database.

to the dividend tax will be increased to 1,630.[11] While the MOF continues to argue that the dividends paid by state-owned companies should be part of the state budget and available to fund programs that improve public well-being, it continues to face opposition from SASAC. At the time of this writing it is not clear whether dividends paid by state-owned enterprises will begin to flow at least in part to the state budget or continue to be subject to the basic control of SASAC through the extrabudgetary State Capital Management Budget.

While government economic rebalancing policy initiatives focusing on taxes have been weak, those focusing on government expenditures have been more robust. As reflected in table 3.1, combined fiscal outlays in 2010 on education, health, social security, and employment were RMB2,600 billion, more than triple the level of 2004. In nominal terms social expenditures grew between 2004 and 2010 at an annual rate of 22 percent, well ahead of the growth of nominal GDP over this period. Thus these expenditures have grown from 5.0 to 6.6 percent of GDP. The government is not only more rapidly building out the social safety net in urban areas, which had frayed in the 1990s as the government restructured state-owned firms and many workers lost their access to social services provided by these enterprises, but also extending programs to segments of the population that historically had received few benefits from government social programs.

In rural areas the most impressive new government program to deliver social services is a rural cooperative medical insurance scheme. First introduced in some localities on a trial basis in 2003, this is a voluntary health insurance

---

11. "Why China Collects Earnings from More SOEs?" People's Daily Online, November 5, 2010, available at http://english.people.com.cn (accessed on September 13, 2011).

program administered by county-level units financed by contributions from individuals, local governments, and the central government.[12] Initially individuals had to pay RMB10 per year to enroll in the program, and the central and local governments each contributed an additional RMB20 per enrollee. The program provides partial reimbursement of health care costs. The average reimbursement rate for in-patient medical care in 2007 was estimated to be about 30 percent (World Bank 2008, 89).

Central government outlays on this program rose rapidly in the mid-2000s, allowing the scheme to be rolled out in an increasing number of counties. By 2009 it was available in 95 percent of China's county-level administrative units and had 833 million enrollees, 10 times the number participating in 2004. Moreover, the per capita premiums financing the program more than doubled between 2004 and 2009, which made possible better-quality care and higher rates of reimbursement for inpatient care (National Bureau of Statistics of China 2010f, 873). In 2010 the government's contribution to the program jumped to RMB120 per enrollee, up by 50 percent from the level in 2009, and this amount rose to RMB200 in 2011. The ramp-up in government funding for the program is intended to bring the reimbursement rate for medical treatment under the insurance program to 70 percent or more, up dramatically from the 30 percent rate only a few years earlier (Ministry of Finance 2010, Wen Jiabao 2011).

A second major government initiative to build up the social safety net in rural areas is a new pension program. The government began this program, also administered at the county level, as a pilot in limited locations in 2008, a few years after the launch of the new rural cooperative medical insurance system. The program's geographic coverage expanded to include 10 percent of county-level units in 2009, 24 percent in 2010, and 40 percent of all counties in 2011 (Wen Jiabao 2009, 2011). By the end of 2010 there were 103 million rural residents participating in the scheme (National Bureau of Statistics of China 2011c).

Like the rural medical insurance scheme, participation in the rural pension program is voluntary and is financed by annual individual and government contributions.[13] The minimum annual individual contribution is RMB100 but rural residents can opt for higher contribution levels, up to RMB500 in many provinces.[14] The annual government contribution to the individual pension

---

12. County-level units include counties, autonomous counties, county-level cities, and districts under city jurisdiction. There were about 2,860 county-level units in China in 2009 (National Bureau of Statistics of China 2010f, 3).

13. An earlier rural pension program, launched in the 1990s, failed. In large part this was because there was little incentive to participate because there was no government subsidy (Shen and Williamson 2010, 241).

14. Contribution levels are typically in increments of RMB100. Jilin and Hebei provinces, for example, have a program with five annual contribution levels ranging from RMB100 to a maximum of RMB500. But in Fujian the program has 12 contribution levels ranging from RMB100 to a maximum of RMB1,200.

accounts of participants during the accumulation period ranges from RMB30 to RMB50. Beginning at age 60, the rural retirement age under the scheme, the monthly payout to individuals is the sum of a fraction of the balance accumulated in the individual's account plus an additional government contribution of a minimum of RMB55.[15] And rural residents age 60 or over when the plan was launched can enroll in the program and receive RMB55 per month even though they have made no contributions to the scheme.[16]

In addition to these initiatives to improve rural health conditions and to provide pensions to rural residents, the government eliminated tuition and miscellaneous school fees for 150 million rural primary school students in 2006 and 2007. In 2008 the central government launched a pilot program to provide subsidies to farmers to renovate their dilapidated homes. Total outlays for this program in 2008–10 were RMB11.7 billion with an additional RMB10 billion earmarked for the program in 2011.[17]

Between 2004 and 2010, the number of workers in urban areas covered by different kinds of insurance expanded: by 58 percent for basic retirement, 113 percent for medical, 26 percent for unemployment, 136 for workers' compensation, and 181 percent for maternity.[18] These increases resulted in a substantial increase in the share of workers in urban areas covered by these programs. For example, the share of the urban workforce covered by the urban basic health insurance program increased over this period from less than a third to just over half.[19]

However, almost half the urban population is not covered by the health insurance scheme, which is largely limited to workers in the formal sector. Those individuals who are self-employed, unemployed, or retired from work units that did not provide insurance coverage, along with many others, had no health insurance coverage until recently. The government in 2007 unveiled a new pilot program to provide basic health insurance to these individuals in

---

15. The fraction is 1/139 based on an average life expectancy in rural areas at age 60 of about 71 years. Government contribution levels are substantially higher in relatively wealthy areas than in less wealthy jurisdictions, presumably in large part because prices and thus the cost of living are higher. In suburban Beijing the government contribution to the monthly pension payment to individuals is reportedly RMB280 per month (Shen and Williamson 2010, 243).

16. To receive this benefit all younger family members must enroll in the program (Shen and Williamson 2010, 243).

17. Xinhua, "MOF Funds Renovation of Unsafe Rural Homes," People's Daily Online, March 24, 2011, available at http://english.people.com.cn (accessed on March 24, 2011).

18. The data are from National Bureau of Statistics of China (2010f, 910) and ISI Emerging Markets, CEIC Database.

19. These estimates understate the share of the workforce in urban areas that is covered by pensions because the numbers in the numerator of the calculation do not include those covered by separate pension schemes for civil servants, the military, and workers in state-run schools, hospitals, and so forth. These groups, however, are included in the numbers on the urban workforce (with the possible exception of some military staff).

two or three cities in each province (Ministry of Human Resources and Social Security 2007). The availability of this program was subsequently expanded geographically and by the end of 2010 there were 195 million participants (National Bureau of Statistics of China 2011c).

Like its rural counterpart, the urban basic medical insurance program for those urban residents not working in the formal sector is voluntary and funded through individual and government contributions. Initially the government contribution was set at a minimum of RMB40 per enrollee. By 2009 this contribution had doubled; it rose further to RMB120 in 2010 and to RM200 in 2011 (Ministry of Finance 2009, 2010; Wen Jiabao 2011). This initiative is designed to provide health insurance to an additional 400 million Chinese, bringing coverage to 90 percent of the population by 2011. In addition, government funding was also provided in 2009 to build 34,000 health clinics in towns and townships and 2,000 new hospitals in county-level administrative units.

The net effect of the health insurance reforms in urban and rural areas has been to reduce the out-of-pocket share of health care expenditures substantially. As a result of the initiatives discussed above, by 2009 the out-of-pocket share of total health care outlays had fallen to two-fifths, down substantially from the peak of three-fifths at the beginning of the decade.[20] Of course, in a longer-term perspective the out-of-pocket share of outlays is still twice what it was when reform was getting underway in the late 1970s and early 1980s. So there is room for substantial further increases in government funding of the new medical insurance schemes.

In addition to accelerating the build-out of the social safety net, the government is also rapidly increasing transfer payments through both pensions and programs to support low-income households. For example, the State Council in August 2007 approved a three-year program to substantially increase old age pensions to workers retired from enterprises. The government increased monthly pension payments, which averaged RMB963 in 2007, to an average of RMB1,063 beginning in January 2008, and to RMB1,173 in January 2009.[21] By 2010 the average pension was RMB1,400 per month, making the cumulative increase since 2007 45 percent. Because consumer prices rose less than 10 percent cumulatively over this period, the average annual increase in pensions was just over 10 percent in real terms. Pension payments rose by an additional RMB140 per month in 2011 (Ministry of Finance 2011).

The second example of growing transfer payments is the minimum living standard guarantee (*dibao*) program. When this program began in urban areas in the mid-1990s it provided a guaranteed minimum income to less than a million people. But by the early part of the last decade the program expanded to cover more than 20 million urban residents. As shown in table 3.2, the

---

20. ISI Emerging Markets, CEIC Database.

21. "Next Year Basic Old Age Pension Payments Are Planned to Rise by RMB110," People's Online Daily, available at http://finance.sina.com.cn (accessed on September 13, 2011).

Table 3.2 Minimum living standard guarantee (*dibao*), 1999–2010

	Urban				Rural			
Year	Number of beneficiaries (millions)	Average minimum cost of living level (renminbi per person per month)	Average government subsidy level (renminbi per person per month)	Total expenditure (billions of renminbi)	Number of beneficiaries (millions)	Average minimum cost of living level (renminbi per person per month)	Average government subsidy level (renminbi per person per month)	Total expenditure (billions of renminbi)
1999	2.66			1.54	2.66			
2000	4.03			2.72	3.00			0.73
2001	11.71				3.05			
2002	20.65		54	11.26	4.08			
2003	22.35	149	59	15.30	4.05			
2004	22.01	159	65	17.29	4.96			
2005	22.33	155	72	19.07	8.25	76		2.53
2006	22.41	170	83	22.21	15.09	68	33	4.16
2007	22.71	182	102	27.48	34.52	69	37	10.41
2008	23.35	205	141	38.52	42.84	82	49	22.23
2009	23.48	228	165	46.14	47.59	101	64	34.51
2010	23.11	251	179	49.59	52.28	117	70	42.30

Sources: Ministry of Civil Affairs (2008, 2009, 2010, 2011); National Bureau of Statistics (2010f, 74–83); State Council (1997, 1999, 2001, 2007); World Bank (2008, 78); Xinhua News Agency, "Rural Minimum Assistance Program Expanding in 2007 to Cover the Countryside," February 9, 2007, http://news3.xinhuanet.com (accessed on August 15, 2011); Xinhua News Agency, "Rural Minimum Assistance Program Sets Sail, Will Help More Poor People Overcome Daily Hardships," May 28, 2007, http://news.xinhuanet.com (accessed on August 16, 2011); Xinhua News Agency, "Minimum Assistance Program is Determined by Assistance Requirements, Subsidies Differ According to Conditions," January 29, 2008, http://xinhuanet.com (accessed on August 16, 2011).

program subsequently expanded substantially in two dimensions. First, the average monthly subsidy paid to eligible urban residents increased dramatically, from about RMB55 in 2002 to RMB180 by 2010. This was primarily because the government steadily increased the targeted minimum income level for program recipients. Second, the program was extended to rural areas and grew rapidly to cover more than 50 million individuals by 2010. As a result, annual expenditures on this program in urban and rural areas combined rose to RMB90 billion in 2010, a vast increase from only RMB3.5 billion in 2000.

Financial Reform

A second policy domain to promote economic rebalancing is in the financial system. The key element of financial reform is not the introduction of ever more complex financial instruments, the accelerated liberalization of capital account restrictions, or expanded access by foreign financial services companies to the domestic market. Rather it is the elimination of remaining government controls on interest rates on both deposits and loans. Throughout the reform period the authorities have controlled interest rates in a manner that has led to a relatively low average real rate of return on household bank savings (Lardy 1998, 10). In effect depositors have been taxed so that borrowers, historically mostly state-owned companies, can have access to cheap credit.

This implicit tax on depositors appears to have increased significantly around 2004.[22] Figure 3.1 charts the real one-year deposit rate (the nominal one-year deposit rate minus the consumer price index) for a 14-year period ending in 2010. The average real return on a one-year deposit for the years 1997 through 2003 was 3.0 percent. Strikingly, the real one-year deposit rate was never in negative territory during this period except during the last two months of 2003. In contrast, during the years 2004 through 2010 the real one-year deposit rate was in negative territory more than half the time and the average real rate for the seven-year period fell to –0.3 percent. Thus the negative returns earned by savers in China today are not explained by the low interest rate policies many central banks around the world adopted in 2009–10 to promote recovery from the global financial and economic crisis. Low real deposit rates in China are a phenomenon dating back to 2004.

These low real rates are the direct result of a change in the central bank policy on the adjustment of nominal deposit rates. From 1997 through 2003, when inflation picked up the central bank raised nominal deposit rates with a very short time lag. The inverse was true when the pace of inflation ebbed.

---

22. While this study argues that financial repression, as reflected in the level of real deposit rates, the required reserve ratio, and other indicators, increased after 2003, Huang and Wang (2010) use six variables to construct an index of financial repression and find that from the mid-1950s through 2006 there was a long-term decline in financial repression followed by a rise in the following two years. They attribute the rise to China's response to the global financial crisis.

Figure 3.1 Real return on household one-year deposits, 1997–2010

percent

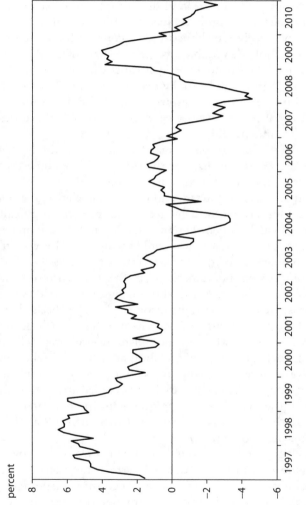

Sources: ISI Emerging Markets, CEIC Database.

In contrast, beginning in 2004 whenever inflation picked up the central bank raised the nominal deposit rates with a lag, and the upward adjustment was substantially less than the increase in inflation. When inflation ebbed the bank adjusted the nominal deposit rate downward rather quickly.

The direct result of the way the central bank has set nominal rates since 2003 is that household interest earnings on average have been far less than they would have been in a more liberalized financial environment, where market forces play a major role in determining interest rates. As noted in chapter 2, the decline in property income (of which more than four-fifths is interest income) received by households accounted for about one-fifth of the decline in household disposable income as a share of GDP between 1992 and 2008. This is particularly noteworthy because the stock of household savings relative to GDP grew substantially over these years.[23] In short, because of negative real interest rates the growth of household income since 2003 has been slower than would have occurred in a more liberalized (less repressed) financial environment.

The indirect effect of negative real deposit rates in China seems to be that households increased the share of their disposable income that they saved. The response of households generally to a change in interest rates reflects the combination of offsetting substitution and income effects. While there is no theoretical presumption of which effect will dominate, empirically the substitution effect is usually larger. Thus a reduction in the real interest rate would be expected to lead to a lower household saving rate. However, if the primary motivation for savings is to achieve a certain target level of financial assets, the income effect would dominate, i.e., as the real return to savings declined, in order to achieve their target level of savings, households would save more (consume less) from their current income. The hypothesis that the primary motivation for Chinese households to save is to achieve a target level of savings makes sense in a society where medical insurance coverage is limited, hospital access usually depends on paying cash in advance, and relatively high down payments are required to qualify for a mortgage on a residential property. There is also empirical support, based on a detailed analysis of Chinese household data, for the hypothesis that a decline in the real interest rate leads to an increase in the household saving rate (Chamon and Prasad 2008, 19; IMF 2011c, 34; Nabar, forthcoming).

The aggregate data on household savings from the flow of funds are shown in figure 3.2. In 1997–2003, when the real one-year deposit rate averaged 3.0 percent, household savings averaged 29 percent of disposable income; after 2003, when the average real rate of return on one-year deposits turned negative,

---

23. Household savings deposits rose from RMB1,175 billion, or 44 percent of GDP, in 1992 to RMB21,790 billion, or 69 percent of GDP, in 2008 (China Banking Society 1997, 464; National Bureau of Statistics of China 2010f, 38, 733).

Figure 3.2 Household savings from disposable income, 1997–2008

percent

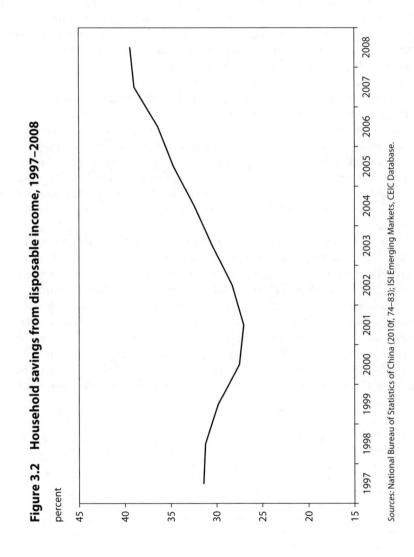

Sources: National Bureau of Statistics of China (2010f, 74–83); ISI Emerging Markets, CEIC Database.

household savings jumped to an average of 36 percent of disposable income.[24] Thus the aggregate data also support an inverse relationship between the real interest rate and the household saving rate. As noted in chapter 2, the rise in the household saving rate accounted for about one-quarter of the long-term decline in household consumption as a share of GDP.

Market determination of deposit rates would eliminate the element of financial repression that imposes a high implicit tax on Chinese savers. Interest rate liberalization would raise household consumption as a share of GDP through two mechanisms. First, higher real deposit rates would increase household income and, for any given saving rate, also increase household consumption as a share of GDP. This might be thought of as the direct effect.

Liberalization of deposit rates would also spur household consumption indirectly. Since household saving is to a substantial extent motivated by precautionary demand, when the government suppresses real interest rates on deposits, households that are seeking to achieve a certain target level of savings will increase their saving rate to make up for the lower real return. If the government were to liberalize deposit interest rates, the household saving rate would likely decline, i.e., households would choose to spend a higher share of their income. This might be thought of as the indirect effect of interest rate liberalization.

Thus the combined direct and indirect effect of liberalizing deposit rates could be to raise the share of private consumption in GDP by as much as 5 percentage points.[25] That alone would reverse about two-fifths of the long-term decline in the share of household consumption in China's GDP.

In addition to low deposit interest rates, financial reform should also address other elements of China's financial system that reflect financial repression. These elements include the very high required reserve ratio, discussed in the next section of this chapter, and compulsory quotas imposed on banks requiring them to hold both large quantities of government bonds issued by the MOF and bills issued by the central bank. The low yields on

---

24. At the time of this writing, the flow of funds data, which give household disposable income and savings based on national income data, are available only through 2008. Household saving rates reported in the aggregate flow of funds data are substantially higher than those reported in the household surveys. For example, in 2004 the household saving rate calculated from household survey data was 24 percent of disposable income, while the flow of funds reported that household saving was 32 percent of disposable income. This differential between survey-based measures of saving and national income–based measures of saving are common and stem largely from low survey response rates from high-income households that have high saving propensities (Chamon and Prasad 2008, 7).

25. For the period covered by the flow of funds data, 1992 through 2008, the decline in interest income received by households was about 2 percentage points of GDP (the direct effect of declining real deposit rates) and the increase in the household saving rate as a percentage of GDP was about 3 percentage points of GDP. Note that the rise in the household saving rate as a share of disposable income was much greater than the rise as a share of GDP, since household disposable income is much smaller than GDP and over this period fell by 9 percentage points of GDP.

government bonds and central bank bills and the fact that these financial instruments are held predominantly by banks are two further indicators of financial repression, in addition to the negative real interest rate on household deposits. In the earliest days of the government bond market in the 1980s continuing into the 1990s, individuals were the dominant bond investors and the MOF and corporate bond issuers (almost all state-owned companies) had to pay market-oriented interest rates to sell the bonds (Lardy 1998, 132). But over the past decade, the MOF increasingly placed government bonds directly with the banks at interest rates dictated by the MOF, which were designed to lower the ministry's interest expense. The funds raised by the MOF thus came indirectly from household depositors via the banks, rather than directly from the households. By 2009 individuals held only 1 percent of all outstanding bonds, while banks held over 70 percent of all fixed-income securities, including 50 percent of all MOF bonds and almost all central bank bills. These low-yielding bonds accounted for an unusually high 20 to 30 percent of total bank assets (Walter and Howie 2011, 103–09).[26]

While substantially increased government social expenditures, increased pension payments, and increased transfer payments to the lowest-income urban and rural residents are potentially contributing to economic rebalancing, the government has discussed but not yet adopted financial and banking reforms that would support the transition to consumption-led growth. Indeed, in two respects financial policy has retrogressed since 2004. First, a policy of gradual liberalization of interest rates on loans and deposits initiated in 1997 was largely abandoned after 2004.[27] Second, as already noted, from the perspective of households the financial system has become more—not less—repressive since around 2003. Following a brief summary of the history of interest rate liberalization I turn to a more detailed estimate of the implications of financial repression for households.

The People's Bank of China initiated a program of market-oriented interest rate liberalization in 1997 when, for the first time, it allowed financial

---

26. According to Walter and Howie (2011) banks hold these bonds only because they are required by the party to do so. I believe that banks are willing to hold large amounts of low-yielding government bonds and central bank bills because they are in effect compensated in the form of low-cost deposits from households. The low cost of deposits is, of course, a direct consequence of the central bank's control of the structure of interest rates, particularly the ceiling it places on the rates that banks can pay on deposits (Lardy 2008). This is discussed further in the next section of this chapter.

27. This is in contrast to policy continuity allowing increasing market determination of very short-term interest rates. In January 1996 the central bank launched a unified interbank lending market where interest rates on short-term loans could be freely set by market participants. Spot bond trading and repo transactions in this market were allowed starting in 1997. Later the issuance of and trading in short-term commercial paper and other short-term financial instruments was introduced in the interbank market and the number of market participants grew substantially. In 2007 the central bank introduced the Shanghai Interbank Offer Rate (SHIBOR) System in an attempt to build a benchmark yield curve on maturities of up to one year. For details see Porter and Xu (2009).

institutions the flexibility to set interest rates on loans at a level somewhat higher than the benchmark rates set by the central bank. For example, the flexibility that commercial banks had in setting lending rates to small enterprises was increased. Prior to 1998 the margin was limited to 10 percent above the benchmark rates set by the central bank.[28] In 1998 this margin was increased to 20 percent. Thus, for example, in the second half of 1998, when the benchmark interest rate on a one-year working capital loan was 6.93 percent, banks were allowed to set rates as high as 8.32 percent. Subsequently the People's Bank granted commercial banks this kind of flexibility to set lending rates for all types of borrowers. Rural credit cooperatives were given even greater flexibility and were allowed to charge interest rates on loans as much as 50 percent above central bank benchmark rates as early as 1998. Flexibility for rural credit cooperatives rose to 100 percent starting in September 2002. In 2000 the central bank also decontrolled foreign currency lending rates and rates on foreign currency deposits over $3 million.

This liberalization of interest rates on loans and deposits peaked in 2004. At the beginning of the year the People's Bank raised the upper limit on the lending rates that could be charged by commercial banks and urban credit cooperatives, from 1.3 times the benchmark to a new limit of 1.7 times. Finally, in late October 2004 the central bank raised the flexibility of lending rates for both urban and rural credit cooperatives to a maximum of 2.3 times the benchmark and completely removed the cap on lending rates charged by commercial banks. These gradual steps marked an important relaxation of central bank control of interest rates. They were part of the government's effort to encourage banks to operate on a commercial basis. A key aspect of such operation, of course, is the pricing of risk. Prior to 1997 banks had little incentive to develop sophisticated risk pricing skills, since every loan had to be made at the same benchmark interest rate.

But in two critical respects these steps fell short of full liberalization. The central bank maintained the cap on deposit rates for all institutions and also mandated that lending rates could not fall below 0.9 times its established benchmark rates.[29] Thus banks, in effect, were guaranteed a minimum interest rate spread. October 2004 marked the end of market-oriented interest rate reform (*lixi shichanghua gaige*), first announced by the central bank in 1996. The central bank has not further widened the bands around the benchmark interest rates for loans and deposits. But Premier Wen used the same "market-oriented interest rate reform" phrase in his speech to the National People's

---

28. The central bank sets specific benchmark lending rates for loans of varying tenors and purposes. For ordinary loans the central bank sets rates for tenors of six months or less, six months to a year, one to three years, three to five years, and over five years. There are different rates for individual mortgage loans, and in earlier periods the central bank set specific interest rates for a variety of other special purpose loans, for example, for loans financing technical transformation.

29. Details on the program of market-oriented interest rate reform are available in China Banking Society (1999, 7; 2005, 4–5).

Congress in 2009, putting market-oriented interest rate reform back on the policy agenda (Wen Jiabao 2009).

If financial repression has increased since 2003, what are the concrete implications for households? One way to measure the implicit tax imposed on households by the decline in the real rate of interest that banks pay households on their savings deposits is to ask how much more households would have earned on their savings if the real interest rates prevailing at some point after 2003 had been the same as in 2002. I measure the decline from 2002 for two reasons. First, on February 21, 2002, the central bank set the interest rate that banks could pay on demand deposits at 0.72 percent and then left that rate unchanged until November 2008, despite a substantial pickup in price inflation over the period. Second, as will be argued in the next section of this chapter, negative real interest rates on deposits are closely related to China's exchange rate policy, and 2002 predates the emergence of an undervalued exchange rate of the renminbi. As previously noted, the real rate of interest on one-year bank deposits was continuously positive until the closing months of 2003. For example, starting in February 2002, the central bank set the interest rate on one-year deposits at 1.98 percent; given that the consumer price index declined 0.8 percent that year, the real rate of interest was 2.78 percent. That is close to the average real interest rate of 3.0 percent on one-year deposits that prevailed in the years from 1997 through 2003.

By contrast, after 2002 consumer price inflation rose, and the central bank adjusted nominal time deposit rates upward by only small amounts and left the nominal interest rate on demand deposits unchanged for more than six years. In the first half of 2008 consumer price inflation was 7.9 percent, meaning that the real rate of return on demand deposits had fallen to –7.18 percent, a decline of 8.7 percentage points. The central bank did increase the nominal interest rate that banks could pay on term deposits of various maturities. For example, the central bank had moved up the rate on one-year deposits by mid-year 2008 to 4.14 percent. But in real terms the rate was –3.76 percent, a decline of 6.54 percentage points compared with the real return on one-year deposits in 2002.

To measure the implicit tax on household savings in the first half of 2008, start by noting that household bank deposits during that period averaged RMB18,680 billion.[30] Almost two-fifths of this was in the form of demand deposits, and the balance was in term deposits of maturities ranging from as short as three months to as long as five years. If these deposits had earned the same real rates as in 2002, household income in the first half of 2008 would have been RMB690 billion greater than it actually was, an amount equal to 5.3 percent of China's GDP in the first half of the year. That means that the average negative real deposit rates prevailing after 2003 significantly retarded

---

30. This is the average of the end-December 2007 amount of RMB17,575 billion and end-June 2008 amount of RMB19,781 billion.

the growth of household income, making the contribution of household consumption to economic growth less than it would have been in a system with market-determined interest rates.

In addition to contributing to economic imbalances by constraining the growth of household income and consumption, the central bank's low interest rate policy also has contributed to another dimension of China's economic imbalance, its exceptionally high rate of investment since 2003. The simplest explanation is that there was a marked decline in real lending rates after 2003. In 1997–2003 the real rate on a one-year loan averaged 6.8 percent.[31] But since the beginning of 2004 the real interest rate on a one-year loan has averaged only 1.7 percent, encouraging investment in projects that have much lower returns and thus boosting the investment share in GDP.

The government's policy of low interest rates on deposits indirectly depresses interest rates on loans. This occurs largely because of competition among banks. The low benchmark rate the central bank set on deposits gives commercial banks a very cheap source of funding. Bank profitability in recent years has been quite high, even though the banks do not take much advantage of the flexibility they have had since the fall of 2004 to set lending rates at any point above 0.9 times the benchmark rates.[32] Except for borrowers that are unusually risky, banks are unable to set loan rates much above the benchmark, because other banks would undercut their rates. The contribution of competition among banks to low lending rates is reinforced by the large savings-investment imbalance that emerged after 2003, reflected in China's large current account surplus. With the country awash in liquidity, market forces pushed down lending rates.

The influence of low interest rates on investment is particularly noticeable in investment in residential real estate. The increase in residential real estate investment is responsible for a large share of the increase in the average investment share of GDP after 2003, discussed in chapter 2 (Anderson 2011a). The analysis of China's macro prudential regulation in chapter 1 showed how China's financial regulators have had some success in limiting the buildup of financial leverage that could substantially exacerbate the economic effect of a collapse of property prices. But the authorities have been much less successful in controlling the macroeconomic risk that GDP growth could decelerate significantly as a result of a marked slowdown in the pace of property investment. As reflected in figure 3.3, investment in residential real estate by property development companies averaged only 2.4 percent of GDP in the early

---

31. The real rate on a one-year loan is calculated as the nominal rate minus the rate of price inflation as measured by the ex factory price of producer goods.

32. In 2010, for example, about three-quarters of all loans were made at the benchmark rate or within 10 percent of the benchmark (People's Bank of China Monetary Policy Analysis Small Group 2011a, 5).

Figure 3.3 Investment in residential housing, 1996–2010

percent of GDP

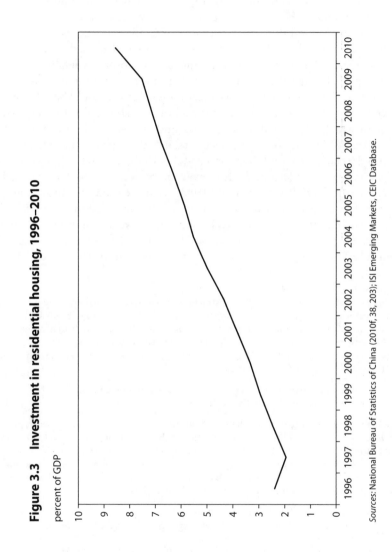

Sources: National Bureau of Statistics of China (2010f, 38, 203); ISI Emerging Markets, CEIC Database.

years of the housing boom, 1996–99.[33] In 2000–2003 this rose to an average of 4.1 percent. Subsequently, as real returns to financial saving fell into negative territory, investment in residential real estate soared, reaching 8.6 percent of GDP in 2010. For the years 2004–10, investment in residential real estate averaged 6.8 percent of GDP.[34] Investment in residential real estate grew by a further 36 percent in the first half of 2011 to reach RMB1,864 billion, or 9.1 percent of GDP (People's Bank of China Monetary Policy Analysis Small Group 2011c; National Bureau of Statistics of China 2011d).

This rise in residential real estate investment in China does not appear to be the result of either a rapidly rising rate of home ownership in urban areas or rapidly rising urbanization.[35] The sharpest rise in home ownership in China occurred in the mid-1990s as a result of a massive, probably historically unprecedented, privatization of the urban housing stock, almost all of which had been owned by government agencies and state-owned enterprises. This housing was sold to then-current residents, mostly at prices that were heavily discounted relative to replacement cost. In 1998, when this privatization process was near completion, the home ownership rate in urban areas reached 80 percent, up from 9.7 percent in 1983, when economic reform was just getting underway. Most of this increase must have occurred in 1996–98, at the height of the privatization process. In subsequent years the homeownership rate rose very gradually, albeit to very high levels—82.1 percent by 2002, 87.0 percent by 2006, 87.8 percent by 2008, and 89.3 percent by the end of 2010.[36]

---

33. The measure of residential real estate investment used here is completed investment in residential real estate by property development companies. Since about four-fifths of residential housing investment in rural areas is undertaken by farm households, this measure largely excludes residential housing investment in rural areas. For data for the years 1998 through 2009 see National Bureau of Statistics of China (2010f, 203). The complete time series from 1996 onward is available from ISI Emerging Markets, CEIC Database.

34. Including investment in residential property undertaken by rural households, total residential property investment averaged 8.0 percent of GDP in 2004–10.

35. The focus here is on urban China because housing in rural areas has always been privately owned. Even during major political campaigns, such as the Great Leap Forward in the late 1950s and the Cultural Revolution in the 1960s, rural housing was not collectivized. Equally important, it remained an inheritable asset. In contrast, in the early 1950s most private urban housing was taken over by the state, and for several decades thereafter almost all new urban housing investment was undertaken by local governments or state-owned enterprises.

36. "The Burden of High House Prices on Housing Consumption Culture and Consumption Psychology," December 31, 2009, available at www.gygov.gov.cn (accessed on April 12, 2011); "The Home Ownership Rate for Households Living in Urban Areas Is 89.3 Percent," March 9, 2011, available at www.hzrei.gov.cn (accessed on April 12, 2011); "In What Ways Are People's Living Standards Improving After All?" March 19, 2008, available at www.gov.cn (accessed on April 12, 2011); "Last Year the Urban Home Ownership Rate of Urban Households Reached 82.1 Percent," March 27, 2003, available at www.jiangxi.gov.cn (accessed on April 13, 2011); "Real Estate Reform is Exceeding an Important Landmark," March 11, 2011, available at www.lhfgc.gov.cn (accessed on April 13, 2011). These homeownership rates presumably only apply to urban residents who have the legal right to live permanently in a city, i.e., have an urban household registration (*hukou*).

Similarly rapid urbanization is not a satisfactory alternative explanation of the long-term rise in the share of GDP allocated to residential real estate investment. In 2000–2003 China's urban population was rising by about 24 million per year, and these new urbanites were being accommodated with residential investment equal to an average of 4.1 percent of GDP and residential housing starts that rose from 240 million square meters per year in 2000 to 440 million square meters in 2003. After 2003 the urban population increased by an average of only 19 million annually, but average residential housing investment of 6.8 percent of GDP was two-thirds larger than in 2000–2003, and annual residential housing starts soared from 490 million square meters in 2004 to 1,290 million square meters in 2010.[37]

Thus the rise in residential real estate investment in China in the previous decade was not the result of a rapidly rising rate of home ownership or an accelerating pace of urbanization. Rather it was the result of residential real estate's becoming a preferred asset class, particularly for urban residents. There were several reasons for this. First, the real returns to bank deposits declined dramatically, and on average for one-year deposits were negative in real terms after 2003. In contrast, returns to newly constructed residential property, though varying widely by location, averaged 2.3 percent per annum in real terms in 1998–2003 but rose to 4.6 percent in 2004–10.[38] In other words, the average real return on a one-year bank deposit exceeded the average house price appreciation by 0.7 percent in 1998–2003, but in 2004–10 the relationship flipped, and in real terms the average house price appreciation exceeded the one-year deposit rate by an average of 4.9 percent.

Second, the financial terms for individual mortgages were favorable for two reasons. First-time property buyers were able to borrow at a discount of 15 or 30 percent to the benchmark lending rate set by the central bank for the tenor of their mortgage. In addition, by taking out a mortgage, a household could reduce its share of the implicit tax levied on household bank deposits. This was because a household that secured a mortgage to purchase a residential property reduced its net deposits (equal to deposits minus loans) in the banking system. This reduction came about both because some of the funds the household previously had on deposit in the banking system were

---

37. The estimate of the average annual increase in the urban population in 2000–2003 and 2004–10 takes into account the results of the 2010 census, released in May 2011. The census reported an urban population of 665.6 million in 2010, a very sharp increase of 43.7 million above the previously reported 2009 urban population, which the statistical authorities estimated based on an annual sample survey on population changes. To calculate the average annual increase in the urban population in the two periods, I have adjusted the previous estimates of the annual population in 2001–09 upward, by 3 million in 2001, 6 million in 2002, and so f~ · 27 million in 2009.

38. Real returns were calculated as the 70-city price increase for newly const property minus the consumer price index, using annual data for the years 199 terly data for the years 2001–10. Data are from ISI Emerging Markets, CEIC Dat

converted into a down payment and because the household further reduced its net deposits by taking out the individual mortgage loan.

Third, there was no property tax, so the carrying costs of owning an empty flat were modest.[39]

Fourth, because the Chinese currency remained largely inconvertible on capital account transactions, most households had no legal opportunity to shift part of their savings into higher-yielding, foreign currency–denominated financial assets. The State Council did approve the introduction of a qualified domestic institutional investor (QDII) program in 2006 that allows households to place renminbi funds with licensed domestic financial institutions that invest the funds on their behalf in foreign currency–denominated financial assets. But by the end of 2010 the total approved amount of QDII funds was only $68.4 billion, equivalent to only 1.5 percent of the value of household bank deposits (Lardy and Douglass 2011, 11; People's Bank of China 2011a).

Fifth, weak governance as well as the high price volatility typical of immature equity markets led to a lack of confidence among many retail investors in the Shanghai Stock Exchange. As early as 2001 Wu Jinglian, China's leading academic reform economist, characterized the Shanghai Stock Exchange as a "casino" in which household investors inevitably would lose money over the long run; his views reflected widespread concerns about front running, insider trading, and other trading abuses.[40] A massive run-up in prices, pushed the Shanghai Stock Exchange A-share market index to a peak of 6,251.5 in October 2007. Subsequently, even before the onset of the global financial and economic crisis, the market sold off, with the index falling by more than half by mid-year 2008. The market then plunged further, with the index hitting a low of about 1,800 at the time of the Lehman collapse in the fall of 2008. Despite China's relatively strong economic growth during the global economic crisis and a particularly rapid recovery in corporate profits in 2010, by end-June 2011 the A-share market index stood at only about 2,800, less than half its peak level in October 2007. Most Chinese households, having been burned by the stock market, have limited their equity investments. UBS estimates that equities accounted for only a little more than 10 percent of urban household wealth in 2010, while bank deposits and real estate accounted for 42 and 40 percent, respectively. Furthermore, the corporate bond market is tiny and government bond yields so low that bond are not an attractive investment for individual investors. It is therefore not surprising that bonds accounted for only about 1 percent of urban household assets in 2010 (Wang Tao 2011b, 12).

The extent to which real estate has become a preferred asset class in urban China is reflected not only in the run-up in investment in residential property

---

39. The pilot property tax programs in Shanghai and Chongqing were not introduced until 2011.

40. "Stock Market Causes Heated Debate," *China Daily*, March 13, 2001, available at www.china.org.cn (accessed on April 12, 2011).

as a share of GDP but also in the surprisingly high share of urban households that own multiple homes. For example, according to a survey of the Chinese central bank for the fourth quarter of 2010, 18.3 percent of all households in Beijing owned two or more properties (People's Bank of China Business Management Office 2010). Much, if not most, of this property is vacant, in part because the rental yields on property in tier-one cities such as Beijing, Shanghai, and Shenzhen are very low.[41] But ownership of multiple properties is not limited to tier-one cities. At mid-year 2010 the share of all residential properties purchased in all Chinese cities as investments hit a peak of over 40 percent, and (despite the various measures introduced starting in December 2009 to discourage property investors) at mid-year 2011 more than 20 percent of all purchases of residential property still were for investment purposes (Ulrich 2011).

The pervasiveness of property as a desirable investment class has a further important implication for the evolution of the household saving rate. As noted earlier in this chapter, one motive for household saving is to accumulate the funds necessary to make the down payment for a mortgage on a residential property. That could support the conjecture that the household saving rate might fall as the share of urban residents who have already purchased a home rises to relatively high levels. But property ownership among permanent urban residents had already reached very high levels by the early 2000s, and the household saving rate nonetheless began to rise at that time. Perhaps this rise reflects the rise of property as a preferred asset class. If, after a first-time property purchase, a growing share of homeowners desires to own a second property, the household saving rate might even rise, as a growing share of households not only was paying down a first mortgage (which counts as savings) but also began to save for a down payment on a mortgage to acquire an additional residence.

The main risk that China faces is not that borrowers will default on their mortgages as the result of a correction in property prices, leading to a financial crisis—as occurred in several advanced industrial countries during the global financial and economic crisis. As discussed in chapter 1, the Chinese bank regulator requires banks to collect substantial down payments as a condition for issuing a residential mortgage, particularly for property investors, and although household mortgage debt has risen sharply in recent years it is a relatively low share of household disposable income. The risk arises instead because at some point households may no longer perceive housing as a preferred asset class. That would mean a sharp drop in residential investment. Since residential investment by 2010 accounted for a substantial share of national investment, that drop would lead to a substantial slowdown in economic growth.

---

41. Rental yields (the ratio of annual rental income to the price of a dwelling) in Beijing, Shanghai, and Shenzhen in 2010 ranged from 2.3 to 2.9 percent (Wang Tao 2011b, 7). In a survey of 59 cities around the world only 3 cities in 2008 had rental yields under 3.7 percent. "Buy-to-Let Yields," *Economist*, August 8, 2008, available at www.economist.com (accessed on April 19, 2011).

As Wang Tao (2011a, 7) has pointed out, housing could lose its preferred asset class status for a number of reasons: a sharp rise in interest rates;[42] the liberalization of portfolio capital outflows for households; improved regulation of the Shanghai Stock Exchange, which would give investors confidence in equities as a viable long-term investment class; the emergence of another asset class that draws investment away from property; or a price decline that leads to negative real returns on property investment.

I might add to this list more widespread and higher taxation of property that increases the carrying cost of investing in property, the eventual desire on the part of households for greater diversification in their wealth holding, and limits on the level of prudent leverage by households. As already noted, prior to the mid-1990s, urban households held little of their wealth in the form of property. By 1997, after the housing privatization campaign was well underway, property accounted for a fifth of the estimated wealth of urban households.

But by 2010 the property share of urban household wealth reached two-fifths (Wang Tao 2011b, 4). Three factors account for the doubling in the real estate share of household wealth in a period of just over a decade. First, as already noted, residential investment as a share of GDP rose ever higher as urban residents moved to ever larger and higher-quality residences. Second, real estate price appreciation on average picked up starting in 2004, while beginning in late 2007 equity prices fell sharply and by mid-2011 had recovered only very partially. Third, a significant share of urban households purchased a second or even third property. At some point households may decide that they have enough exposure to property as an asset class and thus seek to diversify the composition of their wealth. When this happens the demand for property could slump, causing prices to fall.

While household debt relative to disposable income in China is still well below the extraordinarily elevated levels observed in the United States, the United Kingdom, and a few other advanced industrial countries on the eve of the financial crisis, this ratio in China rose by almost 20 percentage points between the end of 2008 and the end of 2010. This jump substantially exceeds the pace of accumulation of household debt in the United States in the run up to the global financial crisis.[43]

The macro risk of a residential property slump arises not because of high leverage in the property sector, though some property developers could be

---

42. Mortgage interest rates in China are reset annually on the basis of changes to the benchmark lending rates set by the People's Bank of China in the previous year. Thus, as in the United Kingdom and Hong Kong, mortgage interest rates are generally floating.

43. The debt of US households peaked at 132 percent of disposable income in 2007. In the prior decade the average annual increase in indebtedness was 5 percentage points of GDP. Flow of Funds of the United States, Table 2.1, available at www.federalreserve.gov (accessed on September 15, 2011).

forced into bankruptcy in a property downturn.[44] It arises because property investment accounts for a large share of total national investment, residential real estate accounts for three-quarters of all property development, and a very large share of economic activity in China is linked to property development, either directly or indirectly. Forty percent of steel output goes directly into real estate, and when steel used in appliances—the sales of which are highly correlated with housing development—is added, the share rises further. Taking into account the entire upstream supply chain connected to property, UBS estimates that property accounts for as much as one-quarter of final demand in China (Wang Tao 2011b, 2). When these connections between property and other sectors are considered, it becomes clear that a property slump immediately would have widespread adverse macroeconomic consequences.

The adverse effect of a significant residential property price correction likely would be long-lived for three reasons. First, anecdotal information suggests there is a large overhang of vacant residential properties purchased by investors that expect ever rising property prices. If this is true, in a significant, sustained price correction a large number of these properties would come back onto the market, pushing prices down further and depressing the level of new construction. Second, since residential property is a large share of urban household wealth, a sharp price correction would reduce household wealth and thus have an additional adverse effect on economic growth through its negative effect on household consumption expenditure. Third, a property slump would have large negative fiscal consequences for local governments. A sharp drop in new housing starts would cause income from land sales and leasing to plummet, impairing the ability of local governments to provide social services and finance local infrastructure projects, further reducing aggregate demand. Moreover, a sharp decline in revenues from land leasing could impair the ability of local governments to repay the debts of local investment companies, an issue discussed in chapter 1. A significant share of this debt is secured by land or income from land leasing (Green 2010). This result, in turn, could lead to the reemergence of large-scale nonperforming loans in the banking system.

Very few if any emerging-market economies devote as large a share of GDP to residential property investment as does China. In the 1970s and 1980s when Taiwan was undergoing similarly rapid economic growth and urbanization, investment in residential housing peaked at 4.3 percent of GDP in 1980 and

---

44. Property developers at the end of 2010 had RMB832.6 billion outstanding in bank loans for the purchase and leasing of land and RMB2.3 trillion in bank loans outstanding for property development. Individual mortgage loans outstanding were RMB6.2 trillion. Thus total property lending was RMB9.35 trillion and accounted for 20.5 percent of all loans outstanding from the banking system (People's Bank of China Monetary Policy Analysis Small Group 2011a, 45–46). However, these numbers understate the debt of property developers. As property lending by banks tightened up in 2010–11, developers sought other sources of finance, notably trust products and offshore bond issuance. In 2010 the total issuance of property-related trust products was RMB286 billion (Green 2011). And in the first half of 2011 Chinese companies raised $21.5 billion in international bond markets. Most of these companies are from the property sector. Robert Cookson, "Fears Rise of Defaults by Chinese Companies," *Financial Times*, June 30, 2011, 26.

averaged only 3.1 percent of GDP over the two-decade period.[45] Investment in residential property in India rose from 3 percent of GDP in 2000 to 5.2 percent in 2008, presumably reflecting the acceleration of economic growth during this period.[46] Thus China is currently investing roughly twice as large a share of GDP in residential real estate than these two economies did when their allocation of resources to housing peaked.

A comparison with the United States also is instructive. During the 2002–06 US real estate boom, investment in residential real estate averaged 5.5 percent of GDP, up less than a percentage point from the long-run average of 4.7 percent of GDP in 1950–2001 (Council of Economic Advisors 2010, 121). At the peak of the bubble in 2005, about 2 million new housing units were constructed, and housing investment accounted for 6 percent of GDP. The burst of the property bubble led not only to the global financial and economic crisis but also to a long period of subpar growth in the United States. Even after the US economy began to recover in the second half of 2009, economic growth was subdued, largely because investment in residential real estate continued to fall. According to the analysis of Michael Mussa (2011), "The failure of residential investment to show a substantial rebound after six quarters of general economic recovery is a special feature of the present recovery." By the final quarter of 2010, investment in real estate in the United States had fallen to just 2.5 percent of GDP and an annualized rate of only half a million housing units, a level barely sufficient to replace the old units that were being removed from the housing stock. Mussa forecasts that residential real estate investment, after reaching a low in the first quarter of 2011, will begin to grow later in the year and will expand by an additional 20 percent in 2012. However, he does not see housing starts recovering to what he regards as the long-term sustainable level of 1.7 million units until 2016. The clear lesson is that the real estate boom was responsible for pushing up US growth in the years 2002 through 2005 and that the bursting of the property bubble drove the economy into the deepest recession since the Depression. Most important, it now looks like working through the aftermath of the burst will be a drag on US economic growth for two or more years from the time general economic recovery began, and that it could be as long as seven years from the time general economic recovery began until the United States reaches the point where housing is making what might be considered a normal contribution to economic growth.

Exchange Rate Policy

More flexibility with respect to the exchange rate of the renminbi is a third domain in which government policy could contribute to China's desired transition to a more consumption-driven growth path. As reflected in figure 3.4,

---

45. Council for Economic Planning and Development (1997, 27, 52).

46. IHS Global Insight, *Global Construction Outlook*, September 7, 2011. Data on file with authors.

Figure 3.4   Change in foreign exchange reserves, 2001–10

billions of US dollars

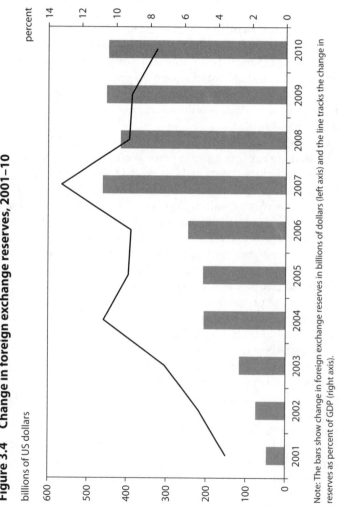

percent

Note: The bars show change in foreign exchange reserves in billions of dollars (left axis) and the line tracks the change in reserves as percent of GDP (right axis).

Sources: State Administration of Foreign Exchange, www.safe.gov.cn; ISI Emerging Markets, CEIC Database.

since 2003 the central bank has engaged in systematic, large-scale intervention in the foreign exchange market, selling domestic currency and buying up foreign exchange, thus leading to a vast buildup of foreign exchange reserves. Starting in 2004 and continuing through 2010, the annual increase in reserves averaged 10 percent of GDP. The average annual absolute increase in official reserves exceeded $400 billion in 2007–10, taking reserves at year-end 2010 to $2.9 trillion.[47] In the absence of this unprecedentedly large, one-way, and continuous exchange market intervention, the renminbi would have appreciated substantially more than the modest cumulative 24 percent real, trade-weighted appreciation that actually occurred in 2004–10.[48] The government could achieve greater flexibility in the exchange rate of the renminbi by gradually eliminating official intervention in the foreign exchange market, allowing the value of the currency to be determined by supply and demand in the market. This approach also would eventually end the build-up of foreign exchange reserves.

Renminbi appreciation would contribute to economic rebalancing in two ways. First, by making exports more expensive and imports cheaper, currency appreciation would reduce the growth of exports and increase the growth of imports, reducing China's large global external surplus. Arguments that China is different and thus that renminbi appreciation is not likely to have much effect on its global current account position do not stand up to careful scrutiny (Goldstein and Lardy 2009, 55–57).

The second reason that currency appreciation would contribute to the desired transition to a more consumption-driven growth path is as important as the first but frequently overlooked: Greater exchange rate flexibility is a precondition for the introduction of market-determined interest rates. The reason is that central bank control of interest rates at very low levels appears to be part and parcel of the policy of keeping the renminbi undervalued. This is certainly suggested by the sharp decline in the real returns to savers after 2003, just when China's current account surplus began expanding sharply (as a result of the increasing undervaluation of the currency starting a year or two earlier), and central bank intervention in the foreign exchange market increased significantly.

If domestic interest rates were liberalized, the costs incurred by the central bank to maintain a significantly undervalued exchange rate would increase dramatically. This is because, for almost a decade, China's political leadership has saddled the People's Bank with two potentially conflicting objectives— keeping the currency undervalued and maintaining domestic price stability. By keeping deposit rates low the central bank, in effect, mitigates this conflict.

---

47. $2.9 trillion does not include official reserves of $200 billion that were transferred to the China Investment Corporation, China's sovereign wealth fund, and much smaller amounts that were injected into other financial institutions, notably several securities firms.

48. Bank of International Settlements, BIS Effective Exchange Rate Indices, updated April 15, 2011, available at www.bis.org/statistics/eer/index.htm (accessed on April 18, 2011).

When the central bank intervenes in the foreign exchange market, buying up foreign exchange with domestic currency, it can directly control the rate of appreciation of the renminbi. But in so doing it increases the domestic money supply. Given the unprecedented scale of central bank intervention in the foreign exchange market since 2003, without offsetting monetary actions by the central bank domestic price inflation would have become a serious problem. Instead average annual consumer price inflation was a modest 3 percent in 2004–10 (National Bureau of Statistics of China 2010f, 307; 2011c).

The central bank takes two types of monetary actions, referred to as sterilization, to offset the increase in the domestic money supply associated with the bank's intervention in the foreign exchange market. First, the central bank issues bills to commercial banks. This involves a straightforward commercial bank purchase of interest-bearing paper issued by the central bank, resulting in a reduction in the domestic money supply.[49] Second, the central bank raises the required reserve ratio, the share of deposits that banks must place at the central bank. Raising the required reserve ratio reduces the money supply below the path it would otherwise take because it limits banks' ability to expand their lending operations.

In a flexible interest rate environment, a central bank's sterilization costs usually rise along with increases in the magnitude and duration of its intervention in the foreign exchange market. As the stock of sterilization bonds rises, investors in these bonds, anticipating that the central bank ultimately may be less than fully successful in controlling inflation, typically will demand increasingly higher interest rates to be willing to hold large quantities of the central bank's paper. On the other hand, the interest rate the central bank earns on the foreign currency–denominated financial assets that comprise its official foreign exchange reserves will likely be stable. Eventually, as these opposing trends play out, the central bank likely will begin to lose money on its foreign exchange operations, i.e., the amount it pays in interest to holders of central bank bills may come to exceed the amount of interest the central bank earns on its reserves.

Setting interest rates administratively at very low levels allows the People's Bank of China to minimize or even avoid these potential financial losses altogether (Ljungwall, Yi, and Zou 2009). At the end of 2010 there was RMB4 trillion outstanding in central bank bills, almost all of which was held by commercial banks. Average interest rates paid by the central bank in 2010 were 1.692 percent for three-month bills and 2.136 percent for one-year maturities (People's Bank of China Monetary Policy Analysis Small Group 2011a, 8). The alternative use of these funds by banks would have been much higher-yielding loans to customers; requiring banks to hold central bank bills thus constitutes an implicit tax. In 2010 the average interest rate banks earned on their

---

49. Large-scale issuance of bills by the central bank began in late 2003 because by that time the central bank had sold its entire holdings of MOF bonds.

loans was 6.11 percent, more than 4 percentage points higher than what banks earned on central bank bills (People's Bank of China Monetary Policy Analysis Small Group 2011a, 4).[50] Thus, ignoring the additional risk associated with loans, as opposed to presumably risk-free central bank bills, the tax associated with bank holding of central bank bills in 2010 was about RMB170 billion, or 0.4 percent of GDP.[51]

Central bank sterilization, via hiking the required reserve ratio, also constitutes an implicit tax on banks. By the end of 2010 the People's Bank of China had raised this ratio to 18.5 percent, up 12.5 percentage points from the 6 percent required reserve ratio that applied from 2000 through August 2003. Given that average bank deposits during 2010 were RMB73.3 trillion, the 12.5 percentage point increase in China's required reserve ratio meant banks had to place an additional RMB9.2 trillion on deposit with the central bank, compared with what would have been required if the required reserve ratio had remained unchanged. The interest rate the central bank pays on these reserves was 1.89 percent from February 2002 through October 2008 and has been 1.62 percent since then. On the same methodology used to calculate the implicit tax imposed on banks by requiring them to hold central bank bills, in 2010 the additional implicit tax on banks associated with the increase in the required reserve ratio can be estimated as RMB450 billion, about 1 percent of GDP.

Thus, whether by requiring banks to hold ever larger amounts of central bank bills or raising the required reserve ratio, ultralow interest rates allow the central bank to sterilize on the cheap.

While the central bank's intervention in the foreign exchange market and related offsetting sterilization operations impose a substantial implicit tax on banks, the central bank offsets this tax through its control of deposit rates that banks pay to savers. As already noted, the ceiling that banks are allowed to pay on deposits is quite low, so low that for one-year deposits the average real interest rate during the years 2004 through 2010 was negative. In short, while it is not described this way by official sources, it appears as if the banks are willing to put massive quantities of funds into low-yielding deposits at the central bank and to hold a significant amount of low-yielding central bank paper in part because they are implicitly compensated in the form of a very low cost of funds on the deposit side of their business. The low ceiling that the central bank sets on deposits, combined with the floor that is set on lending rates, allows banks to earn very generous spreads on their deposit taking and lending business (Lardy and Douglass 2011). The generous spread more than compensates the banks for the implicit tax imposed on them by

---

50. This was the average weighted interest rate banks received on loans of all maturities, excluding short-term discounted bill lending.

51. The calculation assumes that bank earnings on central bank bills were an average of the yield on three-month and one-year maturities.

the requirement to hold low-yielding central bank bills and to place funds in low-yielding accounts at the central bank (Lardy 2008).

A closely related reason the central bank has kept interest rates low since 2003 is to minimize the magnitude of so-called hot money inflows from abroad. Private investors outside of China, observing China's rapidly growing external surplus beginning in the middle part of the last decade, widely anticipated that the renminbi would appreciate, either through the central bank moving the nominal exchange rate or through the emergence of higher price inflation in China than in the rest of the world. To capitalize on this anticipated appreciation, these investors want to hold renminbi-denominated financial assets. They attempt to do this by evading Chinese controls on inflows of portfolio capital. These foreign investors expect to earn an amount equal to the interest they would earn on renminbi bank deposits or the gains they could achieve by investing in real estate plus any appreciation of the renminbi that occurred between the time they get their funds into China and the time they take them out. The central bank tries to mitigate the volume of these capital inflows by keeping domestic interest rates on deposits low relative to foreign interest rates and placing increasingly strict limits on the ability of non-Chinese to invest in residential property. In 2006 Wu Xiaoling, a vice governor of the central bank, stated explicitly that the central bank was keeping domestic interest rates low to maintain a negative spread between domestic and international interest rates but that this entailed a risk since "the low interest rate environment is prone to resulting in asset bubbles, which we are closely watching and are worried about."[52] More recently Li Daokui, a member of the Monetary Policy Committee of the People's Bank of China, explicitly reiterated this concern, stating "if China's interest rates are too high...hot money will flow in."[53]

Thus the central bank had two closely related reasons to keep deposit interest rates low after 2003. First, low rates enabled the central bank to sterilize on the cheap, mitigating the conflict between its two assigned policy goals. Second, low rates helped hold down the volume of speculative capital inflows and thus reduced the magnitude of foreign exchange purchases the bank had to undertake to keep the currency undervalued and thus also reduced the size of sterilization operations required to maintain price stability.

In addition, the central government, and particularly the Ministry of Finance, had yet another reason for the central bank to set a ceiling on the interest rates banks paid on deposits and a floor on the rates they could charge on loans. The government wanted to maintain a wide spread in order to assure that China's commercial banks would be profitable. The government in a series of steps starting in the late 1990s undertook a major recapitalization of several of the largest state-owned banks. By 2005 the total cost of this recapitalization

---

52. "China PBOC Concerned about Possible Asset Bubbles," Dow Jones Newswires, November 26, 2006, available at http://online.wsj.com (accessed on November 27, 2006).

53. "China Central Bank Adviser Backs Interest-Rate Rises," Dow Jones Newswires, May 16, 2011, available at www.wsj.com (accessed on May 16, 2011).

reached an estimated $4 trillion (Ma Guonan 2006). The funding arrangements for this multistep recapitalization process were elaborate and far from fully transparent, but it appears that the People's Bank of China and the MOF split some 85 percent of the total cost. The balance, in effect, was born by strategic foreign institutional investors that took equity stakes in the banks prior to their public listings. Both the ministry and the central bank wanted to protect their investment by ensuring that these banks remained profitable. Since Chinese commercial banks have very little fee income, they depend for their earnings very largely on the spread between their deposit and lending rates, i.e., the net interest margin. Thus the key to ensuring high levels of bank profitability was to place a low ceiling on the interest rate that banks could pay on deposits and a floor on the interest rate they could charge on loans to borrowers.

The Ministry of Finance's desire to ensure profits in the banking sector only increased in later years, when the China Investment Corporation (CIC) gained control from the People's Bank of China of Central Huijin, a financial institution that owns large stakes in several of China's largest banks. CIC, which is controlled by the MOF, also assumed responsibility for paying the interest on a special RMB1.55 trillion bond that the MOF had issued in 2007 to acquire funds used to purchase $200 billion in foreign exchange from the State Administration of Foreign Exchange. The MOF then injected this $200 billion into CIC as the agency's initial registered capital (China Investment Corporation 2011, 9). CIC is dependent on dividend payments from bank profits in order to service this debt. Liberalization of interest rates on loans and deposits would reduce bank profitability and perhaps require the ministry itself to assume responsibility for the interest payments on its bond issue, which would place an additional claim on fiscal revenues (Walter and Howie 2011).

Explicit support for the view that liberalization of the financial system would raise interest rates on loans and deposits comes from Xiao Gang, the chairman of Bank of China, China's fourth largest commercial bank. In early 2010 he stated that interest rate liberalization would reduce bank spreads by almost half, implying that deposit rates would rise but that banks would not be able to fully pass on the higher cost of funds to their customers.[54] This, of course, is an explicit admission that the central bank, by setting ceilings on deposit rates but floors on lending rates, artificially boosts bank profitability. Nonetheless Xiao Gang has been a consistent advocate for liberalization of interest rates, seeing it both as a means of avoiding asset bubbles that accompany negative real deposit rates and as a prerequisite for increasing competition in the banking system, deepening China's capital markets, and improving the monetary policy transmission mechanism.[55]

---

54. The alternative that would also reduce bank spreads would be a fall in deposit rates but a larger fall in lending rates, which is most implausible in the current environment. Xiao Gang, "Don't Blame It on the Government," August 6, 2010, available at www.boc.cn (accessed on August 27, 2010).

55. Xiao Gang, "Liberalize Interest Rates Further," *China Daily*, January 7–9, 2011, 12.

Market-determined interest rates would lead to lending rates that on average are higher in real terms than has been the case in recent years, thus potentially reducing China's extraordinarily high rate of investment of recent years. That reduction would contribute to the leadership goal of reducing China's dependence on investment as a source of economic growth. Greater interest rate flexibility also would allow the central bank to mitigate macroeconomic cycles by raising real lending rates to moderate investment booms, thus reducing the cyclicality of economic growth. At present the authorities still rely in part on direct controls on the quantity of loans that banks can extend, an imperfect instrument that banks and firms seek to evade through a variety of practices.

Given these direct and indirect contributions that greater exchange rate flexibility could make to economic rebalancing, how has China's exchange rate policy evolved in recent years?

On July 21, 2005, China introduced a new currency regime that ended the policy of a fixed nominal exchange rate of the renminbi vis-à-vis the dollar, which it had adopted in the mid-1990s (People's Bank of China 2005b). The new policy had several dimensions. First, the central bank immediately revalued the official bilateral exchange rate against the US dollar from RMB8.28 to RMB8.11, an appreciation of 2.1 percent. Second, it stated that the renminbi henceforth would be managed with respect to a basket of currencies, rather than being pegged to the dollar. Third, and potentially most important, the central bank said that the exchange rate of the renminbi would become "more flexible" with its value based more on "market supply and demand."

It is important to note that by the time the People's Bank announced this policy change in mid-2005, the renminbi was already significantly undervalued on a real, trade-weighted basis, perhaps by as much as 20 to 25 percent (Cline and Williamson 2008; Goldstein and Lardy 2009, 25). This assessment is based both on various technical methodologies and on a qualitative analysis of the evidence from the prior decade, when the renminbi was pegged to the dollar. It is analytically useful to divide this decade into roughly two periods. From the middle of 1994, when China abandoned its dual exchange rate system in favor of a single, unified exchange rate and began pegging to the dollar, to February 2002, the dollar was appreciating on a real, trade-weighted basis. Thus the Chinese currency, again on a trade-weighted basis, also was appreciating by an average of about 3.5 percent per annum, as shown in figure 3.5.[56] As pointed out in chapter 2, this pace of real appreciation seems to have been

---

56. The dollar and the renminbi, of course, did not appreciate on a trade-weighted basis at exactly the same pace because the relative importance of various countries as trading partners of the United States and China is not the same. Appreciation of the US dollar vis-à-vis the Canadian dollar and the Mexican peso, for example, would be far more important in determining the trade-weighted value of the US dollar, since Canada and Mexico are the largest trading partners of the United States but considerably less important trading partners of China.

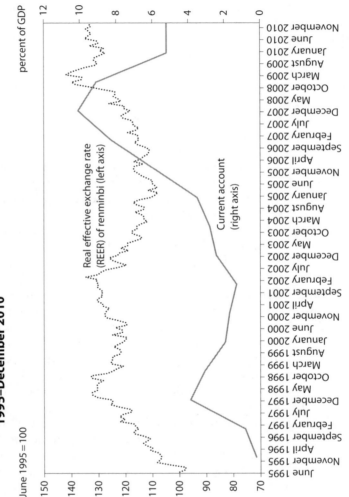

Figure 3.5   Real effective exchange rate and current account, June 1995–December 2010

June 1995 = 100

percent of GDP

Real effective exchange rate (REER) of renminbi (left axis)

Current account (right axis)

Sources: Bank for International Settlements; State Administration of Foreign Exchange, www.safe.gov.cn; ISI Emerging Markets, CEIC Database.

roughly equal to the differential growth of productivity in China's tradable goods sector compared with that of China's trading partners.

The real effective exchange rate of the renminbi from the mid-1990s through 2001 should be regarded as an equilibrium exchange rate. Several factors underlie this judgment. First and perhaps most important, as already noted, China's average current account position in this period averaged a very modest 2 percent of GDP and showed no secular trend.[57]

Second, as mentioned above, prior to mid-1994 the Chinese operated a dual exchange rate system in which privileged importers could buy foreign currency at a favorable rate, and others purchased foreign exchange in what were referred to as swap centers, where exporters were the source of foreign exchange offered for sale.[58] The large gap at year-end 1993, between the official rate of RMB5.8 to the dollar and the swap market rate of RMB8.7 to the dollar, reflected the substantial overvaluation of the currency at the official rate. But when the People's Bank of China unified the rates on January 1, 1994, it did so by moving the official rate to the then-prevailing swap market rate. At that point the official rate was probably a bit undervalued, but this was corrected when the authorities gradually appreciated the rate over the next 18 months to RMB8.3 to the dollar and then by October 1997 to RMB8.28 to the dollar, the point at which it was rigidly pegged until July 2005.[59]

The third reason for regarding the exchange rate prevailing from the mid-1990s through 2001 as an equilibrium exchange rate is that following the unification of the two exchange rates in January 1994, the central bank substantially reduced exchange controls on current account transactions. This led in late November 1996 to China's formal acceptance of the obligations imposed by Article VIII of the International Monetary Fund (IMF), meaning that China had achieved convertibility on all current account transactions and

---

57. In the discussion of the sources of growth in chapter 2, the metric was the surplus on goods and services. This is appropriate because by definition GDP is equal to the sum of consumption, investment, and net exports of goods and services. In this chapter the metric to measure the external position is a somewhat broader measure, the current account. In addition to trade in goods and services, the current account also includes investment income and transfers. However, arithmetically the difference between the two in recent years in China has been small, at least through 2009. Net exports of goods and services have accounted for the vast majority of the country's net current account position, while net foreign income and profit and net current transfers have been much smaller components. In 2007, for example, the shares of these three components in the net current account were 83, 7, and 10 percent, respectively (State Administration of Foreign Exchange International Balance of Payments Analysis Small Group 2008, 9).

58. Starting in 1979 the central government gave up its monopoly on foreign exchange and allowed exporting firms to retain a part of their earnings from exports rather than surrendering them entirely to the government. The amounts of foreign exchange so retained grew rapidly over time (Lardy 1992, 52–57).

59. The move from RMB8.7 to RMB8.28 represented a cumulative nominal appreciation of 5 percent.

that the government would approve all bona fide requests for foreign exchange for current payments and transfers (IMF 1997, 132). Absent current account convertibility, the current account balance might be small, but this could reflect limited access to foreign exchange by would-be importers rather than a true equilibrium exchange rate.

After February 2002, however, the US dollar began to depreciate on a sustained basis. As a result of the peg to the dollar, the renminbi also depreciated in value and thus diverged systematically from its previous equilibrium rate. By the middle of 2005, when the People's Bank of China announced the change in its currency policy, the renminbi had depreciated by 15 percent in real, effective terms according to the index compiled by the Bank for International Settlements. But compared with the trend line of appreciation over the previous six or seven years, the degree of undervaluation was greater, about 20 to 25 percent (Goldstein and Lardy 2009, 10–26).

The undervaluation of the renminbi was also reflected in the gradual expansion of China's external surplus after 2002, also shown in figure 3.5, and an increasingly rapid buildup of foreign exchange reserves, discussed earlier in this chapter and shown in figure 3.4.

The Chinese authorities allowed the renminbi to appreciate about 25 percent on a real, trade-weighted basis between June 2005 and the end of 2008. However, China's current account surplus continued to expand rapidly, tripling in absolute terms between 2005 and 2008. The current account surplus reached 10.1 and 9.1 percent of GDP in 2007 and 2008, respectively, historically unprecedented levels for a large, trading economy.

The reasons why China's external surplus continued to expand after the currency began to appreciate are very straightforward. First, currency appreciation will begin to reduce a country's external surplus below the path that would have occurred in the absence of appreciation. But this will occur with a lag of several quarters. Second, as already pointed out, the starting point in July 2005 was not an equilibrium renminbi exchange rate but a currency that was significantly undervalued. Third, while the currency appreciated about 6 percent in the second half of 2005, subsequently the pace of appreciation was very modest. The real, trade-weighted value of the renminbi actually depreciated over the course of 2006 and changed little in the first half of 2007. Not until the closing months of 2007 through the end of 2008 did the People's Bank allow the currency to appreciate much more rapidly.

During the global financial and economic crisis the government repegged the renminbi to the dollar for about a 22-month period that ended in late June 2010. Then the People's Bank of China allowed the currency to appreciate gradually vis-à-vis the dollar, much as it had between July 2005 and April 2009. By June 2011 the renminbi had appreciated by about 5 percent vis-à-vis the dollar in nominal terms. But on a real, trade-weighted basis the renminbi depreciated between June 2010 and June 2011 and over the two and a half year period ending in June 2011.

While the value of the renminbi depreciated over the two years ending in December 2010, the current account surplus came down by almost half from its peak of 10.1 percent of GDP in 2007 to 5.2 percent of GDP in both 2009 and 2010. What accounts for this reduction? Is China's external economic rebalancing well underway? If so, will this external rebalancing be sustained? The official answer advanced by the Chinese government is yes to both these questions. In the course of China's annual consultation with the IMF in the spring of 2010, government officials stated that "they view the level of the renminbi right now as much closer to equilibrium than at any time before" and that "they anticipate that the current account surplus will settle at about 4 percent of GDP over the medium term" (IMF 2010b, 16, 19). The IMF's interlocutors credited ongoing structural reforms, rising wages, and the recent appreciation of the currency as factors underlying the transition to an even smaller surplus than recorded in 2009.

The staff of the IMF (2010b), on the other hand, underlined the "potential for larger current account surpluses to reassert themselves." The staff pointed to three factors underlying this view. First, they noted that reserve accumulation continued to be rapid and that, given the large absolute size of China's reserves, the income component of the current account would grow rapidly as global interest rates returned to more normal levels. Second, they pointed out that the real level of China's trade-weighted exchange rate in mid-2010 was little different from what it was in the late 1990s but that over the decade China had experienced substantially higher productivity growth in the production of tradable goods than its trading partners. Third, the IMF staff attributed the reduction of the current account in 2008 and 2009 primarily to the global slowdown. Using different methodologies the IMF staff suggested that as global growth recovered China's underlying competitiveness would become more apparent and that the current account would expand to around 8 percent of GDP by 2015. The IMF's view was reaffirmed in the spring 2011 *World Economic Outlook*, which forecast that China's current account would rise to 5.7 percent of GDP in 2011 and to 7.6 and 7.9 percent of GDP by 2015 and 2016, respectively, and again in the Fund's 2011 Article IV Report (IMF 2011a, 2011c).[60]

Some independent estimates advance views consistent with those of the IMF. Joseph Gagnon (2011) forecasts that if China continues to accumulate foreign exchange reserves at roughly the same pace as in 2004–08 its average current account surplus in 2011–15 will rise to an average in excess of 8 percent of GDP, two-fifths higher than the 2009–10 level. William Cline's (2010) analysis shows that because of the usual two-year lag between an exchange rate change and a change in a country's external balance, a substantial portion of the decline in China's current account surplus—between the peak 10.1 percent

---

60. The detailed year-by-year current account forecasts are available in IMF (2011d).

of GDP in 2007 and the 5.2 percent level in 2009–10—can be explained by the sizeable real appreciation of the renminbi in 2005–08, most of which occurred in the closing months of 2007 and in 2008. But with the renminbi actually depreciating between the end of 2008 and mid-year 2011, China's surplus is likely to begin to rise again when economic recovery strengthens in its main export markets—the United States and Europe.

Price Reform

Price reform offers a fourth policy arena the government could utilize to contribute to the rebalancing of China's economic growth. Over the first two decades of economic reform the government largely relinquished the once pervasive direct control exercised by the State Price Commission over goods prices. By the end of the 1990s the state directly controlled the prices involved in only 4, 9, and 10 percent, respectively, of retail, agricultural, and producer goods sales (Lardy 2002, 25). But the state retained price-setting authority for a few critical factor prices such as capital (already analyzed), power (fuels and electricity), water, and land. The prices the state sets for these items as well as environmental charges are not currently in accordance with relative scarcities and the environment (He and Kuijs 2007). Appropriate pricing at a minimum means full cost recovery; more ambitiously it would mean marginal opportunity cost pricing—i.e., including both the cost of environmental damage in production and consumption and the opportunity cost of resource depletion (World Bank 2007).

Most of the factors for which the state continues to exercise price-setting power are significantly underpriced. The underpriced inputs are used more intensively in manufacturing than in services. This is clearly the case for capital, since manufacturing is more capital intensive than services. But it is also the case for fuels and electricity because industry accounts for almost two-thirds of final energy consumption in China, compared with about one-quarter in the United States (Bergsten et al. 2008, 142). Underpricing of these inputs has raised profitability in manufacturing and, as noted in chapter 2, contributed to an increase in the share of total national investment flowing into China's manufacturing sector after 2003. It has thus contributed to the global supercompetitiveness of Chinese exports, which are overwhelmingly manufactures, and distorted the domestic pattern of production in which the share of services in GDP languished for much of the last decade.

More appropriate pricing, including the enforcement of existing environmental standards, would raise the cost of production of manufactures, making them less competitive in global markets and thus reducing China's external surplus. It would also mean that economic returns in tradable goods (overwhelmingly manufactures) production would fall relative to economic returns in services. That effect would reduce investment in manufacturing, particularly the most energy-intensive industries, and increase investment in services and thus over time lead to the desired change in the structure of output discussed in chapter 2.

Energy is one of the most important areas where the state has retained price-setting power throughout the reform era. In the first decade of reform, the 1980s, the state set the price of crude oil at a small fraction of the world price, continuing a policy inherited from prereform policymakers. But beginning in the late 1980s, the Chinese government moved gradually to raise the domestic price of crude toward the international level. By 1998, when convergence was complete, the government adopted a formal plan to adjust monthly the domestic price of crude oil so as to keep it in line with the international price. Retail prices gradually reflected the principle of full-cost pricing, and in mid-2000 the government adopted a formal program to adjust these prices monthly as well, so that refined product prices fully reflected the cost of crude, refining costs, and so forth (Lardy 1992, 90–94; 2002, 26). Thus while the prices of both crude and refined products remained government controlled, these prices in principle would diverge only slightly from international market prices.

But, as the cost of crude on the global market began to rise rapidly in 2004, the Chinese government began to modify its pricing policy. The authorities still adjusted upward the domestic price of crude oil to keep it in line with the international price, but the government allowed only part of the rising cost of crude to be reflected in retail prices of major refined products, notably diesel and gasoline. By 2005 the government was paying subsidies to Chinese refiners to compensate them for at least part of their refining losses.

This problem recurred on a much larger scale in the first half of 2008, when global oil prices rose sharply and retail prices in China for gasoline and diesel fuel were both well below retail prices in the United States and the lowest of any oil-importing emerging-market country (Anderson 2008b). China Petroleum & Chemical Corporation (Sinopec), the country's largest oil refiner, saw its net profits plunge by three-quarters in the first half of 2008 as its profits in other lines of business and refining subsidies from the central government barely offset its massive refining losses.[61] In June 2008 the Chinese government finally raised the retail price of gas and diesel by almost one-fifth. Financial pressure on the refiners eased further in the second half of the year as the international price of crude oil fell precipitously; the National Development and Reform Commission (NDRC), the agency responsible for setting energy prices, held the domestic retail prices of gasoline and diesel fuel unchanged until mid-December, when it cut prices slightly.

---

61. Sinopec lost RMB46.0 billion on its refining operations in the first half of 2008, compared with profits of RMB5.7 billion in the first half of 2007. Its overall operating profits plunged from RMB53.6 billion in the first half of 2007 to RMB7.2 billion in the first half of 2008. "Sinopec Corp. Announces 2008 Interim Results," Sinopec, available at http://english.sinopec.com (accessed on September 13, 2011).

Unlike that in 2004, the government's price adjustment in 2008 reduced, but did not eliminate, the operating losses of the refiners. Equally important, it left the refiners with no return on the capital employed in refining. For the year as a whole the three largest refiners incurred RMB165.2 billion in losses on their refining business, of which the government covered RMB63.2 billion in fiscal subsidies and the firms absorbed about RMB100 billion from their profits on their nonrefining operations.[62]

In the first part of 2009 the NDRC continued to reduce refined product prices by less than the decline in the international price of oil. By mid-year 2009, underpricing of gasoline and diesel fuel had been substantially reduced. In fact, retail prices of gas and diesel in China were above the US level, and prices in China were no longer the lowest of a large group of oil-importing emerging-market economies (Anderson 2009). As a result, China's oil majors were no longer losing money on their refining operations.[63]

In January 2009 the government instituted fuel price reforms that went part way to restoring the full-cost pricing policy that had first been adopted in 2000 but then abandoned in 2004. Under the new regime, the domestic price of crude continues to be aligned with the international price, and the NDRC considers adjustments to retail prices of refined products whenever an international crude oil price index changes by more than 4 percent in any 22-working-day period.[64] In principle, there will be full-cost pass-through, including a 5 percent margin for refiners, when the global price of crude is under $80 per barrel, i.e., prices of gasoline, diesel, and other refined petroleum products will move fully in step with global crude prices.[65] However, if the global price of crude rises above $80 per barrel, retail prices of refined products will rise less than would be required under full-cost pass-through. This policy will be achieved by cutting refining and distribution margins and then imposing financial losses on refiners. If the global price of crude rises above $130 per barrel, retail prices will be capped (Stanway 2009). Thus, as long as the global

---

62. "2009 Review of the State Council's State-Owned Assets Supervision and Administration Commission," State-Owned Assets Supervision and Administration Commission, August 3, 2010, available at www.sasac.gov.cn (accessed on May 2, 2011).

63. Sinopec, for example, reported profits on its refining business of RMB23.077 billion in 2009, compared with losses of RMB63.635 billion in 2008. See China Petroleum & Chemical Corporation (2010, 25).

64. The global index is based on prices for North Sea Brent, Middle East benchmark Dubai, and Indonesian Cinta crude oils.

65. In addition to the international cost of crude (including cost, insurance, freight [cif]) and the refining profit margin, costs reflected in the wholesale prices set by the NDRC include domestic freight, value-added taxes, and sales tax. The difference between the wholesale and retail prices for refined products, also controlled by the NDRC, is a fixed margin to cover distribution and marketing costs. This spread is typically 5 to 6 percent for gasoline and about 4 percent for diesel fuel.

price of crude remains below $80 per barrel, the state will neither subsidize domestic users of fuel nor cut the profit margin of refiners.

The shortcomings of this policy approach for a product with as much price volatility as crude oil are obvious. As the global price of crude began to rise in the second half of 2010 on the back of the global economic recovery and then, as a result of political unrest in much of the Arab world, rose sharply to well above $100 per barrel in the first quarter of 2011, the NDRC raised retail prices for refined products in both February and April. But the increases, in each case, were less than two-fifths of the increase in the NDRC's index of international crude oil prices.[66] The International Energy Agency estimated that in February 2011 the price of diesel and gasoline in China were 35 and 14 percent, respectively, below the international price (IEA 2011). The degree of underpricing in China had increased further by April. As a result PetroChina and Sinopec, China's two largest refiners, reported 2011 first half losses of RMB23.4 billion and RMB12.2 billion, respectively, on their refining operations.[67]

A similar pattern occurred in electric power, which in China relative to GDP is twice as important as petroleum. Through the middle of the last decade, full-cost pricing was in effect, companies generating electric power were profitable, and few consumers of electricity were subsidized (Anderson 2008a, 4).[68] In 2004 the government approved a mechanism in which the NDRC would raise the price of electricity if domestic coal prices rose more than 5 percent in a six-month period. But in 2007 and 2008, as the price of coal rose on the domestic market, coal mines were reluctant to fulfill annual supply contracts

---

66. On February 20, 2011, the NDRC announced price increases for gasoline and diesel of 4.1 and 4.5 percent, respectively, although the index of crude oil prices had increased 11.45 percent since the previous price increase in December 2010. On April 6, 2011, the NDRC announced price increases for gasoline and diesel of 5.5 and 5 percent, respectively, although the index of crude oil prices had increased by 14.3 percent since the last fuel price increase on February 20, 2011.

67. Yvonne Lee, "Sinopec Output Boosts Profit," *Wall Street Journal*, August 29, 2011, available at www.wsj.com (accessed on September 16, 2011). Yvonne Lee, "High Oil Prices Weigh on PetroChina Profit," *Wall Street Journal*, August 26, 2011, available at www.wsj.com (accessed on September 16, 2011).

68. The exception to full-cost pricing was that in order to boost economic growth some local governments provided subsidized electric power to some firms producing aluminum, cement, steel, zinc, and other energy-intensive products. The NDRC banned this practice in 2006 in order to achieve the key 11th Five-Year Plan (2006–10) objective of reducing energy consumption per unit of GDP. But in November 2008, as the global financial crisis intensified, some provincial governments resumed these subsidies. By May 2010, when the NDRC stepped up its effort to enforce the ban, it estimated that subsidies to energy-intensive firms exceeded RMB15 billion. It appears these subsidies did not take the form of fiscal transfers to these firms by local governments. Rather local governments forced power generating companies to supply power to these firms at prices less than the official tariff schedule. "China Scraps Preferential Power Rates for Energy-Intensive Firms," People's Daily Online, August 6, 2010, available at http://english.people.com.cn (accessed on September 13, 2011).

that had been struck earlier when prices were much lower. That forced the generators, especially the small, independent power producers that frequently were unable to obtain annual supply contracts, to buy a growing share of their coal on the spot market, where prices were much higher than the contract price. But the price that the electric power generating companies received for delivering power to the electric power grid companies had remained unchanged since 2006. Thus the generating companies were squeezed, and their profits plummeted. To put pressure on the NDRC, the agency responsible for price setting, some generating companies curtailed their power production. This led to localized electric power shortages and protests from large power users.[69] Not until June 2008 did the NDRC belatedly respond to the rising price of coal and increase the price of power that grid companies paid to the generators, but only by 5 percent.

This on-grid price increase turned out to be far too modest to restore the power generators to a profit-making position. The price of coal fell in the second half of 2008 compared with the peaks of the first part of the year, but China's simultaneous economic slowdown (noted in chapter 1) led to much slower growth in the demand for electricity. In some months of the fourth quarter of 2008, electric power demand declined in absolute terms. At least through 2008, the resulting adverse effect of the resulting lower rate of utilization of power generation capacity more than offset the reduction in the market price of coal. The result was that in the first 11 months of 2008 the five largest power generating companies, which account for about two-fifths of China's power generation, posted losses of RMB30 billion, and profits of the power industry as a whole fell 84 percent, compared with 39 percent growth in the same period in the prior year.[70]

Moreover, China's electric power grid companies were not allowed to pass on the modest June 2008 on-grid price increase to final consumers, so the price adjustment simply reduced the losses of the generators at the expense of the power distributors. For example, the profits of the State Grid Corporation of China, responsible for the distribution of electric power in 26 of China's 31 provincial-level administrative units, fell by 80 percent in 2008, to RMB9.66 billion, compared with RMB47.1 billion the prior year (State Grid Corporation of China 2009, 34).[71] Thus electric power remained subsidized for both household and industrial consumers.

---

69. Most large users of electric power had stand-by generating capacity installed in earlier periods of uncertain power supply. But the cost of power from these generators is relatively high, so large users would rather pay somewhat higher prices for power from the generating companies, especially if these higher prices reduced supply uncertainty.

70. Li Qiyan, "Power: Stymied Coal Talks Point to Power Reform," *Caijing*, February 4, 2009, available at http://english.caijing.com (accessed on April 14, 2009).

71. The sharp decline was the result not only of the margin squeeze but also of severe winter storms and a major earthquake in Sichuan Province.

Slowing economic growth reduced the demand for coal in 2009. Moderating coal prices provided some relief to China's generating companies, and in November 2009 the NDRC raised the price of electricity for nonresidential users by 5.4 percent. Nonetheless, the financial situation at China's largest electricity distributor, State Grid, continued to deteriorate. In 2009 profits plummeted another 50 percent from the depressed level of 2008 to only RMB4.52 billion, resulting in a cumulative decline of 90 percent in profits compared with 2007 and a return on assets of only 0.25 percent (State Grid Corporation of China 2010, 4, 29). Moreover, as China's own growth accelerated in 2010 and the global economy began to recover, coal prices rose again, offsetting the effect of the November 2009 price increase. As a result, in 2010 electric power generators suffered a loss of RMB32.9 billion.[72] By contrast, profits of State Grid Corporation rebounded to RMB35 billion, presumably reflecting the November 2009 electricity price increase for nonresidential customers.[73]

It is important to recognize that from an economic point of view the magnitude of subsidy received by users of electric power is substantially larger than simply the losses reported by the electric power generating companies and the size of the subsidies that generators sometimes receive from the state. When profits of the generators and/or the distributors fall to zero, the return on their assets also is zero. Thus the real economic subsidy to users of electric power is the sum of any operating losses plus an allowance for return on capital. Similarly, government subsidies sometimes paid to the generators cover only operating losses and do not take into account a normal rate of return on capital. Thus the real economic cost of the subsidy to users of electric power far exceeds the losses reported by the industry. Even if we assume a relatively low "normal rate of return" on these assets, say 5 percent, the economic subsidy to users of electric power in 2010 was more than eight times the RMB32.9 billion in operating losses reported by the generating industry.[74] To this we would need to also add the implicit subsidy inherent in the low rate of return on assets at the State Grid Corporation. Despite the

---

72. "China's Thermal Power Plants to See More Losses," *China Daily*, February 26, 2011, available at www.chinadaily.com.cn (accessed on April 21, 2011).

73. "China's Top Grid to Cut 2010 Grid Investment 20 Pct," Reuters, January 18, 2010, available at www.uk.reuters.com (accessed on May 3, 2011).

74. The depreciated value of the fixed assets of the electric power industry in 2009 averaged RMB 4.3 trillion (National Bureau of Statistics of China 2010f, 508–09). If we assume their net assets in 2010 were 15 percent greater than in 2009 (the same rate of growth of assets that they reported in 2009), to earn 5 percent on these assets the electric power generating industry would have needed earnings of RMB250 billion. Thus the subsidy received by electric power users in 2010 was not just the RMB32.9 billion reported operating losses of the generating companies but the operating losses plus RMB250 billion, or a total of RMB285 billion. This amount is 8.6 times the reported operating loss.

jump in its profits in 2010, it earned only a paltry 1.7 percent on its assets.[75] The other major grid corporation, China Southern, faced the same operating environment so also almost certainly earned a subpar return on its assets. On an all-in basis the subsidy to electric power users in 2010 was probably about RMB360 billion.[76] While this is only 1 percent of 2010 GDP, the benefit is highly concentrated in a handful of industries that use electric power most intensively. Thus the subsidy substantially reduces the production costs and raises the profits of these industries.

One key point that emerges from this analysis of the government's policy options to promote consumption and reduce external imbalances is that there is a high degree of complementarity and interdependence across the four policy approaches. Appreciation of the renminbi and appropriate pricing of factor inputs are highly complementary since they both would raise the cost of producing tradable goods relative to nontradables, thus leading to a reduction in China's global surplus and a restructuring of its GDP. Perhaps the best example of the interdependence of policies to promote rebalancing is that adopting a more flexible exchange rate policy is an essential precondition for moving toward market-determined interest rates. Thus these two policies should proceed in tandem.

What, if anything, can be said about the relative importance of the four policy domains just reviewed in terms of their potential contribution to reducing imbalances in China? The expenditure approach to measuring imbalances laid out in chapter 2 showed that three-quarters of the decline in the share of household consumption in GDP is due to falling disposable income, and one-quarter due to a rise in the household saving rate. Thus while building up the social safety net is highly desirable for several reasons, including its potential contribution to reducing the household saving rate from disposable income, that reduction in and of itself is not likely to be sufficient to reverse the long-term decline in the consumption share of GDP. Policies that raise household disposable income as a share of GDP are potentially much more important.

This interpretation is borne out by examining the effect that an improved social safety net has had on consumption expenditure in other countries. For example, in Taiwan the introduction of the National Health Insurance

---

75. State Grid reported net assets of RMB1,860 billion in 2009 (State Grid Corporation of China 2010, 4). If these assets grew 10 percent in 2010 the reported RMB35 billion in profits that year represents a 1.7 percent return on assets.

76. RMB360 billion is the sum of the following: RMB32.9 billion in reported losses of the generating companies, an estimated RMB250 billion in profits required to yield a 5 percent return on the assets of the generating companies, an estimated RMB67.5 billion in additional profits that State Grid would have had to earn to yield a 5 percent return on its assets, and an estimated RMB13 billion in additional profits that China Southern would have had to earn to boost its return on assets to 5 percent. In the absence of any information on profits and assets for China Southern, the estimated profit top-up required to reach a 5 percent return on its assets is assumed to be 5/26ths that of State Grid.

program raised the share of the population covered by health insurance from 57 to 97 percent between 1994 and 1998, substantially reducing household uncertainty about future health expenditures and thus reducing the household saving rate. But the effect was to increase household consumption expenditures by only 4 percent. If a comparable effect is achieved in China from the health insurance schemes that have been introduced and are now expanding, it would raise the consumption share of GDP by 1.4 percentage points, reversing only a very small share of the long-term decline.[77]

The most important policy tool for rebalancing the sources of economic growth in China is probably to resume the policy largely abandoned after 2004 of allowing market forces to have a greater role in the determination of interest rates on deposits and loans. There are two reasons for this. First, it is quite likely that declining real return on household savings after 2003 was a more important contributor than the weakening of the social safety net to the rise in the household saving rate. Household savings as a share of disposable income actually declined in the second half of the 1990s, the period when the government pushed through a restructuring of state-owned enterprises and many workers lost the benefits provided by these firms. Rather, the rise in the household saving rate coincides with the onset of sharply declining real interest rates on deposits, suggesting that the latter was a more important reason for the consumption decline.

Moreover, while large numbers of workers lost their jobs in state-owned enterprises in the mid-1990s, it is easy to exaggerate the impact that this had on the condition of the social safety net in China, which was quite minimal. Even at the height of employment in state companies in the mid-1990s, the vast majority of the labor force had no medical insurance, workers' compensation insurance, or retirement programs. For example, in 1995 only 7 million employees out of a total workforce of 680 million were covered by the basic medical insurance scheme (National Bureau of Statistics of China 2010f, 118–19, 910).[78] Moreover, while employment in state-owned firms dropped by 31 million between 1996 and 2000, there was no comparable decline in the number of individuals covered by China's social insurance programs. The number of workers covered by retirement and medical insurance, for example, dipped by only a few million in 1997–98, but by 2000 the number covered was far higher than in 1996. So while many workers who lost their jobs in state-owned firms presumably lost the benefits associated with this employment, within a few years this decline was more than offset by the large number of new workers brought into these insurance schemes. Thus it is far from clear that the restructuring of state-owned enterprises in the second half of the 1990s had a significant effect on the average household saving rate. Negative real

---

77. In 2010 household consumption accounted for 33.8 percent of GDP. A 4 percent increase in this share would boost it to 35.2 percent.

78. In addition to the basic medical insurance scheme covering workers there are separate medical insurance systems for civil servants and other government workers and for the military.

deposit rates beginning in 2004 seem the more likely dominant cause. Thus liberalizing interest rates is likely to lead over time to a decline in the household saving rate, contributing to an increase in household consumption as a share of GDP, a key element in economic rebalancing.

The second reason to identify liberalizing interest rates on deposits and loans as the principal policy instrument to rebalance the economy is that negative rates contribute directly to the decline in disposable income as a share of GDP, which accounts for about three-quarters of the long-term decline in the consumption share of GDP. As explained earlier in this chapter, the central bank's interest rate controls have reduced the contribution of interest income to household disposable income by several percentage points of GDP. Thus the path of household income was several percentage points of GDP lower than what would have been achieved if real deposit rates had not declined so sharply after 2003. Thus liberalizing deposit interest rates will increase household income and, for any given saving rate, lead to a higher share of household consumption in GDP.

A third reason interest rate liberalization would contribute to economic rebalancing is that it would lead to higher lending rates and a reduction in China's superelevated share of investment in GDP. As noted earlier in this chapter the real interest rate on loans dropped dramatically after 2003. The low real interest rates on loans prevailing since 2003 have encouraged firms to undertake more investment than would have been economically viable in an economy with market-determined interest rates on loans and deposits. The more capital-intensive growth process that emerged in the low interest rate environment, in turn, explains in part the slower rate of growth of the nonagricultural labor force after 2003. That, in turn led to a lower share of wages in national income than would have occurred if the policy of interest rate liberalization had not been largely abandoned after 2004. This is critical since about half of the long-term decline in disposable income is accounted for by the decline in the wage share of GDP.

Moving toward a market-determined exchange rate is also essential for achieving economic rebalancing in China because it is almost certainly a precondition for liberalizing interest rates. Continued large-scale sterilization likely would become increasingly costly for the central bank if interest rates were market determined. The reason is that once deposit interest rates are liberalized, the central bank would lose its principal policy instrument for compensating commercial banks for holding low-yielding central bank bills and placing low-yielding required reserves at the central bank. If the central bank continued to require banks to hold massive quantities of low-yielding reserves and central bank bills without raising interest rates on these commercial bank assets, the central bank, in effect, would force commercial banks into a loss-making position, hardly likely to contribute to financial stability. To avoid this outcome the central bank would have to pay higher real rates on required reserves and on central bank bills. Paying higher rates could easily push the central bank into a loss-making financial position, eroding its ability to maintain price stability and forcing the Ministry of Finance to provide fiscal subsidies to offset the central bank's losses (Ljungwall, Yi, and Zou 2009).[79] To reduce the probability of being forced into a position of financial losses, the central bank would reduce the scale of its intervention in the foreign exchange market. Under conditions prevailing in recent years that would, of course, lead to an appreciation of the renminbi that, in turn, would facilitate a reduction in China's still large external imbalance.

Endogenous and "Policy Light" Rebalancing

Some have argued that the government need not adopt policies in any of the four domains just analyzed because the economic imbalances that emerged in the past decade will be self-correcting. Proponents of this view argue, for example, that endogenous rebalancing could occur if labor shortages in China led to rapidly increasing real wages. That would reverse the trend of declining household income as a share of GDP and thus, for any given household saving rate, increase consumption as a share of GDP, and reduce the household contribution to the national savings-investment imbalance. Income accruing to the corporate sector, meanwhile, would decline because of the rising cost of labor. That would most likely lead to a reduction in the contribution of the corporate sector to the national savings-investment imbalance, thus further reducing China's external surplus.

Alternatively, some have suggested that simply increasing the availability of household credit could lead households to increase their consumption significantly. That would contribute to a rise in the consumption share of GDP and to a smaller household contribution to the national savings-investment imbalance, thus reducing China's external surplus. Increasing credit availability might be both politically and economically more feasible than the tougher policy choice of liberalizing interest rates and allowing the exchange rate of the renminbi to appreciate significantly.

Rising Wages as an Automatic Rebalancer?

Ross Garnaut (2006, 2010) has been a strong proponent of the view that endogenous rebalancing is underway. He characterizes China since 2006 as being in a "turning period" in which increasing labor scarcity is leading to increases in real wages and the wage share of national income, an increase in the consumption share of GDP, and a reduction in China's external surplus. He points to anecdotal evidence of labor shortages and rising wages in export processing firms on China's southeast coast starting in the middle of the last decade. This view became much more widespread in the wake of labor actions in a number

---

79. According to Article 38 of the People's Bank of China Law (frequently referred to as the Central Bank Law), passed by the National People's Congress in 1995, the Ministry of Finance is required to offset any central bank financial losses with fiscal appropriations. "People's Bank of China Law," *China Law and Practice*, June 27, 1995, 23–30.

of foreign-funded factories in southeast China in the spring of 2009 that led to wage increases of 30 percent or more.

Others have pointed to the large number of provinces that have imposed significant increases in their minimum wage levels as evidence that average wages must be rising more rapidly than in the past. Minimum wage levels are set locally, and the average increase in 2010 for 30 provinces, regions, and municipalities was 22.8 percent, according to the Ministry of Human Resources and Social Security.[80]

When evaluating the hypothesis that rising wages are already rebalancing or soon will automatically rebalance various dimensions of China's economic growth, we must consider at least five factors. First, while average real wages rose rapidly in the previous decade, major economic imbalances emerged nonetheless. The growth of wages and the growth of nonagricultural employment must accelerate compared with the past trends in order to contribute to rebalancing. Second, China has had a minimum wage program since 1993; this too did not prevent the emergence of large economic imbalances. Third, what really matters for external rebalancing is not the rate of increase in real wages but rather trends in unit labor costs. Real wage growth in China may be rapid but, if offset by increasing labor productivity in factories producing export goods and goods that compete with imports, rising wages will not feed through to increases in prices of these goods and thus not undermine China's global competitive position. Fourth, the growth of unit labor costs in China needs to be assessed not just in absolute terms but also relative to unit labor cost trends among China's trading partners. Even if China's unit labor costs are rising, they must rise by more than unit labor costs in China's trading partners to contribute to external rebalancing. Finally, we must recognize that China has important sources of global competitive advantage that are unrelated to wages. These five factors are examined, in turn, immediately below.

Real wages in urban China in the formal sector have been rising throughout the reform period.[81] By 2010 nominal annual wages for formal-sector workers reached RMB36,540 almost seven times those of 1995. Over the same period the urban consumer price index rose only 34 percent (National Bureau of Statistics of China 2010f, 131, 307). So real wages for these workers, who account for over two-fifths of China's urban labor force quintupled, implying an average annual increase of 11.5 percent.[82]

---

80. "Rising Salaries Drives Firms West," *China Daily*, March 7, 2011, available at www.english.people.com.cn (accessed on September 13, 2011).

81. Wage data published regularly by the National Bureau of Statistics cover workers employed in corporate units (i.e., state-owned units, collective units, and units of other types of ownership) but not in private units or self-employed individuals. I refer to the group for which wage data are published regularly as formal-sector workers.

82. In 2009 the reported urban labor force was 311 million, including 55 million employed in private businesses and 42 million self-employed. The wage data given in this paragraph do not include these two groups (see previous note). In addition, China currently has about 170 million

Formal-sector employment excludes migrant workers (regardless of the ownership status of their employer), workers in private businesses, and the self-employed. The migrant labor force reportedly accounts for about 170 million workers, about four-fifths the size of the formal urban workforce.[83] Although China's statistical authority does not publish data on wages of migrant workers, periodic special surveys by Chinese scholars show their wages grew 80 percent in nominal terms between 2001 and 2008, a period in which prices rose by about a fifth (Cai and Wang 2010). Wages of migrant workers almost certainly were at best static during the 2009 economic slowdown but reportedly expanded by a robust 19 percent in real terms in 2010.[84] These data imply annual real wage growth well below that of formal-sector workers but a still respectable 8 percent.

The first year for which China's statistical authorities provided data on average wages in private firms was 2008. The annual wage level in private firms in 2010 was RMB20,760, just over half the average wage in the formal sector.[85] The growth of the average private real wage in 2009–10 was 9.1 percent, about 2 percentage points less than the growth of real wages in those years in the formal sector.

While there are no readily available data on the incomes of nonagricultural self-employed workers, it seems likely that their earnings must be at least as high, and growing at least as rapidly, as those of migrant workers—otherwise why would employers have to bring in migrant workers from hundreds or even thousands of kilometers away to fill their job vacancies? In urban China workers employed in private firms and the self-employed total about 100 million (National Bureau of Statistics of China 2010f, 117).

Taking into account the shares of the urban workforce accounted for by formal employment, migrant workers, private-sector employment, and self-employment, the average real wage in urban areas has probably been rising by almost 10 percent per year over the decade ending in 2010.[86] This confirms

---

migrant workers who are not counted in the formal urban labor force. Thus the wage data given in this paragraph cover about 215 million of a total of about 480 million urban workers.

83. Currently there are about 200 million migrants in Chinese cities, of which 85 percent are workers, the rest are dependents.

84. Cai Fang, "China's Rising Wages," East Asia Forum, September 5, 2011, available at www.eastasiaforum.org (accessed on September 16, 2011).

85. ISI Emerging Markets, CEIC Database.

86. Based on the discussion in the text, the growth of average real wages in urban areas is estimated as 11.5 percent x 0.45 + 8 percent x 0.35 + 9.1 percent x 0.11 + 8 percent x 0.09 = 9.7 percent, where 0.45, 0.35, 0.11, and 0.09 are, respectively, the shares of formal-sector workers, migrant workers, private-sector workers, and self-employed workers in the urban workforce. This is a rough estimate because it assumes that the rate of growth of wages of private-sector workers for the short period for which we do have data (2008–10) is a reasonable proxy for the growth of wages of these workers in earlier years.

the first point—real wages have been rising rapidly in China throughout the decade in which economic imbalances emerged and grew.

Given the shortcomings in the wage data just analyzed—long time lags before official annual wage data become available, no official data at all on wages of migrant workers or the self-employed, and data for only three years for private-sector workers—it is difficult to judge whether the growth of real wages has accelerated recently. Real wage growth of migrants and private-sector workers in 2010 was at an all time high. But part or perhaps all of this rapid growth in 2010 was catch up from much slower growth of wages of these workers during the economic slowdown of 2009. For the formal sector, for which we have the best data and which accounts for more than two-fifths of the urban workforce, the growth of real wages in 2009–10 was actually slightly below the longer term pace wage growth in 1995–2010. The tentative conclusion is that there is not yet much systematic evidence that the growth of real wages has begun to rise above the long-term trend of real wage growth.

A second factor that needs to be taken into account in evaluating the hypothesis that rising wages will automatically rebalance the sources of China's economic growth is that the minimum wage program is not new but was initiated by the Ministry of Labor almost two decades ago, in 1993 (Ni, Wang, and Yao 2011, 18). But in most jurisdictions, once the local authorities established the initial minimum wage level, they raised it over time at a pace that lagged well behind average wage growth, so that the ratio of the minimum to the average wage fell. For example, in Beijing the ratio of the minimum wage to the average wage fell from 34 percent in 1996 to only 17 percent by 2009.[87] Shenzhen's minimum wage program began in 1992, prior to the rollout of a national minimum wage program, when the local authorities set the minimum wage at RMB245 per month, fully half the average monthly wage of RMB494 at that time. But subsequently the authorities raised the minimum wage very slowly, so that by 2004 it was only a fifth of the average wage.[88] These low ratios in China contrast with many countries, where the minimum wage is typically 40 to 60 percent of the average wage (Ni, Wang, and Yao 2011, 21).

As a result of the decline in the minimum wage relative to the average wage, the fraction of the workforce in most administrative jurisdictions in China earning the minimum wage declined over time, eventually reaching very low levels. For example, in Beijing by 2003 only 1.6 percent of the workforce earned

---

87. "Historical Social Insurance and Related Standards in Beijing Municipality," October 12, 2005, available at www.bjld.gov.cn (accessed on July 10, 2006); data from Ministry of Human Resources and Social Security via ISI Emerging Markets, CEIC Database.

88. "Statistical Report on Wages over the Years," August 14, 2005, available at www.szlabour. com (accessed on July 3, 2006); "The Minimum Wage Standard over the Years," available at www. labourlawyer.cn (accessed on July 3, 2006).

the minimum wage.[89] Presumably this share fell even more in subsequent years as the ratio of the minimum wage to the average wage fell further after 2003.

If Beijing is at all representative, even the record 22.8 percent increase in the average minimum wage across China's 30 provinces, regions, and municipalities in 2010 probably has not had a significant impact on average wages and labor costs.[90] If, for example, 2 percent of the workforce earns the minimum wage, the large boost in the minimum wage in 2010 would have increased the national wage bill by less than 0.5 percent. Moreover, we should also take into account that in 2009, as China's growth slowed due to the global recession, local governments did not raise the minimum wage. Thus the record minimum wage increase in 2010 raised the wage bill by about 0.25 percent per year in 2009–10. While increases in the minimum wage may be an important element in government policy on income distribution and welfare, clearly changes in the average wage are far more important than changes in the minimum wage in determining both the wage share in GDP and the competitiveness of Chinese goods in the global market.

A third factor to be taken into account in evaluating the contribution of rising wages to economic rebalancing is the growth of labor cost per unit of output produced. If output per worker rises as fast as labor costs, then unit labor costs are unchanged, and there will be no tendency for rising wages to feed through to higher product prices. The implication of this for internal rebalancing is that even if real wages increase, the wage share of GDP would not rise; thus rising wages would not lead to an increase in the consumption share of GDP. The implication for external rebalancing is that rising real wages would not lower China's external surplus. If there is no tendency for rising wages to feed through to higher product prices, the competitiveness of Chinese products in the international market would not be eroded, and thus rising wages would not contribute to a reduction in China's large external surplus. The IMF estimates that between 2000 and 2008 labor productivity in the tradable goods portion of the Chinese economy grew at an average annual rate of 9.3 percent (IMF 2010b, 19). If that pace of improvement in labor productivity were sustained in 2009–10, it would be sufficient to almost entirely offset the estimated 9.7 percent average annual growth of real wages, leaving unit labor costs in the production of tradable goods essentially unchanged.

The fourth factor to be taken into account in evaluating the hypothesis that endogenous rebalancing is underway is trends in wages and productivity growth in China's major trading partners. This factor is relevant for external rebalancing but not internal rebalancing. In the previous decade, real wages have risen much more slowly globally than in China. The International Labor

89. "Wages of Workers and Staff in Beijing Steadily Increase; Wage Differentials across Sectors Have Expanded," July 10, 2006, available at www.hebei.gov.cn (accessed on July 10, 2006).

90. "Rising Salaries Drive Firms West," *China Daily*, March 7, 2011, available at www.english.people.com.cn (accessed on March 7, 2011).

Organization (ILO) estimates that annual global wage growth in real terms over the period 2001–07 was 1.9 percent and that global wage growth excluding China was 0.8 percent in 2008 and 0.7 percent in 2009 (ILO 2008, 12; 2010, 3). Since these numbers are a very small fraction of our estimate of real wage growth in China, why hasn't the competitiveness of Chinese goods in international markets already rapidly eroded? The answer is that average annual labor productivity growth in the tradable goods sector in China's trading partners between 2000 and 2008 was only 2.3 percent, four times slower than in China (IMF 2010b, 19). The conclusion is that although real wage growth in China has been relatively high compared with that in the rest of the world, the potential impact of rising real wages on the prices of tradable goods produced in China has been offset by much more rapid productivity growth in China than in its trading partners.

If over the last decade unit labor costs have been roughly constant both in China and in its major trading partners, we are not yet at the point where increasing labor scarcity in China is contributing to a decline in China's external surplus. That point will surely come eventually given the sharp decline in the agricultural labor force and rising urbanization that has already occurred. Official data show that agricultural employment by 2009 had declined by more than 90 million from the peak in 1991. That took the share of agricultural employment from three-fifths down to about two-fifths of total employment over the same period (National Bureau of Statistics of China 2010f, 120).[91] Survey data show that in many areas of rural China most of the prime working-age population has already migrated (Park, Fang, and Yang 2010).

However, it is quite likely that rural to urban migration in China will continue for many years. Even if the number of agricultural workers is not likely to decline as rapidly as in the past, there are almost 200 million nonagricultural workers in rural areas who are self-employed or work in the remaining township and village enterprises or in private enterprises. As modern transportation reaches more rural areas, it seems inevitable that many of these rural residents will migrate to cities, attracted by higher wages offered in modern services and manufacturing activities in urban areas. This migration likely will continue to lead to more moderate growth of wages in urban areas than would occur in the absence of continued migration.[92]

China's global competitive position is not determined solely by the level of real wages or unit labor costs relative to those of other countries. Wages in India have been and continue to be much lower than in China, but India is not yet a major world exporter. Its total exports of goods and services in 2010

---

91. The data are for employment in the primary sector, which includes agriculture, forestry, animal husbandry, and fishery along with services that support these activities.

92. For a more detailed analysis that concludes there is "still an immense rural labor surplus exceeding 100 million workers," see Chan (2010, 521). Similarly the IMF (2011c, 7) concludes that "China continues to have a structural labor surplus with significant unemployment and underemployment."

were $330 billion, less than a fifth of China's exports of $1,750 billion (WTO 2011, 31–32). Thus the fifth element in evaluating the proposition that rising real wages will lead to an automatic rebalancing of the Chinese economy is the nonwage factors that have contributed to China's emergence as the world's number one exporting country.

One key nonwage source of global competitive advantage for China is that foreign firms play an unusually large role in China's export sector. Foreign firms have not only brought modern production technology to China in many industries but have also brought important skills in global brand building, marketing, and distribution. Thus they have played a critical role in China's export expansion. China adopted a relatively liberal foreign direct investment regime early in the reform period. In 1979 and 1980 the government signaled its openness to foreign direct investment by promulgating a law on joint ventures and by establishing four special economic zones, where foreign joint ventures received preferential tax treatment and other benefits. Just as important, in 1979 China established a legal framework for export processing, which provided various incentives for the assembly of imported parts and components to produce finished goods for export. By the mid-1980s these incentives included the duty-free import of all raw materials, parts, and components used in the production of goods for export. That meant that producers of these goods in China operated at international prices, free from distortions caused by Chinese import tariffs, which at that time were relatively high (Lardy 2002, 34).

Initially, foreign direct investment was relatively small in scale, but it grew rapidly in the 1990s. Starting in the early 2000s, China was in most years the largest emerging-market recipient of foreign direct investment. Cumulatively through 2010, foreign direct investment was $1,476 billion (State Administration of Foreign Exchange 2011). The majority of China's inbound foreign direct investment has been in the manufacturing sector, and a substantial portion of this has been exported oriented. As a result, for more than a decade foreign firms have regularly accounted for a large share of China's exports. In 2010, for example, foreign firms exported goods valued at $863 billion, 55 percent of China's total goods exports (National Bureau of Statistics of China 2011c).

India, despite much lower wages than in China, was not as attractive a destination for foreign investment as China in part because until recently its foreign investment regime was much more restrictive than China's and its infrastructure development was weak. As a result, foreign firms make only a minor contribution to Indian exports.[93]

A second important nonwage factor contributing to the international competitiveness of goods produced in China is the substantial investments

---

93. In 2003–05 foreign affiliates accounted for 7.7 percent of India's manufactured exports (Pradhan, Das, and Paul 2011). Since manufactures account for three-quarters of Indian goods exports, foreign firms account for less than 6 percent of India's total goods exports, less than a tenth of the export share of foreign affiliates in China.

China has made in infrastructure. According to the World Bank, China's logistics capacity is far superior to that of India and other countries where wages are lower than in China. The Bank ranked China 27th out of 155 countries in its 2010 logistics performance index, which measures a range of variables including warehousing, border clearance, in-country distribution, and payments systems. China, not surprisingly, ranks behind high-income countries like the United States, Germany, Japan, and Australia. But the World Bank ranks China far ahead of emerging-market competitors such as India (47th), Mexico (50th), and Vietnam (53rd) (Zhang 2011).

Finally, one must recognize that there is a scale factor that must be taken into account when looking at the potential for rising real wages to undermine China's global competitiveness. Even if China's unit labor costs begin to rise faster than in other emerging markets, it is unlikely that China's strong global competitiveness position will be rapidly undermined. If a cost advantage emerges in Vietnam, for example, it may become more profitable for some firms to move their manufacturing operations there. But if this decision is taken by foreign firms on a large scale, Vietnam's cost advantage would be quickly eroded. Vietnam's total exports in 2010 were only about $70 billion.[94] If a tenth of the foreign firms now operating in China, for example, were to decide to move their operations to Vietnam, that country's exports hypothetically would more than double in a short period of time. But long before this doubling could occur, real wages in Vietnam would be driven up rapidly and the country's limited logistics capacity would quickly be overwhelmed, leading to sharply higher costs that would reverse the apparent initial cost advantage of Vietnam compared with China.

In short, though real wages have risen briskly in the formal sector and somewhat more slowly in the informal sector for at least a decade, China's economic growth over the same period nevertheless became more imbalanced in several dimensions. Thus the pace of wage increase was not fast enough to lead to a rise in the wage share of income. A rise in the wage share of income depends not only on trends in real wages but also on the pace of expansion of employment in the modern sector. As will be analyzed in chapter 5, the pace of expansion of nonagricultural employment slowed in the past decade compared with the decade of the 1990s. Nor was the pace of wage increase in the past decade sufficiently rapid to offset the renminbi undervaluation that led to record trade and current account surpluses by 2007–08.

Increase Consumer Credit to Rebalance?

The "policy light" approach to economic rebalancing is to expand credit available to households. The argument is that borrowing allows households to shift their spending forward in time, leading to consumption growth that outpaces

---

94. UNCTAD database, UNCTADStat, available at http://unctadstat.unctad.org (accessed on September 20, 2011).

income growth, thereby increasing the share of consumption in GDP. The McKinsey Global Institute is a proponent of this view, arguing that Chinese households, due to limited access to credit, are forced to accumulate large pools of savings in advance of major expenditures. McKinsey also argues that outstanding consumer credit in China is well below that of other large developing countries (McKinsey Global Institute 2009, 25). This view also has been amplified by other writers who charge that "China lacks the infrastructure of modern consumer finance, and is years—possibly decades—away from building it to the standards of the developed world."[95]

However, these arguments are based on the mistaken perception that China's financial system has not changed over the past decade. The view that China's financial system is dominated by state-owned banks that take deposits primarily from households and then channel loans almost exclusively to large state-owned companies was a reasonable approximate characterization of the financial system in the mid-1990s (Lardy 1998). The Bank of China, one of China's major commercial banks, did not promulgate even provisional regulations on consumer credit until the end of 1998 (Bank of China 1999, 348–52). Banks in the 1980s and 1990s did extend loans to self-employed individuals who ran manufacturing and services businesses. The amounts, however, were extremely small, growing from about RMB5 billion and 0.2 percent of all bank loans outstanding in 1991 to RMB39 billion and 0.5 percent of all loans outstanding by the end of 1997 (China Banking Society 1998, 508). As the housing privatization program gathered steam, banks also began making mortgage loans to individuals, but this was initially on a modest scale. By year-end 1997 total mortgage loans outstanding to households stood at only RMB13 billion. Thus the sum of business and mortgage loans to individuals at year-end 1997 was about RMB50 billion and accounted for only 0.7 percent of bank loans outstanding and 0.6 percent of China's GDP. And household bank debt as a share of household disposable income, a measure of debt burden, was a minuscule 0.9 percent.

From this modest beginning households gained increasing access to bank loans, with the amount of credit extended to households rising dramatically over the next decade or so and then accelerating sharply during China's stimulus program. The share of all new bank loans extended to households rose from 14 percent in 2008, just as the global financial crisis emerged, to 26 percent in 2009, and then 36 percent in 2010 (People's Bank of China 2009, 2010a, 2011a). By the end of 2010, total loans outstanding to households stood at RMB11,258.6 billion (People's Bank of China 20011b).

Before gauging how big a number this is, it is important to outline the scope of household borrowing. What is included in official Chinese data on household borrowing from banks? What should be included? The answer to the first question, in short, is all borrowing by households: mortgage borrowing, loans

95. Joseph Sternberg, "Don't Bank on China 'Rebalancing,'" *Wall Street Journal*, January 20, 2011, available at http://wsj.com (accessed on January 20, 2011).

for cars and education, credit card debt, and, importantly, business borrowing by households. Business borrowing by households includes loans extended to unincorporated family businesses (self-employed workers), as well as loans to agricultural households. Most of the latter are short-term loans, suggesting that they are used on a seasonal basis to finance the purchase of seeds, fertilizer, and other farm inputs. The magnitude of the increase in household business borrowing during the stimulus program was set forth in chapter 1.

Why should household business borrowing be included in a measure of credit to households? Because China in 2009 had 66 million self-employed nonagricultural workers (more than 10 percent of the nonagricultural workforce) and 300 million farm workers, one should not judge the potential for credit to expand household consumption by simply looking at credit card debt or some other narrow measure of consumer credit. The finances of a household running a family business are inseparable from the finances of the business. If an urban household is able to borrow to expand its family business, it will be able to use a larger share of the business income to finance current consumption. If a rural household wants to buy a newer, higher-capacity truck in order to raise profits in its transportation business and can finance it through a business loan, the family will not have to forgo current consumption for a number of years in order to build up a pool of savings prior to making the purchase. Rather, the family can finance the purchase of the truck with a loan and use more of their current income to finance consumption expenditures.

With this understanding in mind, we can answer two more questions: How rapidly has household borrowing increased over time, and how should we assess the RMB11.3 trillion in household bank debt outstanding at the end of 2010? First, by two metrics the long-term growth of household borrowing has been extremely rapid. Bank loans outstanding to households at the end of 2010 were 225 times those of 1997 and accounted for 22 percent of all bank loans outstanding. Bank loans outstanding to households at the end of 2010 stood at 28 percent of GDP, more than 45 times their share at the end of 1997. Second, the growth of household borrowing in recent years has been explosive. Over half of the increase in household borrowing from banks between 1997 and 2010 occurred in the three years 2008 through 2010.[96] Third, this massive increase in borrowing pushed household bank debt outstanding from 32 percent of disposable income at the end of 2007 to 49 percent at the end of 2010.[97]

The structure of household borrowing from banks at the end of 2010 is reflected in figure 3.6. A little over half of all borrowing is to finance housing, a third is to support household businesses, and much smaller amounts, about

---

96. Household borrowing outstanding from the banking system at the end of 2007 was RMB5,067 billion (People's Bank of China 2008).

97. The statistical authorities at the time of this writing have released flow of funds data, which provide information on household disposable income, only through 2008. The 49 percent figure for year-end 2010 is an estimate based on the assumption that household disposable income as a share of GDP after 2008 declined at roughly the same pace as it did between 2003 and 2008.

Figure 3.6 Composition of household borrowing, 2010

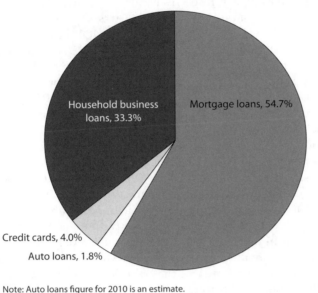

Note: Auto loans figure for 2010 is an estimate.

Sources: People's Bank of China (2011a); ISI Emerging Markets, CEIC Database.

4 and 2 percent, respectively, are credit card debt and car loans. Though credit card debt is a small share of total household borrowing, it tripled in absolute size between the end of 2008 and the end of 2010.

How does the availability of credit to households in China compare with that in other emerging markets? Is it plausible to argue that the extremely low consumption share of GDP in China can be explained by the limited availability of credit to Chinese households compared with households in other countries? Would Chinese households consume more if their access to credit was enhanced?

The IMF periodically analyzes household credit, based on a definition that includes mortgages, credit cards, auto loans, consumer durable financing, and other loans intended to finance directly some form of consumption but excludes business borrowing by the self-employed. Even on this narrow definition, China is an outlier on the high side in terms of consumer credit availability relative to other emerging markets at roughly comparable levels of development. In 2005, before the recent large increase in consumption loans in China, credit outstanding to consumers in China (excluding business loans to the self-employed) was about 11 percent of GDP. That was well above credit availability in the Philippines, Indonesia, and India but well below the levels in Thailand and Korea (IMF 2006, 49). Since there is a fairly strong positive relationship between the ratio of household credit to GDP and per capita income across countries, it is not surprising that consumer credit availability is much higher in Thailand and Korea, where per capita GDP in 2005 was half again as high and ten times higher, respectively, than in China. What is surprising is that consumer credit availability in China was so much higher than in the Philippines and Indonesia, where per capita GDP in 2005 was roughly comparable to and slightly below China's, respectively.[98] The margin by which consumer credit in China exceeds that in other emerging markets at roughly comparable levels of development increased after 2005. For example in 2009 Indonesia's consumer credit outstanding as a share of GDP was unchanged from the 8 percent ratio of 2005 while in China it had increased by 5 percentage points to reach 16 percent (IMF 2010a, 32; People's Bank of China 2010a).

In addition to this comparative analysis, other evidence suggests that consumer spending in China is not credit constrained relative to countries at comparable levels of per capita GDP. Many Chinese households choose not to take on credit. China has the largest car market in the world yet, as shown in figure 3.6, car loans outstanding are quite small. In 2009 only about 20 percent of Chinese car buyers took out loans to pay for car purchases, compared with rates of 50 percent in Japan and 90 percent in the United States.[99] Similarly, credit card debt is a small share of total borrowing by Chinese households. However, it is only about a fourth of the credit lines available to households. At year-end 2010, households were authorized to carry revolving credit card debt of up to RMB2 trillion, while outstanding credit card debt was only RMB449 billion.[100] This evidence, too, supports the view that increasing availability of consumer credit is far from a surefire way to dramatically increase the consumption share of GDP in China.

In summary, the record to date on government policies to promote increased domestic consumption is mixed at best. In the fiscal domain, tax cuts for individuals have been modest, and tax increases on state-owned corporations, in the form of the new requirement to pay dividends to the state, have been mostly inconsequential. But on the expenditure side, the government's fiscal initiatives to build out the social safety net are impressive, particularly in health care. In recent years, increases in government transfer payments, such as pensions paid to retirees and support to individuals with very low incomes, are also quite large. As noted above, however, the potential for this build-out of the social safety net to stimulate an increase in private consumption expenditures is limited.

---

98. Data on per capita GDP are from IMF (2006, figure 2.1).

99. "China Automarket," November 19, 2010, available at http://en.automarket.net.cn (accessed on May 17, 2011).

100. ISI Emerging Markets, CEIC Database. Interestingly, the ratio of credit card debt outstanding to total approved credit card lines of credit in China was almost exactly the same as in the United States at the end of 2010. See Federal Reserve Bank of New York (2011).

In the financial arena, where the potential contribution to rebalancing is probably greatest, policy adjustments thus far have been anemic. More than two years ago Premier Wen promised market-based reform of interest rates that could ease the high implicit tax burden on households and thus contribute significantly to increased consumption expenditure. But thus far there has been no policy follow-through. Indeed, change seems to be moving in the opposite direction: As reflected in a sharp decline in the real return on one-year deposits and an increase in the required reserve ratio to an unprecedented 21.5 percent by mid-year 2011, financial repression, if anything, has increased since the premier's March 2009 speech. In the same speech Premier Wen outlined potentially far-reaching reforms of the pricing of water, electricity, and other important factors of production, but actual implementation of this agenda is still over the horizon.

China's exchange rate policy appears to have made a modest contribution to economic rebalancing. On a real trade-weighted basis from mid-2005, when the dollar peg was abandoned, through the end of 2008, the renminbi appreciated by about 25 percent. That appreciation, combined with the sharp decline in global trade in 2009 and only modest trade recovery in 2010, contributed to the substantial reduction in China's external surplus from the peak of 10.1 percent of GDP in 2007. However, despite the exchange rate policy change announced in June of 2010 there has been no further appreciation of the renminbi. On a real, trade-weighted basis the renminbi actually depreciated between June 2010 and mid-year 2011, and more importantly it has also depreciated over the longer period from the end of 2008 through mid-year 2011. Independent estimates of the degree of undervaluation have ticked up slightly, from 15.3 percent in April 2010 to 17.6 percent in April 2011 (Cline and Williamson 2011). Thus it seems likely that as growth in China's major export markets recovers more fully, China's external surplus will rise.

China's GDP expenditure data confirm that policies adopted to rebalance economic growth since 2004 have been insufficient. Investment growth did moderate somewhat in 2005–07, in line with the government objective of reducing the extraordinarily high share of resources going to investment. But the decline, shown in figure 2.1, was only slight and was reversed beginning in 2008. By 2010 the investment share of GDP rose to an unprecedented 49 percent of GDP.[101] Thus since 2003, the share of China's GDP going to investment has been continuously above two-fifths, well above the share of GDP going to investment in Japan, Korea, and Taiwan during their high-growth periods. Moreover, the large increase in net exports as a share of GDP from 2004 through 2007 also contributed to the fall in the consumption share of GDP, as reflected in figure 2.2. By 2007 government and personal consumption combined accounted for less than half of GDP, the lowest share of any

---

101. ISI Emerging Markets, CEIC Database.

economy in the world, and this share continued to fall through 2010. China is particularly an outlier in terms of personal consumption, which in 2010 accounted for only 34 percent of GDP.[102]

The efforts to rebalance the economy also are not yet reflected in the structure of output. As shown in figure 2.5, in the first two decades of economic reform the share of output originating in the services sector roughly doubled, from about 22 percent in the very early 1980s to 42 percent by 2002. This conforms to the usual pattern of economic growth in which the services share of GDP increases in rapidly growing developing economies. But after 2002, the services share of output essentially stagnated, rising by only 1 percentage point by 2010. The absence, over an eight-year period, of significant growth in the services share of GDP in a fast-growing developing economy is extremely unusual, if not unprecedented. On the other hand, between 2002 and 2010 the share of GDP originating in industry rose by 2 percentage points, returning its share to 47 percent, only 1 percentage point below its level in 1978 on the eve of reform. This too is an unusual pattern for a developing economy.

---

102. ISI Emerging Markets, CEIC Database.

4

China and Global Economic Rebalancing

The focus of the previous chapter was how China can transition to a new economic model that will allow it to sustain rapid growth. The thesis is that this transition is strongly in China's own economic and political interests because the export- and investment-driven growth strategy of the past decade is no longer viable. Given the current global environment, China's growth seems likely to slow significantly if it continues to rely on increasing exports to fuel its growth. External demand is muted and is likely to remain so for some time, given the slow pace of economic recovery from the global financial and economic crisis in the developed countries that have long been the major markets for China's exports.

The unprecedented scale of capital investment in China relative to the size of its economy in recent years also will encounter sharply diminishing returns. The heightened level of investment since 2003 reflects two factors. First, the government decided to accelerate infrastructure investment in 2009–10. Second, financial repression has contributed to a massive increase in real estate investment.

Accelerating infrastructure development to offset the softening of external demand during the global downturn was rational, but a superelevated level of infrastructure investment can't be the basis for sustained long-term economic growth. Indeed, two indicators show the pace of infrastructure investment slowed substantially in 2010 compared with 2009. First, outstanding medium- and long-term bank loans for infrastructure development grew by RMB2.5 trillion, or 43 percent, in 2009 but only by RMB1.65 trillion, or 19 percent, in 2010 (People's Bank of China 2010b, 2011b). Second, completed urban infrastructure investment soared 41 percent in 2009 to reach RMB5.5 trillion, while overall national investment rose only 30 percent. In 2010 this pattern was reversed when the growth of completed urban infrastructure investment was a more moderate 17 percent, well below the 23 percent expansion of national investment.[1]

Similarly, the highly elevated level of real estate investment of recent years also is unlikely to be sustainable in the medium run. As analyzed in chapter 3, weakening of residential property investment could slow China's growth substantially for an extended period of time. Thus China's growth seems likely to slow significantly unless private consumption demand becomes a much more important source of aggregate demand over the next few years. The obvious conclusion is that rebalancing is fundamentally in China's own economic interest.

This chapter examines China's economic rebalancing from a global perspective. What are the gains to the rest of the world, if any, if China is successful in transitioning to more consumption-driven growth and a significantly smaller external surplus? Several possible gains come to mind. First, and perhaps most important, would be a reduction in global economic imbalances. There is a widespread view that the global financial crisis was in part the result of large global economic imbalances. Countries like the United States saved far too little and depended on large financial inflows to finance expenditures, particularly consumption outlays. Emerging-market countries like China saved far too much and became very large creditors to countries with external deficits, such as the United States. If these large global imbalances are eliminated or significantly reduced the risk of another global financial crisis falls.

Second, the world would also benefit from China's transition to more consumption-driven growth because it would mean reduced consumption of energy and enhanced prospects for limiting global warming. While China's energy use was only half that of the United States in 2000, its economic growth in the subsequent decade was so energy intensive that the International Energy Agency estimates that China's energy consumption surpassed that of the United States in 2009 even though its economy is only two-fifths the size of the United States. In the years between 2000 and 2008 the increase in China's energy consumption was more than four times greater than in the previous decade (IEA 2010, 5). China's energy-intensive growth path both adds to global environmental degradation and puts upward pressure on prices of a broad range of global commodities. On its current growth trajectory, China alone likely will account for as much as two-thirds of the growth of total global oil demand and 45 percent of the growth of global primary energy demand over the decade ending in 2020 (IEA 2010, 618–73). Fundamentally changing this trajectory will require China to transition to a growth model with drastically reduced subsidies for energy consumption, with less emphasis on

---

1. National Bureau of Statistics of China, "Systematic Report Number Four on Economic and Social Development Accomplishments in the Eleventh Five-Year Plan," March 3, 2011, available at www.stats.gov.cn (accessed on March 3, 2011); National Bureau of Statistics of China, "Systematic Report Number 16 on Economic and Social Development Accomplishments in the Eleventh Five-Year Plan," March 11, 2011, available at www.stats.gov.cn (accessed on March 14, 2011).

the heavy industry closely associated with investment and urban residential construction, and with more emphasis on light industry and services that will satisfy rising consumer demand.

Third, China's export-led growth has imposed costs and risks on its trading partners. If China's growth is rebalanced and external surplus reduced, the costs and risks imposed upon its trading partners will also be smaller. The *Economist* magazine has frequently noted that in an ex post accounting sense China accounted for a large share of global growth in the previous decade.[2] But this does not necessarily mean that the rest of the world benefited from this outsized contribution. China's global economic surplus was expanding during most of these years, meaning that China was adding more to the supply of goods to the rest of the world than it was adding to the demand for goods from the rest of the world. Thus even as China ex post "accounted for" a large share of global growth, its rising external surplus constituted a potential drag on growth in the rest of the world, because its contribution to demand in the rest of the world was not keeping pace with its rapidly growing economy. Of course, it would be hard to argue that this drag actually slowed economic growth in other countries. The four-year period 2004–07, when China's external surplus was increasing most rapidly, was a period of unusually rapid global economic growth, indeed the most rapid since the early 1970s (IMF 2008, 21–22). But this was largely because the United States and other advanced industrial countries were pursuing expansive monetary and fiscal policies that effectively offset the drag on global growth coming from China. In retrospect, of course, it is clear that these monetary and fiscal policies were not sustainable and were among the principal factors leading to the global financial crisis and the most severe global slowdown in several decades.

In the current environment, the cost to the global economy if China's external surplus were to begin to expand again would be higher than in the last decade. There are three reasons for this. First, much of the developed world is in a "liquidity trap," meaning that monetary policy is not effective in stimulating demand because of the zero bound on the policy interest rate. Second, developed countries' internal debt rose so much during the crisis that cutting budget deficits has become an imperative and has effectively ruled out additional fiscal stimulus in virtually all cases. In short, while previously the rest of the world had some flexibility in using expansionary monetary and fiscal policy to offset China's drag on global growth, after the crisis the economic policy options of governments in the rest of the world are much more constrained. Third, China is now a larger factor in the global economy. In the middle of the

---

2. "Its contribution to global GDP growth since 2000 has been almost twice as large as that of the next three biggest emerging economies, India, Brazil and Russia, combined" (July 28, 2005); "For the first time it is now contributing more to global GDP growth (measured at market exchange rates) than the United States is" (September 27, 2007); "China has become the main engine of the world economy, accounting for one-third of global GDP growth in the first half of this year" (October 9, 2008). Available at www.economist.com (all accessed on May 2, 2011).

past decade it accounted for 9.5 percent of global GDP; by 2010 that share had increased to 13.6 percent (IMF 2011d). The risk of a rising Chinese surplus is that growth would stall in the United States and other advanced industrial countries that are now limited in their ability to offset China's subtraction from growth in the rest of the world. Thus the risk associated with a resurgence of China's global external surplus is an aborted global recovery, making it harder for the United States and countries in Europe to deal with their fiscal challenges.

Global Imbalances

The supercharged global economic growth that preceded the global financial and economic crisis was accompanied by a historically unprecedented buildup of current account imbalances. On the eve of the crisis, imbalances had reached almost 6 percent of global GDP, almost triple the level of 1996 (Blanchard and Milesi-Ferretti 2009, 7).[3] Imbalances are not inherently bad. For example, they may be generated by an expectation of brighter growth prospects in some countries, leading to an inflow of foreign direct investment and portfolio capital seeking to gain a share of anticipated profits. In this situation the countries with relatively high growth prospects generally run current account deficits. This appears to be roughly the position of the United States in 1996–2000. Capital inflows into the United States allowed increased investment linked to the high-tech boom.

In the next period, starting in around 2001, the US current account deficit widened substantially, largely because of a substantial decline in private savings. The composition of capital inflows into the United States changed, with debt assuming a much larger role. The nature of the investors changed as well, with official investors becoming increasingly more important relative to private investors. The widening of global imbalances reflected not only the widening imbalance of the United States but also the decision in many Asian countries in the wake of the Asian financial crisis to run current account surpluses. These countries wanted to build up larger official foreign exchange reserves to serve as a buffer against future financial crises. Additionally, higher global oil prices gave oil-exporting countries larger surpluses, much of which they invested in US debt.

Global economic imbalances subsequently increased sharply after 2004. While the US contribution to global imbalances was unchanged, China's current account surplus, which earlier had averaged only 0.1 percent of global GDP, jumped to an average of 0.6 percent in 2005–08. Surpluses of oil exporters continued to rise sharply, on the back of higher oil prices. European imbalances increased as well, with a group of countries on the periphery

---

3. The measure of global imbalances is the sum of the absolute value of individual country current account imbalances.

(including Ireland, Greece, Portugal, and Spain) experiencing much higher external deficits, while external surpluses rose in "core" Europe (Blanchard and Milesi-Ferretti 2009, 7).

It is relatively easy to describe the trends in global imbalances, identify where they originate, and set forth details of the associated financial flows. It is considerably more difficult, however, to demonstrate the precise linkages, if any, between these imbalances, on the one hand, and the global financial crisis that emerged strongly in 2008, on the other. Thus "controversy remains about the precise connection between global economic imbalances and the global financial meltdown" (Obstfeld and Rogoff 2010, 132). The paragraphs that follow provide a summary of three alternative views. The first is that global imbalances are mostly benign and thus efforts to reduce imbalances are misguided. A second view is that while imbalances may pose challenges, particularly in deficit countries with large capital inflows, these challenges can be overcome with appropriate adjustments in domestic monetary policy. The third view is that global economic imbalances, combined with excessive deregulation of financial markets, weak financial regulation, and distortions in financial markets, led to the global financial crisis.

The view that imbalances are benign is perhaps most strongly advocated by Richard Cooper. He views large current account deficits in the United States as the "natural consequence of the excess savings in the rest of the world, an attractive menu of financial assets from which to choose in the United States, and increasing globalization of financial markets." Thus he argued that "it would be a mistake to try to eliminate the [US] current account deficit in the near future or even to try to reduce it to $200 billion to $300 billion" (Cooper 2005, 6). Cooper's analysis focuses on China when looking at the surplus side of the equation. He argues that China's underdeveloped domestic financial markets limit the opportunities for financial investment within the country. If China were able to liberalize its capital account, citizens likely would put a substantial portion of their savings abroad in the form of foreign currency–denominated financial assets. Given that China is not yet prepared to remove such controls on capital outflows, Cooper argues, China's central bank is playing the positive role of a financial intermediary, in effect taking the surplus of domestic savings over domestic investment and investing it in foreign assets on behalf of China's savers.

The second view, most closely associated with John B. Taylor, is that global imbalances per se were not the problem. Rather he argues that the US Federal Reserve maintained an accommodative monetary policy, first adopted in 2001 in the wake of the bursting of the US technology bubble, for far too long. If the Fed had tightened sooner, in 2002 rather than waiting until 2004, US domestic interest rates would have been higher, mortgage financing would have been more expensive, and the underlying bubble in property prices would have been more modest or likely avoided altogether. On Taylor's calculation, if the Federal Reserve had followed his monetary policy rule, housing starts in the

United States would have peaked at an annual rate of a little over 1.7 million units in 2003 rather than the actual 2.1 million unit rate observed in late 2005 and early 2006 at the peak of the US housing bubble (Taylor 2009, 5).

The third view is that a complex interaction of global financial imbalances, weak financial regulation, credit market distortions, the Fed's monetary policy stance, and other factors "created the toxic mix of conditions making the U.S. the epicenter of the global financial crisis" (Obstfeld and Rogoff 2010, 145). Ouarda Merrouche and Erlend Nier (2010, 27) provide empirical support for the hypothesis that "widening global imbalances and associated capital flows were the root cause of the build-up of financial imbalances across advanced economies" and thus were the proximate cause of the global financial crisis. They find there was a strong link between widening global economic imbalances and associated capital flows, on the one hand, and the buildup of financial imbalances within Organization for Economic Cooperation and Development countries, on the other. Deficit countries with large capital inflows had higher ratios of credit to GDP (i.e., more leverage); higher ratios of financial-sector credit to deposits, reflecting a greater reliance by banks on wholesale funding (which in a crisis could and did dry up); higher ratios of household debt to GDP (i.e., more household leverage); and more appreciation of house prices ahead of the crisis. Consistent with Obstfeld and Rogoff, Merrouche and Nier also demonstrate that the supervisory and regulatory environment affected the buildup of financial imbalances ahead of the crisis.

Merrouch and Nier (2010), however, specifically reject the view that overly accommodative monetary policy fueled the buildup. They note that on a cross-country basis there is little association between measures of monetary policy and house price increases. Some countries with low real interest rates had large house price appreciation; other countries had rapid increases in housing prices with relatively high real interest rates; others had both low real interest rates and little house price appreciation. Rising house prices, however, were strongly associated with surges in capital inflows from abroad, supporting the view that the proximate cause of the global financial crisis was economic imbalances, not failures of monetary policy.

While the debate over the precise linkages between the expansion of global economic imbalances and the global financial crisis will undoubtedly continue for years, several broad if somewhat tentative conclusions can be drawn. First, the view that global economic imbalances are benign seems largely discredited. All too frequently these imbalances are the result of domestic distortions, which if eliminated would reduce imbalances. In the United States the household saving rate in the middle part of the last decade fell to a historic low because of "financial innovations," such as subprime loans and home equity lines of credit. These led to levels of household debt that ultimately proved destabilizing in the extreme. In China household savings as a share of disposable income rose sharply after 2003. This was not because domestic financial markets were undeveloped; these markets had been underdeveloped since the onset of economic reform in 1978, and household savings from disposable income prior to 2004 were not out of line with those in other developing countries. Rather, the rise in household savings as a share of disposable income after 2003 coincides with increased financial repression that dramatically reduced the real return to savings. It appears that a primary motive for household savings is to achieve a target level of savings. Thus the income effect of lower real rates dominated the substitution effect causing savings to rise relative to disposable income. Therefore, eliminating the distortions imposed by financial repression would allow China's ultralow consumption share of GDP to rise and its external imbalance to shrink.

Second, the view that the United States would not have precipitated the global financial crisis had the Federal Reserve tightened earlier seems unpersuasive. While the Fed controls short-term interest rates, long-term rates are determined by the market. Large capital inflows into the United States, a substantial portion of which originated in China, in the middle years of the previous decade reduced longer-term rates. This reduction, in turn, reduced the spread between long and short rates. Since bank earnings are strongly correlated with the spread between long and short rates, spread compression reduced bank earnings. Lower earnings, in turn, led banks to lever up their balance sheets and to create ever riskier financial products. On the demand side, low long-term rates made mortgage borrowing cheaper and fueled the housing bubble.

Third, at this stage it is difficult if not impossible to assign precise weights to the relative roles of global imbalances and weak financial supervision as causes of the crisis. They are obviously inextricably interlinked. Thus it seems appropriate that reforms at both the national and international levels should try both to improve financial regulation and supervision and to eliminate distortions that lead to large global imbalances.

The Group of Twenty (G-20), which is now the premier forum for international economic cooperation, has embraced this dual mandate. At the G-20 meeting in Pittsburgh in September 2009, the leaders adopted the G-20 Framework for Strong, Sustainable, and Balanced Growth. This framework agreement called specifically for G-20 members with sustained, large external deficits to undertake policies to support private savings and to undertake reductions of fiscal deficits in order to reduce their external deficits. And in a symmetric fashion the framework called for G-20 members with sustained, large external surpluses to strengthen domestic sources of growth.[4] The G-20 enlisted the IMF to oversee a mutual assessment process to evaluate the implications of national economic policies for strong, sustainable, and balanced growth of the world economy. Among the factors identified for analysis are foreign exchange developments and the growth of foreign exchange reserves.

This process underwent a significant step forward at the meeting of G-20 finance ministers and central bank governors in Washington in April 2011.

---

4. Leaders' Statement: The Pittsburgh Summit, G-20, September 24–25, 2009, available at www.g20.org (accessed on May 5, 2011).

At this meeting, members "agreed on a set of indicative guidelines that complete the first step of our work to address persistently large imbalances."[5] A country's current account position is one of the key indicators. The G-20 finance ministers and central bank governors outlined a two-stage process that starts by using four separate empirical approaches to measuring whether a country has a "persistently large imbalance." In the second, more analytical stage, a country that is judged to have a large external imbalance by two of the four methodologies will be subject to more in-depth analysis both to determine the nature and root causes of the imbalance and to identify impediments to adjustment.

Since China has been a key member of the G-20 from the outset and approved the indicative guidelines approach to reducing large external imbalances, there now appears to be a happy congruence of China's domestic and international economic policy objectives. Reducing imbalances, including China's still large external imbalance, is a top domestic objective embraced by China's top leadership and enshrined in many Chinese policy documents, including the 12th Five-Year Plan. With the G-20 agreement China has also acknowledged that reducing external imbalances will contribute to strong and sustainable global economic growth. The next chapter addresses the internal political constraints that could continue to prevent China from adopting policies to achieve these national and international objectives.

---

5. Communiqué: Meeting of Finance Ministers and Central Bank Governors, Washington, DC, April 14–15, 2011, G-20, available at www.g20.org (accessed on May 5, 2011).

5

The Politics of Economic Rebalancing

The Chinese Communist Party officially adopted the policy of economic rebalancing in December 2004 at the annual Central Economic Work Conference.[1] As noted in chapter 2, Premier Wen Jiabao has frequently characterized China's economic growth as "unsteady, imbalanced, uncoordinated, and unsustainable" and has urged the adoption of policies to correct these problems. In his report to the National People's Congress in March 2009 Premier Wen indicated that a comprehensive reform of pricing of resources, such as coal, electric power, and water, would be undertaken in a timely fashion. The promised reforms were to incorporate the cost of environmental damage in power production into power prices. Premier Wen also vowed that China would undertake market-based reform of interest rates, suggesting that the extent of financial repression would be eased and perhaps even eventually eliminated (Wen Jiabao 2009).

However, the reforms aimed at economic rebalancing that have been implemented to date in these and other domains (discussed in chapter 3) range from cautious and incremental to nonexistent. Pricing reforms for electric power and refined petroleum products, for example, fall clearly into the first category. The National Development and Reform Commission (NDRC) has adjusted the prices of these factors of production only slightly in response to rising production costs. Instead of following its own announced policy of raising electricity prices to reflect the rising market price of coal, the NDRC has attempted to impose price caps on coal producers to limit the financial losses of the electric power generating companies. The NDRC's administrative

---

1. "Central Economic Work Conference Convenes in Beijing December 3 to 5," December 6, 2004, available at www.people.com.cn (accessed on September 14, 2011).

approach to pricing continues to be partially successful at best, with lagging periodic price increases leaving oil refiners, power generators, and power distributors with minuscule or highly negative profits. As a result, power generating companies frequently cut production, leading to shortages that are reflected in power rationing and blackouts, as in the first half of 2011.[2] Eventually the government feels compelled to provide fiscal subsidies to offset losses. But these subsidies encourage excess consumption of energy, increase China's greenhouse gas emissions, and subsidize the production of tradable goods.

The government's record on rebalancing in the financial arena has been even more disappointing. The central bank has done little to ease financial repression. Despite five upward adjustments in deposit interest rates between October 2010 and July 2011, the real one-year deposit rate fell further into negative territory as inflation outpaced the rise in the benchmark one-year deposit rate.[3] And although nominal lending rates have moved upward in response to central bank tightening, in real terms lending rates were in negative territory in the first half of 2011.[4] Negative real deposit rates impose a high implicit tax on households, which are large net depositors in the banking system, and lead to excessive investment in residential housing. Negative real lending rates subsidize investment in capital-intensive industries, thus undermining the goal of restructuring the economy in favor of light industry and services.

The central thesis of this study is that the evidence from the past seven or eight years shows that modest, marginal, incremental economic reforms will not lead to a fundamental rebalancing of China's economy. Underlying financial distortions—including administrative controls that keep deposit interest rates low, an undervalued exchange rate, subsidized energy, and so forth—are contributing to a significant ongoing misallocation of resources throughout the Chinese economy. These distortions contribute to a low share of wages and a high share of corporate profits in national income; a low share of household disposable income in GDP; a high share of savings and a low share of consumption in household disposable income, and thus a low share of private consumption in GDP; a high share of household savings allocated to housing; an elevated share of investment in GDP; and a still large external surplus.

---

2. When encountering operating losses, power generators cut production much more rapidly than refiners. This is probably because the generating companies have no other source of revenue, whereas the oil companies have substantial profits from their nonrefining operations that they can use temporarily to offset refining losses. See the discussion in chapter 3.

3. The one-year deposit rate has been adjusted upward by 1.25 percentage points, while consumer prices, which rose by 4.4 percent year-over-year in October 2010, rose by 6.5 percent in July 2011. Thus the real deposit rate over this period fell by 0.85 percentage points to reach –3 percent.

4. In March, for example, the average loan rate (a weighted average across all tenors) was 6.91 percent, up 72 basis points from the beginning of the year (People's Bank of China Monetary Policy Analysis Small Group 2011b, 6). But year-over-year ex factory prices of producer goods rose by 8.2 percent in March. So the real lending rate was –1.3 percent.

A much more concerted and sustained effort is needed to remove underlying financial distortions if China's economic imbalances are to be reversed.

What are the perceived obstacles to such an approach? There are several, nonexclusive, answers to this question. The most prominent, perhaps, is that while China's top leadership understands the case for rebalancing it is equally or even more focused on maintaining political stability by keeping inflation low and ensuring steady growth of nonagricultural employment.

A second possible obstacle to a more aggressive economic rebalancing program is that good intentions and good economic policies at the central level are all too frequently thwarted at lower levels of government administration by local leaders, who have their own policy priorities and objectives. In this view, the center is not strong enough to realign the incentive structure at the local level in such a way that central government policies are effectively implemented.

One example of this inability to realign local incentives is policy with respect to residential property development. The central government has correctly assessed the macroeconomic risks of excessive investment in residential real estate and has promulgated regulation after regulation to moderate the boom. These policies include mandates to local governments to limit the rise in land prices, a contributor to the rising cost of residential housing. But local political leaders, particularly at the municipal level, have sometimes ignored or undermined these mandates because they are heavily dependent on revenues gained from the leasing and sale of land to finance local programs.[5] In 2010, when both land prices and the volume of land transactions soared, these revenues reached an all-time high of RMB2.9 trillion. This is equal to 70 percent of all tax revenues collected by local governments and 40 percent of total local government budgetary revenues, including fiscal transfers from the central government (Ministry of Finance 2011). Equally important, these land revenues are still not included in local fiscal budgets and thus not subject to even a pro forma review by local people's congresses. The absence of any oversight, of course, maximizes the flexibility local leaders have in deciding how these monies are spent. Local leaders are naturally less than enthusiastic about enforcing guidelines on land prices promulgated by Beijing that would moderate the housing boom but reduce the resources available to them to finance pet projects in their own jurisdictions.

A related argument is that China's political leadership has become weaker over successive generations, and therefore one should not be surprised if policy in many domains—including economic policy—increasingly becomes subject to the influence of special interest groups that lobby to shape policy to their ends (Kennedy 2005). Mao's leadership was, for much of his era, unquestioned. Deng Xiaoping was a strong successor but nonetheless had to devote some time and political capital to forming coalitions to support his policy objectives. Jiang Zemin, who became secretary general of the party shortly after

---

5. Zhang Yanling, "Real Estate: No Trespassing," *Caixin Weekly,* May 2, 2011, 32–33.

the Tiananmen movement and was subsequently designated as China's core leader by Deng, operated in what was becoming a collective leadership system. Nonetheless he was still regarded as the paramount leader. His successor Hu Jintao, by contrast, is widely seen only as the first among equals in an even more strongly collective leadership system. Xi Jinping, Hu's presumptive successor at the time of this writing, is very likely to be in a similar position of needing to build consensus on major policy initiatives. This decline in the ability of Chinese leaders to push through tough reforms reflects the rapid emergence of powerful interest groups in China, including formal and informal groups representing manufacturers. These groups gained an increasingly influential voice in arguing that currency appreciation is not in China's interest and would have negative economic consequences. Opposition from these groups may explain why the central bank, which has favored more rapid currency appreciation, has been unable to win the policy debate on this issue in the Standing Committee of the Politburo.

The Economic Challenge

The reduction of China's savings-investment imbalance necessarily requires both structural reforms and a real appreciation of the renminbi that would lead to an expansion of domestic demand relative to domestic supply. That, in turn, requires a reallocation of domestic capital and labor resources away from exports and goods that compete with imports toward nontradable goods, primarily services. China's leaders appear reluctant to undertake this adjustment in large part because they fear it could lead to a loss of jobs and ultimately to political instability.

The leadership's extreme concern over the potential adverse effect of more rapid appreciation of the renminbi on employment seems misplaced on three levels. First, the investment- and export-intensive growth path that emerged in the early years of the past decade appears to have led to a slower growth of nonagricultural employment than in the 1990s, when services grew much more robustly and investment and exports were less important drivers of China's economic growth. In the decade 1991 through 2001, when a relatively more balanced economic growth strategy was in place, the nonagricultural labor force grew at a 3.0 percent annual rate. That growth occurred despite the loss of tens of millions of jobs during the restructuring of state-owned companies in the mid-1990s. By contrast from 2001 through 2009, when the export- and investment-intensive growth strategy prevailed, modern-sector employment grew at an average annual rate of only 2.7 percent.[6] Although some manufactured exports are quite labor intensive, on average services are far more labor intensive than manufacturing. As a result of the languishing share of services

---

6. The calculation is based on data in Brandt, Hsieh, and Zhu (2010, 690) with updates kindly provided by Professor Brandt. These data include estimates of employment of migrant workers in the modern sector.

output in GDP in the last decade, the share of the labor force employed in services is relatively low in China compared with other countries with similar levels of per capita income. And this shortfall in services sector employment has been rising in recent years (Guo and N'Diaye 2011, 106). Therefore, contrary to what is frequently said, China's period of export- and investment-oriented growth was not particularly favorable for expanding nonagricultural employment. If anything the opposite was true.

Second, the rebalancing of China's economy should occur over a period of years during which time the nontradable sector expands rapidly while the tradable sector grows very slowly, if at all. Thus rebalancing need not imply an absolute shrinkage of exports and consequently a decline in manufacturing employment. Net job loss is much more likely if the adjustment process is compressed into a short period of time. This would likely require a large initial step appreciation of the currency, leading to a sharp contraction of exports and thus an absolute shrinkage of employment in the tradable goods sector. Given the time lag before employment in the production of nontradable goods would pick up, this compressed adjustment would increase the possibility of a significant net loss of jobs in the transition period. Concern about the potential contractionary effect of renminbi appreciation on employment led Morris Goldstein and myself to reject a large one-off appreciation to eliminate a sizeable renminbi undervaluation in a single step. Rather we recommended that China pursue a "three-stage approach" to currency appreciation and rebalancing that would include a more gradual pace of appreciation combined with increased government infrastructure spending to offset any transitional job loss in the export sector (Goldstein and Lardy 2009, 94–96).[7] In the long term, there seems little doubt that, given the enormous scope for employment generation in the nontradable sector, "rebalancing China's growth toward domestic demand would likely raise aggregate employment" (Guo and N'Diaye 2011, 99, 112).

Finally, even if there is some loss of jobs in the transition to domestic demand-driven growth, there are several reasons for believing that delaying rebalancing makes the ultimate costs of adjustment substantially higher. To begin with, delaying liberalization of interest rates and moving toward a more market-determined exchange rate has led to a massive buildup of official foreign exchange reserves—$3.2 trillion at mid-year 2011.[8] Although the Chinese authorities do not report any information on the currency composition of their foreign exchange reserves, it is widely believed that about two-thirds are held in dollar-denominated financial assets, such as US Treasury bonds

---

7. Earlier, when the degree of undervaluation of the renminbi was smaller, we advocated a "two-stage approach" that began with a step appreciation that would substantially reduce the undervaluation. Morris Goldstein and Nicholas Lardy, "Two-Stage Currency Reform for China," *Asian Wall Street Journal*, September 12, 2003.

8. People's Bank of China, "Report on Financial Statistics for the First Half of 2011," July 12, 2011, available at www.pbc.gov (accessed on July 12, 2011).

and bonds issued by US government–supported agencies like Fannie Mae and Freddie Mac. These large holdings of US dollar-denominated financial assets entail two risks. First, the gradual depreciation of the US dollar from 2003 to the end of 2010 reduced the value of China's foreign exchange reserves, measured in renminbi, by $271 billion.[9] Some argue that such paper losses are irrelevant from the point of view of central banks generally. But these losses have become a sensitive political issue within China as critics question why the government is accumulating an ever growing stock of foreign exchange reserves that seem destined to decline in value. The State Administration of Foreign Exchange has been forced to defend its management of the country's reserves, arguing that the losses that result from the depreciation of the dollar are only paper losses and do not represent a loss of external purchasing power of the reserves.[10] However, there is an additional real risk that even if the US dollar does not continue to depreciate, the purchasing power of China's dollar-denominated reserve assets could be reduced in the future if the US government is unable to reduce its fiscal deficit, potentially leading to above-average rates of inflation in the United States for a sustained period of time.

The second reason that delaying the liberalization of interest rates and moving toward a more market-determined exchange rate makes the ultimate cost of adjustment even higher is related to the buildup of central bank sterilization liabilities. As outlined in chapter 3, to sterilize the domestic monetary effects of the increase in official foreign exchange reserves, the People's Bank of China both issues central bank bills and raises the required reserve ratio. By year-end 2010 there were RMB4 trillion in central bank bills outstanding, and the central bank had boosted the required reserve ratio to an extremely elevated level of 18.5 percent of deposits.[11] These liabilities expanded further in the first half of 2011 as the central bank raised the required reserve ratio six times to an all-time high of 21.5 percent of deposits, more than offsetting a runoff in the stock of central bank bills outstanding.[12]

---

9. Wang Xiaotian, "China Loses $271b from Debt Holdings," *China Daily*, May 6, 2001, available at www.chinadaily.com.cn (accessed on July 6, 2011). Wang's article is based on a study by Zhang Anyuan, head of the Fiscal and Financial Policy Research Division of the NDRC's Institute of Economic Research.

10. "SAFE: No Direct Forex Loss from Yuan's Rise," Xinhua, July 20, 2011, available at chinadaily.com.cn (accessed on July 20, 2011). Aaron Back and Liu Li, "China Regulator Defends Handling of Forex Reserves," July 20, 2011, available at wsj.com (accessed on July 20, 2011).

11. In 2010 the central bank exempted rural credit cooperatives and other small banks from three of the six 50-basis-point increases in the required reserve ratio. Thus the 18.5 percent required reserve ratio mentioned in the text applies to large banks. The ratio for the small banks was 17.0 percent.

12. Bank deposits by end-June 2011 were RMB80.3 trillion, so the 3 percentage point increase in the required reserve ratio in the first half of 2011 required banks to place an additional RMB2.4 trillion on deposit at the central bank. The reported outstanding amount of central bank bills at end-June 2011 was RMB2.4 trillion, down RMB1.6 trillion from year-end 2010 (People's

But before the authorities can move to liberalize deposit interest rates, they will have to begin to unwind these sterilization instruments by not rolling over the bills as they mature and by reducing the required reserve ratio back to the mid-single-digit level that prevailed from the late 1990s to the mid-2000s. For example, for most of 2003, before China's annual current account surpluses and accumulated stock of foreign exchange reserves exploded, the required reserve ratio was only 6 percent. The 15.5 percentage point increase in this ratio since then has required banks to place an additional RMB12.5 trillion on deposit at the central bank. Unwinding this increase without giving rise to inflation will be a challenge for the central bank. But if the central bank continues to be charged with maintaining both an undervalued exchange rate and price stability, China's current account surplus will remain large; and to maintain price stability the central bank will have to continue sterilizing. If the central bank is forced to continue to raise the reserve requirement at the pace of 2010 and the first half of 2011 (six increases totaling 300 basis points), sterilization liabilities will balloon further. The lesson is fairly obvious: Delaying reforms only increases the challenge of rebalancing.

The third reason delaying the implementation of policies to rebalance the sources of economic growth is costly involves the real side of the economy. Not allowing market forces to play a greater role in the determination of the value of the currency distorts the allocation of investment resources and thus raises the ultimate costs of real readjustment. This is because the exchange rate is a critical price in all open economies, but particularly in China, where the ratio of traded goods to GDP is unusually elevated for a large, continental economy.[13] An undervalued currency raises profitability in tradable goods industries and reduces profitability in nontradable goods production. Thus one would expect undervaluation to increase the share of investment going to manufacturing, which produces 95 percent of China's exports and a very large share of import-competing goods, and to reduce the share of investment going to services.

Bank of China Monetary Policy Analysis Small Group 2011c, 10–11). The required reserve ratio for small financial institutions at mid-year 2011 was 20 percent.

13. Exports plus imports of goods and services rose from 43 percent of GDP in 2001 to a peak of 73 percent in 2006, and then fell to 50 percent in 2009 before recovering to 56 percent in 2010. For the 10-year period the ratio of trade to GDP averaged 60 percent. For the same period in the United States the trade ratio averaged 26 percent. See US Trade in Goods and Services, 1992–Present, US Census Bureau, Foreign Trade Division, available at www.census.gov/foreign-trade/data (accessed on May 10, 2011). China's trade ratio is very high in part because of processing trade (trade in which imported parts and components are assembled into finished goods that are then exported). These processed exports have a very high import content. However, if we calculate China's trade ratio in 2010 on the extreme assumption that both imports and exports comprising what the Chinese call processing trade were zero, China's trade ratio would still be 35 percent, substantially higher than the 28 percent ratio for the United States in the same year. Moreover, US exports also have a large import content as reflected in an estimate that domestic value added accounts for 77 percent of US exports (Johnson and Noguera 2011). Making an adjustment parallel to the one for China mentioned above, the trade ratio of the United States would be 18 percent in 2010, half China's ratio.

This is precisely what happened in China over the last decade. The share of urban fixed asset investment flowing into manufacturing rose from 23 percent of total investment in 2003 to 31 percent in 2010, while the share going to services fell from 38 to 32 percent.[14] The longer the currency remains undervalued, the longer the allocation of investment resources will remain distorted and the greater the ultimate costs of economic rebalancing will become.

The Political Challenge

What about the political constraints to adopting policies to rebalance growth, particularly the argument that even if the policies are adopted by the central government they will not be implemented at the local level, because the incentives of local political leaders are not aligned with those of the top political leadership? In many domains the central government depends critically on provincial and local governments to carry out its policies. The case of policies to moderate the housing boom has already been mentioned. Protection of intellectual property is another obvious example. The central government does not have the boots on the ground in the localities to raid the firms producing goods embodying pirated intellectual property; to identify, locate, and arrest the owners of these firms; and then prosecute these owners for violations of the provisions of China's intellectual property laws. Each of these steps must be carried out by local authorities. But local government officials often are interested primarily in the employment and tax revenues generated by firms producing pirated products and seem unconcerned that these firms are in violation both of China's international trade commitments and Chinese domestic law. In some cases these interests are reinforced by personal connections between the local officials and owners of the firms producing pirated products. Thus enforcement of China's laws on intellectual property is episodic, usually in response to massive periodic campaigns organized in Beijing to require local officials to enforce such laws. Once the campaign is over it is business as usual in the localities. This largely explains why despite the codification of a more than adequate set of national intellectual property laws, protection of intellectual property has been a major irritant in China's economic relations with the United States, Europe, and other advanced industrial countries for more than two decades.

This line of argument, however, is not a very persuasive explanation of why the central government can't successfully rebalance China's sources of growth.

---

14. National Bureau of Statistics of China (2010f, 180–82). ISI Emerging Markets, CEIC Database. The coverage of these data on manufacturing investment excludes investment in mining, utilities, and construction. These three subsectors of the broader category the Chinese call "secondary industry" do not produce tradable goods. Investment in fixed assets in manufacturing in urban areas accounts for more than four-fifths of investment in fixed assets in manufacturing in urban and rural areas combined.

The primary drivers of imbalances, low interest rates, currency undervaluation, and underpriced factors of production are under the exclusive control of the central government. Once it eliminates these financial distortions, economic rebalancing will be carried out by private agents, not local government officials. When the central government reduces its intervention in the foreign exchange market and allows the exchange rate to appreciate significantly, investment in tradable goods industries inevitably will decline. The reason is that exports are produced overwhelmingly by private firms, both foreign-funded and indigenous, which are highly sensitive to market signals.[15] If profits in tradable goods industries decline, these private firms will invest less; if profits decline further, they will shrink their businesses or even exit from export- and import-competing industries. Local first party secretaries, governors, and mayors may wring their hands over the loss of employment, tax revenues, and other benefits generated by these export- and import-competing industries in their jurisdictions, but by and large they will be powerless to offset the actions of these profit-oriented, private firms.

Similarly, market-oriented interest rate liberalization is a policy that will be approved by the State Council and be implemented by the People's Bank of China. It will generate predictable results by private actors at the local level. Local political authorities will have very limited possibilities for taking offsetting action. When the People's Bank of China allows supply and demand in the market to determine interest rates, real returns on bank deposits will move back into positive territory (as in the pre-2004 period), and the preferred asset class status that residential housing has enjoyed since 2003 will erode. As suggested in chapter 3, this will mean the demand for housing might shrink absolutely in the short run and will certainly moderate substantially in the short and medium term. On the demand side, nothing local political leaders can do will lead private households to purchase more property than they wish to own. Similarly, on the supply side, since residential property development in China is overwhelmingly in the hands of private firms, when the demand for residential housing moderates or declines, residential property development and construction will inevitably grow more slowly or shrink. This could only be partially offset by an accelerated development of what is called social or affordable housing, a program more directly controlled by local governments.

State-owned companies once had a significant role in both the real estate development and construction industries, but these roles have shrunk dramatically in the past decade or so. In 1998 state-owned firms accounted for a third of the companies and two-fifths of employment in the real estate development industry (National Bureau of Statistics of China 2000, 217–18). By 2009 they accounted for only 5 percent of the firms and 6 percent of the employment in the industry (National Bureau of Statistics of China 2010f, 199–200). Indigenous private companies and foreign firms now dominate

---

15. In 2010, of China's total exports of $1,577.9 billion, state-owned firms accounted for only $234.6 billion, or 15 percent. ISI Emerging Markets, CEIC Database.

China's real estate development industry. China's single biggest residential property developer is China Vanke Co., Ltd., a listed Shenzhen company.

The story is similar in the construction industry. In 1996 state-owned construction companies were responsible for 55 percent of construction measured by value; by 2009 their share was only 20 percent, and private firms dominated the industry (National Bureau of Statistics of China 1997, 483; 2010f, 591).[16]

Again, if residential property loses its status as a preferred asset class and private demand for property shrinks, first party secretaries, particularly at the municipal level, will decry the loss of revenue from land leasing, the loss of the local employment and tax revenues generated by a booming residential construction sector, and so forth. But, given that these activities are overwhelmingly in the hands of private, profit-oriented firms, once the central government unwinds existing distortions of interest rates, the result is highly predictable. It does not depend on a prior overhaul of the incentives facing local party officials or more fundamental political reform.

The emergence of a collective leadership system and the rise of special interest groups is a much more compelling explanation of China's failure to pursue economic rebalancing policies more aggressively since 2004. Limited progress in reforming China's exchange rate regime, liberalizing deposit and lending interest rates, and requiring large state-owned enterprises to pay dividends to the MOF reflect the nature of economic policy making in China today—without a consensus it is difficult to change policy.

Economists at the Chinese central bank and a handful of independent scholars have been the most persistent advocates for greater exchange rate flexibility and liberalization of interest rates. They were strong advocates of the depegging of the renminbi to the dollar, a policy adopted in mid-2005. Guo Shuqing, at the time a deputy-governor of the central bank and concurrently head of the State Administration of Foreign Exchange (SAFE), in a five-part article published in *China Daily* in October 2004 argued that "exchange rate flexibility within a reasonable range would not pose a serious threat to China's employment" (Jun Ma and Folkerts-Landau 2004).[17] In the same time frame Li Ruogu, also a deputy-governor, acknowledged that the central bank "has made a lot of progress in preparing for currency flexibility" (Jun Ma and Folkerts-Landau 2004).[18] Support for the policy shift also came from economists such as Wang Zhao at the Development Research Center of the State Council. In May 2005 he

---

16. These figures almost certainly overstate the role of state-owned companies in residential real estate construction. A large share of state-owned construction companies' activities are focused on infrastructure. For example, the Ministry of Railroads has two affiliated companies, China Railway Construction Corporation and China Railway Engineering Corporation, that are responsible for almost all rail construction.

17. Guo Shuqing is now chairman of China Construction Bank, China's second largest commercial bank.

18. Li Ruogu is now chairman and president of the Export-Import Bank of China.

wrote an article that was widely covered by the media, including People's Daily, which argued that the Chinese currency is "obviously undervalued" (Green 2005).

After China's exchange rate policy changed in mid-2005 economists associated with the central bank, notably Yu Yongding, the long-time director of the Institute of World Politics and Economics, persistently promoted accelerated exchange rate appreciation. When he served as a member of the central bank's monetary policy committee for a few years in the mid-2000s, Yu Yongding publicly advocated that faster appreciation of the renminbi was the most effective policy tool for solving China's economic imbalances.[19] Since he rotated off the committee he has continued to argue forcefully that persistently running balance of payments surpluses "is not in China's best interests" and that "lending to the world's richest country for decades" by accumulating large amounts of dollar reserves "is not reasonable."[20]

The central bank governor Zhou Xiaochuan, given his ministerial rank, has been more circumspect in public comments on the exchange rate that run contrary to policy determined by the State Council. But his widely reported assertion in a speech at Tsinghua University in September 2011 that China's reserves in excess of $3 trillion "have exceeded a reasonable level," is a lower-key way of making exactly the same points as those made by Yu Yongding.[21]

Similarly the central bank has been the main advocate for liberalization of deposit and lending rates. The monetary policy department of the bank drafted the proposal that led to the widening of the bands around the bank's benchmark rates in the late 1990s, as analyzed in chapter 3 of this study. The bank, in its 2004 annual report (published in April 2005) recounted in detail the progress of market-based interest rate reform and asserted that these reforms would be continued "to guide the financial institutions to improve the interest rate term structure, strengthen the pricing mechanism for loan risk and appropriately apply pricing strategies to discourage highly risky investment demand" (People's Bank of China 2005a). In addition to his support for exchange rate appreciation, Governor Zhou has persistently advocated for market-oriented interest rate liberalization, even after the central bank was forced to abandon this policy after 2004.[22] And a current outside member of the central bank's monetary policy committee, Xia Bin, has particularly

---

19. "Yu Yongding: Renminbi Appreciation Is the Most Effective Means of Solving China's Imbalances," Xinhua, July 14, 2006, available at www.xinhuanet.com (accessed on September 23, 2011).

20. Yu Yongding, "China's Moment to Break Free of the Dollar Trap," *Financial Times*, August 5, 2011, 7.

21. "Zhou Xiaochuan: Foreign Exchange Reserves Have Already Exceeded a Reasonable Level," April 19, 2011, available at http://finance.sina.com.cn (accessed on September 23, 2011).

22. "Zhou Xiaochuan Discusses Envisaged Market Oriented Interest Rate Reform," *People's Daily*, March 28, 2005, available at www.people.com.cn (accessed on September 23, 2011). Aaron Back and Liu Li, "China PBOC Governor: To Liberalize Interest Rates Gradually," Dow Jones Newswires, available at http://online.wsj.com (accessed on December 17, 2010).

focused on the desirability of making deposit rates positive, echoing the view of Deputy-Governor Wu Xiaoling that negative real deposit rates entail the risk of encouraging asset bubbles.[23]

However, the Ministry of Commerce, the NDRC, and various industry associations, presumably supported from behind the scenes by a coalition of first party secretaries in key coastal regions, have successfully blocked a more rapid appreciation of the currency for almost a decade. The Ministry of Commerce and its allies persistently have made two arguments. The first is that profit margins in export industries are thin and that any pace of annual appreciation of the renminbi above the low single digits will push a significant share of export firms into a money-losing position, resulting in significant job losses. In a report issued in the fall of 2006, the NDRC cited 3 percent margins in the domestic textile industry.[24] The same message has been repeated frequently since. The Ministry of Commerce and the Ministry of Industry and Information in 2010, for example, conducted a stress test to determine the effect of renminbi appreciation on profitability in China's labor-intensive industries. They concluded that the net profit rate in the garment, shoe, toy, and other labor-intensive industries would fall by 1 percent for every 1 percent appreciation of the renminbi. Pointing out that the average profit margin of these industries was only 3 to 5 percent, the two ministries argued that an appreciation of 2 percentage points would "push the enterprises [in those industries] to the limit of their capability."[25] A month or so later the China Chamber of Commerce for Import and Export of Machinery and Electronic Products weighed in on behalf of its member firms, which account for nearly 60 percent of China's exports. Their refrain was identical: "We would be hurt by an appreciation of the yuan."[26]

Within weeks of the government's announcement in June 2010 that ended the tight pegging of the renminbi to the dollar, a policy initiated in August 2008, China's main textile industry association weighed in strongly against significant appreciation. Gao Yong, the vice president of the China National Textile and Apparel Council, argued that "if the yuan actually appreciates 5 percent against the dollar, over half of China's textile companies will go bankrupt." According to Gao, since the industry employs 20 million people, "a large upward revaluation of the yuan could cost millions of jobs."[27]

---

23. "Increasing the Strength of Proactive, Targeted Controls," *People's Daily* (overseas edition), July 27, 2011, available at www.paper.people.com.cn (accessed on September 23, 2011).

24. "Face the Rise of Yuan," *China Daily*, September 6, 2006.

25. "Ministries Design Exchange Rate Stress Test for Labor-Intensive Industries," *People's Daily*, February 26, 2010, available at http://english.people.com.cn (accessed on September 14, 2011).

26. Terrence Poon, "Chinese Exporters Lobby for Stable Yuan," *Wall Street Journal*, March 23, 2010, available at http://blogs.wsj.com (accessed on September 14, 2011).

27. Yang Ning, "Currency Moves May Imperil Textile Firms," *China Daily*, July 13, 2010, 14. Note that Gao's pleading appears to be based on a substantial exaggeration of employment in the

Yet the evidence is that these pleas from various interest groups lack merit because they ignore the reality of rapid productivity growth in the production of tradable goods, analyzed in chapter 3. Profit margins in many of China's exporting industries were low in the middle part of the previous decade, when the authorities allowed the renminbi to begin appreciating. But there is little evidence that this policy led to a squeeze on margins that threatened the industry and thus might have had negative employment implications. For example, in the garment and footwear industry, return on sales in 2005 was a modest 4.3 percent (National Bureau of Statistics of China 2006b, 512–13). Four years later, in 2009, despite the continuous rise in real wages and about a 20 percent real effective appreciation of the renminbi, sales had more than doubled, employment was up 30 percent, and return on sales in the industry had increased to 6.0 percent (National Bureau of Statistics of China 2010f, 510–11). The industries opposing any appreciation of the renminbi present a static view, systematically ignoring the historical trend in and potential for future productivity growth in their industries, and thus systematically mislead Chinese policymakers.

The second argument persistently advanced by the Ministry of Commerce is that globally balanced trade for China is just around the corner and thus that exchange rate appreciation is unnecessary or would be counterproductive. In 2003–04 it was increasingly apparent that the Chinese currency was becoming significantly undervalued, resulting in pressure from the US Treasury Department, the European Union's Commissioner for Economic Affairs, Japan's Cabinet Office, the Organization for Economic Cooperation and Development, and others for an appreciation of the renminbi and China's eventual transition to a floating exchange rate system.[28] By 2005 the judgment of undervaluation was confirmed in spades, when China's trade surplus tripled to exceed $100 billion; and in July that year the government finally announced the depegging of the currency to the dollar, as outlined in chapter 3. Yet only a few months later the Ministry of Commerce forecast that China's trade structure would improve, that imports would grow relatively faster than exports, and that this would "facilitate the country's pursuit of balanced trade" over the course of the 11th Five-Year Plan (2006–10), which at the time was just getting underway.[29] Needless to say, this projection was wildly wrong, as China's net

---

industry. According to official data, employment in 2009 in the textile and apparel industries combined was 10.7 million (National Bureau of Statistics of China 2010f, 508–11).

28. "EU Official Urges China to Adopt More Realistic Yuan Rate," Dow Jones Newswires, May 22, 2005, available at http://online.wsj.com (accessed on May 23, 2005); "China Needs Transitional FX Regime—Japan Cabinet Office," Dow Jones Newswires, June 6, 2005, available at http://online.wsj. com (accessed on June 6, 2005); "OECD Urges China to Hike Rates, Reform Foreign Exchange," Dow Jones Newswires, November 30, 2004, available at http://online.wsj.com (accessed on September 13, 2011).

29. "Focus on Trade Balance," China Daily, October 13, 2006, 4; "Outline of the Eleventh Five-Year Plan for China's Economic and Social Development," Xinhua, March 16, 2006, available at www. xinhuanet.com (accessed on May 11, 2011).

exports of goods and services continued to soar until they were interrupted in 2009 by the collapse of world trade brought on by the global financial and economic crisis.

Five years later, in February 2010—just months before pegging of the renminbi to the dollar was ended—the Ministry of Commerce was back for a repeat performance. Yao Jian, the spokesman for the ministry, argued in February that "stability of the yuan exchange rate is the top policy target." He backed up this priority by arguing that China "may face a foreign trade deficit in the next six months" and that in any case "it will take 2 to 3 years before China's exports recover to the precrisis level."[30] Again, the ministry's forecast was wildly wrong. China's trade was in surplus in five months out of six in the first half of the year and in the entire second half; exports for the year as a whole recorded a stunning recovery of more than 30 percent over the level of 2009, pushing the level of exports up well above the precrisis level.

The second domain in which the disproportionate influence of interest groups has thwarted sensible national economic rebalancing is China's dividend policy, analyzed briefly in chapter 3. Prior to the approval of this policy by the State Council in 2007, the central government received very modest dividends from large, centrally administered state-owned companies. This was extremely unusual. In most countries where the state is a key owner or shareholder of a company, the state receives dividends (World Bank 2005, 1; 2009, 23–27). While the requirement to pay dividends eliminated this anomaly, it did not result in significant funds being transferred to the government budget, where they would have been available to support greater spending on social programs or other public priorities.

The collection and retention of these revenues by the State-Owned Assets Supervision and Administration Commission (SASAC), and its control of how the monies are spent via the State Capital Management Budget, reflect the power wielded by Li Rongrong, the chairman of SASAC. All state-owned enterprise profit and privatization proceeds are public financial revenue and should be managed as such. "Nobody has the legal power to decide on their spending without approval of the National People's Congress (NPC) through the budgeting process" (World Bank 2005, 7). Given the urgent need of the government to build out the social safety net, the World Bank correctly argues that the isolation of SOE dividends from the normal budgeting process "is hardly justified" (World Bank 2005, 7). Not only is the norm internationally for state-owned enterprise dividends to go to the finance ministry for general public use, State Council document number 26, which established the dividend policy, specifically mandated that the State Capital Management Budget be integrated with the general state budget, which is submitted to the National People's Congress for approval (World Bank 2009, 43). Li Rongrong initially said that he would work closely with the Ministry of Finance and follow the

---

30. "Ministries Design Exchange Rate Stress Test for Labor-Intensive Industries," *People's Daily*, February 26, 2010, available at http://english.people.com.cn (accessed on September 13, 2011).

strategy set by the State Council (World Bank 2005, 1). But, as explained in chapter 3, he did not follow through on this commitment but rather seized control of the funds, used them to further SASAC's own narrow purposes, and bypassed the National People's Congress.

The ability of narrow groups to aggressively pursue their own special interests is somewhat surprising, given that in some cases these narrow interests run counter to the announced policy priorities of the top political and economic leadership of China, led by Hu Jintao and Wen Jiabao. While China's collective leadership system may not allow the Hu-Wen team or its successors to control the formulation and execution of economic policy across the entire spectrum of issues, outside observers generally believe that China's top leadership can be successful in achieving a limited number of its highest priority policies. The signature issues of Hu-Wen include the development of what is called a "harmonious society," widely interpreted as making growth more inclusive, reducing inequality, and reducing economic insecurity (Naughton 2007, 108–10). Thus they have assigned much higher priority to agriculture and rural China more generally as well as to the economic and social development of central and western China than did their predecessors, Jiang Zemin and Zhu Rongji. They have signaled this priority by rolling out national initiatives, for example, eliminating primary school fees in rural areas in the poorer western part of China.

Yet China's foreign trade and exchange rate policy in the Hu-Wen era has undoubtedly imposed a massive redistribution of income and wealth in favor of coastal China. China's exports are generated overwhelmingly in a handful of coastal provinces. In the first four months of 2011, for example, 7 coastal provincial-level administrative units (out of a total of 31 such units)— Guangdong, Jiangsu, Shanghai, Beijing, Zhejiang, Shandong, and Fujian— accounted for more than four-fifths of China's total exports.[31]

China's undervalued exchange rate in effect constitutes a subsidy for these large coastal exporting jurisdictions and a tax on the rest of the country. This study does not attempt to determine empirically the magnitude of the internal geographic redistribution of income and wealth imposed by the renminbi's undervaluation, but it would not be surprising if the subsidy for coastal regions implicit in renminbi undervaluation more than offset all of the fiscal transfers from the central government to the localities, which are designed in part to allow local governments in poorer, inland regions to increase the provision of public services beyond the level that could be financed from revenues available to local governments.[32]

---

31. "Exports and Imports Exceed US$1 trillion in the First Four Months," May 10, 2011, available at www.customs.gov.cn (accessed on May 10, 2011).

32. Fiscal transfers from the central government to provincial and subprovincial governments were RMB3.2 trillion in 2010 and were budgeted at RMB3.71 trillion in 2011 (Ministry of Finance 2011).

In the first half of 2011, China reiterated and seemed to strengthen its commitment to rebalancing the sources of its economic growth. The report of the NDRC at the 11th National People's Congress in March emphasized achieving growth through expanding domestic consumption demand, accelerating the development of the services sector, and reforming factor prices (National Development and Reform Commission 2011). The central theme of the 12th Five-Year Plan (2011–15), published shortly after the conclusion of the National People's Congress, is economic rebalancing. While the plan has very few specific quantitative targets, some of them are directly related to the rebalancing agenda. For example, the plan calls for an increase in the personal income share of national income and a rise in the share of wages in primary distribution. It also calls for a 4 percentage point increase over five years in the services share of GDP. The 12th Five-Year Plan also calls for market-oriented reform of interest rates and market-oriented reform of factor prices for resources such as water, electricity, refined petroleum products, and natural gas.[33] Many of the same rebalancing measures were also reiterated by Vice Premier Wang Qishan in the economic track of the Third US-China Strategic & Economic Dialogue in Washington on May 9–10, 2011.[34]

Similarly, China's goal of gradually realizing the convertibility of the renminbi on capital account transactions seems to signal a commitment to liberalizing steps that are essential to rebalancing the sources of economic growth. As early as 2004, China launched an initiative to promote the internationalization of the renminbi by allowing Hong Kong residents to open renminbi deposit accounts in Hong Kong banks. Subsequently the government has taken a number of steps to encourage the use the renminbi in cross-border trade settlement. Ultimately this could be an important step on the path to full convertibility, a goal that People's Bank of China Vice Governor Yi Gang has identified as the ultimate goal for China's exchange rate reform. Moving from the use of the renminbi as an international settlement currency to capital account convertibility will require market-oriented interest rate reform, the development of a much larger and more liquid domestic bond market, and a much more flexible exchange rate, all steps that would move the rebalancing agenda forward (Lardy and Douglass 2011).

But there are important counterindicators as well. First, while embracing the goal of economic rebalancing, the plan has no specifics on what policy instruments will be deployed to achieve the goal. Second, the previous plan, the 11th Five-Year Plan, included many of the same goals just discussed, but

---

33. Outline of the Twelfth Five-Year Program for National Social and Economic Development (complete text), March 17, 2011, available at www.npc.gov.cn (accessed on March 18, 2011).

34. US-China Comprehensive Framework for Promoting Strong, Sustainable and Balanced Growth and Economic Cooperation, US Department of the Treasury, May 10, 2011; Third Meeting of the US-China Strategic & Economic Dialogue Joint U.S. China Economic Track Fact Sheet, US Department of the Treasury, May 10, 2011; both available at www.treasury.gov/press-center (accessed on May 10, 2011).

government policy in support of these objectives was weak at best, and most economic imbalances expanded during 2006–10. Third, conventional wisdom among outside observers suggests that the Hu-Wen team is too weak to push aggressively on the rebalancing agenda in the waning months of their time in office. Little is known about the economic policy views of the new political leadership that will be ushered in at the 18th Party Congress in the fall of 2012. Even if these leaders turn out to be more reform oriented than their predecessors, it is likely that it will take a minimum of a year for them to consolidate their power and put their mark on economic policy. So the risk is that China will continue for another two or more years on the path of slow incremental economic reforms that are not aggressive enough to result in economic rebalancing.

Implications for the United States

If China does not accelerate the pace of reforms that would support rebalancing the sources of its economic growth, the economic challenge for the United States and, in turn, the global economy, becomes much greater. The challenge for the United States is to reduce its large fiscal deficit and put the trajectory of its government debt on a sustainable path. Based on the savings-investment framework set forth in chapter 2, if there is no change in its external position, the United States can reduce its fiscal deficit only if there is an offsetting change in either the household or the corporate sector. Households are currently paying down debt—i.e., their spending is less than their income. Since household indebtedness has come down only slightly from the peak of 130 percent of disposable income in 2007, it seems likely that deleveraging will persist for some time. The alternative is an offsetting change in the corporate sector, which is also running a surplus. But that would require an increase in business investment, not likely given weak aggregate demand and a prospective fiscal tightening, or a decline in business income. But a decline in corporate profits would presumably accompany a recession, which would reduce government revenues and raise the government deficit.[35] Thus if China fails to rebalance its economy over the next several years, it will be more difficult for the United States to reduce its large fiscal deficit and put the trajectory of its government debt on a more sustainable path.

If China was successful in transitioning to a more consumption demand–driven pattern of growth, its external surplus would shrink, adding to US aggregate demand and thus reducing the US external deficit. The resulting improvement in the savings-investment imbalance of the United States would make possible the improvement in the US fiscal position. From a growth perspective the reduction in the US external deficit would partially offset the adverse effect of fiscal consolidation on US economic growth. If China does not make this transition and its external imbalance increases in size over the

---

35. Martin Wolf, "Why Austerity Alone Risks a Disaster," *Financial Times*, June 29, 2011, 9.

next few years, China will be subtracting from economic growth in the rest of the world, including in the United States. That outcome would undermine the ability to put US debt on a more sustainable path and would exacerbate the negative effect of fiscal consolidation on US economic growth. Thus the United States would face a more difficult trade-off between sustaining economic growth (via less fiscal consolidation) on the one hand and increased risks associated with a rising level of government debt on the other.

Appendix A
Statistical Issues

This appendix addresses three important potential shortcomings of Chinese statistics that bear on the issues taken up in the text.

Services Data in GDP Production-Side Data

It is sometimes suggested that the relatively small share of services in China's GDP reflects inaccurate measurement of services output. Arthur Kroeber, for example, argues that "China does a very poor job of measuring services" and that the upward revision in services following the first national economic census in 2004 (analyzed below) "was too low" (Kroeber 2007, 1–2). Services clearly were significantly undercounted in the past, but it is unlikely that this remains the case today. This judgment is based on an analysis of the results of China's first national economic census, carried out in 2004, its second economic census, carried out in 2008, and the more recent annual revisions of GDP data by the National Bureau of Statistics of China.

The magnitude of the effort involved in the first economic census and the second economic census should not be underestimated. In each census the government recruited over 3 million enumerators and supervisors and mobilized another 10 million statisticians and accountants from government agencies, enterprises, and institutions to participate in the year-long effort. A main goal was to more accurately measure the output of private and individual-run services activities, which historically had not been fully captured by the regular statistical system.

The authorities announced the results of China's first national economic census in late 2005 (State Council Leading Small Group Office on the First National Economic Census and the National Bureau of Statistics of

China 2005). On the basis of the census the statistical authorities revised 2004 GDP upward by RMB2,300 billion, a 16.8 percent increase. This increase was highly concentrated in services. Services output was revised upward by RMB2,129.7 billion, or more than nine-tenths of the total additions to GDP. The restatement led to a 50 percent increase in the size of the services sector in China's 2004 GDP. The balance of the undercount was in agriculture and industry, where the restatement led to increases of 1 and 2 percent, respectively, in the size of the two sectors. The result of these adjustments was a substantial change in the reported structure of GDP. The services share of output in 2004 increased from 31.9 to 40.7 percent, an increase of 8.8 percentage points, while the shares of agriculture and industry fell by 2.1 and 6.7 percentage points, respectively (Li Deshui 2005).[1] In short, the census provided the basis for a better understanding of the level and structure of China's GDP.

Subsequently, in January 2006, the National Bureau of Statistics used the information gathered in the first census to revise production-side GDP and its three components all the way back to 1993. The revision made use of the trend deviation method, widely adopted by the Organization for Economic Cooperation and Development (National Bureau of Statistics of China 2006a, Li Deshui 2005).[2] Later in the year the authorities published a new series on GDP by expenditure for the years 1978 through 2004. On average about 70 percent of the additions to GDP were to the consumption component. For 2004 the adjustments raised GDP by 13 percent. The revisions raised the consumption share of GDP by 1.3 percentage points, lowered the investment share by 1.0 percentage point, and reduced the share of net exports of goods and services by 0.3 percentage points (National Bureau of Statistics of China 2006b, 68; 2005, 63).

The authorities announced the results of China's second economic census in December 2009 (State Council Leading Small Group Office on the Second National Economic Census and the National Bureau of Statistics

---

1. Technically GDP is divided into primary, secondary, and tertiary industry. Primary industry encompasses agriculture, forestry, animal husbandry, and fishery; secondary industry encompasses manufacturing, mining and quarrying, utilities (electricity, water, and gas), and construction; tertiary industry encompasses all economic activities not included in primary and secondary industry. I follow the not uncommon practice of identifying these three components of GDP as agriculture, industry, and services.

2. The initial revisions went back only to 1993, apparently because the authorities carried out the first national services sector census in 1992. On the basis of that census they revised GDP data from 1978 through 1992. In short, they assumed that the undercount of services that they found in the 2004 national economic census had emerged largely since 1992, and that any prior undercount of services and thus GDP was largely corrected by the adjustments made after the services census of 1992. However, the GDP series contained in the *China Statistical Yearbook* published in the fall of 2006 did reflect some very small changes in services output for year years prior to 1993. The absolute amounts added to services output for the years 1978 through 1986 led to an increase in the absolute size of the services sector and of GDP of 2 to 3 percent and 1 percent or less, respectively.

of China 2009). On the basis of the second economic census the authorities revised China's 2008 GDP upward by RMB1,337.5 billion, or 4.4 percent (National Bureau of Statistics of China 2009c). Just over eight-tenths of the addition was in the services sector, increasing its size by almost a quarter. This was much less than the 50 percent upward revision in 2004 services output, but it nonetheless did lead to changes in the reported structure of output. The services share of GDP in 2008 was revised upward by 1.7 percentage points (from 40.1 to 41.8 percent), while the shares of agriculture and industry fell by 0.6 and 1.1 percentage points, respectively.

Since 2003, when the National Bureau of Statistics revised its system for calculating and reporting its annual GDP numbers, China has followed the practice of many other countries by releasing preliminary, revised, and final GDP data (National Bureau of Statistics of China 2003). The preliminary accounting (*chubu hesuan*) of annual GDP is usually released three weeks after the end of the calendar year. Next, around mid-year, the statistical authorities release preliminary verified (*chubu heshi*) data, and even later final verified (*zuizhong heshi*) data. The final verified number usually is now released about a year after the preliminary estimate, although in earlier years the lag was longer.

To date the revisions to the annual preliminary GDP data have all been upward and disproportionately concentrated in the services sector. In 2006, for example, between the preliminary accounting and the final verified number, the National Bureau of Statistics revised GDP up by RMB251.6 billion, a little over 1 percent. Four-fifths of the added GDP came in services. Similarly in 2009, more than nine-tenths of the RMB555 billion that was added to GDP between the preliminary accounting and the final verified number came in services.

Thus while services may still be somewhat undercounted, the statistical authorities in China have made what can only be described as herculean efforts to improve GDP data, focusing on the services sector. These improvements, plus the more modest adjustments following the second economic census compared with the first, suggest that the degree of undercount of output in the services sector has been very substantially reduced, though probably not eliminated.

Housing Consumption in GDP Expenditure Data

A second area of concern about the accuracy of Chinese economic data is the measurement of housing consumption. The decline in private consumption as a share of GDP after 2002 coincides with an enormous boom in residential real estate, which is shown in figure 3.3 in chapter 3. One component of private consumption is housing services. Could it be that official statistics have fallen behind in accurately measuring housing services? This is a not unreasonable worry since measurement of housing services is complex. Outlays on housing are not a good measure of housing services, except for rental units. For example, a family living in a house they own on which the mortgage has been fully amortized may have zero housing outlays. But they are receiving housing services. Thus statistical authorities in most advanced economies impute a rental value for all owner-occupied housing, regardless of whether or not there is a mortgage on the property.

Expert statisticians from China's National Bureau of Statistics Department of National Accounts have written a number of articles proposing improvements in the methods used to measure housing services. Both Xu Xianchun (2002) and Liu Liping (2008) assert that the reported value of housing services as a share of GDP in China was extremely low not only relative to the share in advanced industrial countries but also compared with other countries at levels of economic development comparable to China. But their critiques do not appear to apply to data for years close to the dates at which their articles were published, but rather to much older data.

The statistical authorities originally estimated the value of housing services included in household consumption in China's GDP expenditure accounts as the sum of rents paid on nonowner occupied dwellings plus depreciation of owner-occupied dwellings plus the value of construction materials purchased for housing maintenance and repair. Depreciation rather than an imputed rental value was used to estimate housing services provided by owner-occupied housing in part because the market for rental housing in rural areas is quite limited. Even in urban areas the vast majority of housing is owner occupied. This methodology had two main weaknesses. First, it made no allowance for housing services provided by dwellings owned by the government, enterprises, or institutions. In 1996, 56 percent of the urban population lived in housing units of this type (Xu 2002, 206). Second, depreciation of owner-occupied housing was calculated on the basis of the historical cost of building houses rather than current construction costs. Given the upward trend in the prices of construction materials in China, this approach led to an underestimate of the level of housing services in GDP.

Liu (2008) made his own estimate of housing services for the years 1990–2000 in which he corrected for these problems and derived numbers that averaged 5.3 percent of GDP, compared with an average of 1.6 percent of GDP in the methodology used by the National Bureau of Statistics in compiling GDP statistics for those years. However, unlike the official series, which showed an upward trend in housing services as a share of GDP (presumably because privatization of state-controlled housing in urban areas in the second half of the decade reduced the degree of undercount in the official series), Liu's estimated series showed a declining trend—from 7.2 percent in 1990 to 4.9 percent in 2000.

Curiously, though Liu's article was published in 2008, his analysis of housing services was restricted to the years 1990–2000. And he did not explicitly indicate whether any of the problems he was analyzing had been addressed or were still outstanding.

What is the current methodology used by the National Bureau of Statistics to estimate housing services? To what extent have the historical problems been addressed? First, the problem of undercounting the value of housing services provided by the government, state-owned enterprises, and institutions was largely solved by the privatization of the stock of housing controlled by these units, a process that was completed in the second half of the 1990s. As noted above, this is probably the reason that the value of officially calculated housing services under the old methodology rose from 1.1 percent of GDP in 1990 to 2.2 percent of GDP in 2000. Second, according to another member of the National Accounts Department of the National Bureau of Statistics, following the first economic census in 2004 the statistical authorities began to calculate depreciation of owner-occupied buildings based on current construction costs rather than historical prices (Jin Hong 2009, 6).[3]

Data on housing services for the years 2004–09 as a share of GDP are shown in table A.1.[4] Housing services in these years as a share of GDP are several times higher than the average of 1.6 percent reflected in official data for the years 1990–2000. So if there is still an underestimate in these data for more recent years, the degree of underestimation has been substantially reduced by the factors mentioned above. However, several questions remain. First, what is the effect of using depreciation, rather than an imputed rental value, as a proxy for housing services provided by owner-occupied housing? The depreciation rates reportedly in use, 3 percent in rural areas and 2 percent in urban areas, imply lives of structures of 33 and 50 years, respectively, for rural and urban housing. If these lives are too long then the estimated value of housing services will be understated.[5]

Second, given the housing boom in recent years, isn't it surprising that housing services as a share of GDP did not rise somewhat over 2004–09, the years shown in table A.1? And what in particular explains the decline in the share of housing services, from 6.6 percent of GDP in 2006 to only 6.1 percent in 2009? The vast increase in the stock of urban housing is evident even through casual observation and confirmed by the data underlying figure 3.3, which shows completed investment in urban residential housing from 1996 through 2010. But there also have been vast improvements in the housing stock in rural areas. Per capita floor space increased by 10 percent between 2006 and 2009; the share of the rural housing constructed of reinforced concrete rather than brick and wood rose; the share of rural housing with running water and even air conditioning and central heating went up significantly. Presumably these and

---

3. At the same time, the authorities modified the depreciation rates used to impute the value of housing services. In urban areas the rate was reduced from 4 to 2 percent, and in rural areas the rate was raised from 2 to 3 percent (Jin Hong 2009, 6).

4. These are the only data on housing services that the National Bureau of Statistics has ever included in its annual statistical yearbook. The data for 1990–2000 appear in Liu Liping (2008) but not in the yearbook.

5. Ma and Yi (2010, 4) point out that rural household survey data report both total and cash housing expenditures and argue that the difference between the two is imputed rent. But the difference between these two annual numbers in 2007 was only RMB34, or less than $5, which they regard as implausibly low.

Table A.1 Housing services, 2004–09
(percent of GDP)

Year	Urban	Rural	Total
2004	4.2	1.8	6.0
2005	4.1	1.8	5.9
2006	4.8	1.7	6.6
2007	4.6	1.7	6.3
2008	4.6	1.6	6.2
2009	4.7	1.4	6.1

Source: National Bureau of Statistics of China (2010f, 57).

other qualitative improvements are reflected in the estimate of the statistical authorities that the value of the rural housing stock per square meter increased by 25 percent between 2006 and 2009 (National Bureau of Statistics of China 2008a, 352; 2010f, 376). The decline in housing services as a share of GDP in rural areas reflected in table A.1 seems inconsistent with these trends.

More generally, the decline in total housing services after 2006 seems inconsistent with other data. For example, investment measured in current prices in completed residential buildings in both urban and rural areas rose by 90 percent between 2006 and 2009, well ahead of the 60 percent pace of expansion of nominal GDP. Thus the share of GDP going to residential construction has risen over time, from 6.8 percent of GDP in 2004, to 7.5 percent of GDP in 2006, and then to 9 percent of GDP in 2009.[6] Trying to determine why reported housing services as a share of GDP declined between 2006 and 2009 despite these developments would require constructing a perpetual inventory of China's housing stock, an exercise that lies beyond the scope of this study and which, in any case, to be reasonably accurate would require more data than are readily available.

How does China's share of housing services in GDP compare with this measure in similar countries? In India in recent years housing services have constituted about 8 to 9 percent of GDP.[7] It is a bit surprising that India records housing services in its national accounts as a larger share of GDP than China. First, given the positive relationship between per capita income and the share of GDP contributed by housing services, one would expect that in India, where per capita GDP is substantially lower than in China, housing services would be

---

6. Measurement is the value of completed residential construction in both rural and urban areas divided into GDP (National Bureau of Statistics of China 2008a, 213–14; 2010f, 38, 197–98). These data differ from the data underlying figure 3.3 because they include investment in residential property undertaken by farm households. In 2009 this amounted to RMB499 billion, or 1.5 percent of GDP (ISI Emerging Markets, CEIC Database).

7. Housing services in India rose from 8.2 percent of GDP in 2004 to 9.0 percent of GDP in 2009. Housing services data from ISI Emerging Markets, CEIC Database. GDP data are from *World Development Indicators,* available at http://databank.worldbank.org (accessed on September 19, 2011).

a lower share of GDP than in China. Second, as noted in chapter 3, from 2000 through 2008 investment in housing in India averaged about 4 percent of GDP, substantially less than investment in housing in China in the same years. India's housing consumption could be higher as a share of GDP than in China only if the value of its housing stock relative to GDP prior to 2000 was much higher than in China. This seems unlikely.

The tentative conclusion is that despite the methodological improvements, China's National Bureau of Statistics probably still underestimates the level of housing services, perhaps by a few percentage points of GDP. Moreover, the degree of underestimation appears to be increasing over time. This judgment is based on three factors: first, the likely overestimate of the assumed lives of housing, on which the estimates of housing services for owner-occupied dwellings are based; second, the difficulty of reconciling the declining share of housing services in GDP in 2006–09 with the boom in housing construction and investment; and third, the fact that officially reported housing services in China are a smaller share of GDP than in India, where both per capita GDP and investment in housing as a share of GDP have been well below that in China for at least a decade.

Since housing services are a component of household consumption, the important corollary is that household consumption as a share of GDP also probably is understated by a few percentage points of GDP. Likely the degree of undercount has increased over time, so not only do the official data on household consumption understate the level of household consumption, they probably overstate the decline in the consumption share of GDP in recent years.

Shares in National Income

The National Bureau of Statistics does not publish national data on the wage, capital, and government shares of GDP. But it does publish provincial data on the same variables, so national data can be derived by adding up the provincial figures on employee compensation, net taxes on production, depreciation of fixed assets, and operating surplus. The first of these represents the share of labor, the second the share of government, and the sum of the third and fourth the share of capital.

Two problems arise. First, there are substantial discrepancies between the sum of the provincial data on regional product and national data on gross domestic product. Moreover, the direction of the discrepancy has reversed. In the 1990s, the sum of regional product across all provincial units was as much as 9 percent below the reported national gross domestic product. Starting in 2003 the sum of regional product across all provincial units was greater than the reported national gross domestic product. This discrepancy has increased over time, reaching 4 percent by 2007.[8] The sources of this discrepancy are not

---

8. The discrepancy rose to 7 percent in 2009, the most recent year available. But the data for the most recent year are frequently revised, so it is possible that the final numbers for 2009 will reflect a smaller discrepancy.

clear but are presumably related to the inflation of production-side provincial GDP data in recent years.

The second problem is that these provincially disaggregated data on income shares appear to have been compiled on an inconsistent basis over time. In all countries the question arises of how to classify the income of self-employed individuals. Since self-employed workers own their own capital, part of their income reflects a return to their labor and part a return to their capital. This is an important issue in China, since in 2009 there were 66 million nonagricultural self-employed workers.[9] In the Chinese data published prior to 2010, the year 2004 shows a major discontinuity in the labor share of national income; specifically this measure declined by 4.7 percentage points, while the share of national income accruing to corporations (the capital share) rose by 6.1 percentage points.[10] This is an extremely abrupt change. In the 10 years prior to 2004, the annual absolute change in the labor share of national income averaged only 0.7 percentage points. It seems that the large change in 2004 compared with 2003 resulted from recategorizing some or all of the income of nonagricultural self-employed individuals. In 2003 and prior years, their income was counted entirely as labor income. Starting in 2004, the statistical authorities appear to have imputed the capital share of the income of these self-employed workers and shifted this amount to the operating surplus of enterprises, i.e., capital income.[11] That is the only logical explanation of the large simultaneous drop in the labor share of income and the rise in the capital share of income in 2004.

After 2004 the pattern of annual very small incremental changes in the shares of income accruing to labor, capital, and the government resumed. But in the 2009 data, published in 2010, there was another large discontinuity. Between 2007 and 2009, labor income as a share of GDP jumped 6.8 percentage points, while the share of corporate income dropped 7.1 percentage points.[12] That put the labor share of income back to the 46 percent level of 2003. Similarly, the capital share of income in 2009 was very close to the share in 2003. It appears that in their presentation of the 2009 data, the statistical authorities shifted the income of self-employed nonagricultural workers back into the labor income category. Unfortunately, the statistical authorizes have not released comparable data for the years 2004 through 2007, which would provide a consistent time series. But I believe we can judge long-run trends since, except for 2004–07, the reported labor income share appears to include

---

9. This number includes nonagricultural self employed workers in both urban and rural areas.

10. A 1.6 percentage point decline in net taxes makes these changes sum to zero.

11. According to Hua Sheng, a professor of economics at Beijing Normal University, the entire amount of the income of nonagricultural self-employed people was placed in the category of the operating surplus of enterprises. Hua Sheng, "Debate: Workers' Income," *China Daily*, November 8, 2010.

12. As of the time of this writing the authorities had not published data on income shares for 2008.

all of the income of nonagricultural self-employed individuals, including the return to their own capital.

Another reason to believe that the statistical authorities in 2009 returned the imputed capital income of self-employed workers to the labor income category is a comparison with data contained in China's flow of funds accounts. These data, unlike the data on the shares of income derived from the provincial data, do not show any abrupt decline in the labor share of income in 2004; indeed, the flow of funds data show a slight increase in the labor share of income in 2004. Moreover, the decline in the labor share of income between 1993 and 2007 published before 2010 reflected in the provincial data is much larger than the decline reflected in the flow of funds accounts. The decline in the labor share of income between 1993 and 2007 is 9.8 percentage points of GDP. This is the source of the frequently cited large decline in the labor share of income in China over the long run. In contrast, the decline in the labor share of income in the flow of funds accounts between 1992 and 2007 was only 4 percentage points.

In contrast, the provincial data on the wage share of GDP published beginning in 2010 line up much more closely with the flow of funds data. They show a decline in the labor share of income of 3 percentage points between 1993 and 2009, close to the 5 percentage point decline in labor compensation between 1992 and 2008 reflected in the flow of funds accounts.

The main implication of the analysis above is that some earlier writing on imbalances in China, particularly as it concerns the relatively small share of private consumption expenditure in GDP, appears to have been based on data that overstated the decline in labor compensation as a share of GDP. From the data in table 2.1 one can calculate that the decline in labor compensation accounted for only two-fifths of the long-term decline in household consumption as a share of GDP. Other factors accounted for the balance.

References

Amos, Paul, Dick Bullock, and Jitendra Sondhi. 2010. *High-Speed Rail: The Fast Track to Economic Development?* Beijing: World Bank China Country Office.

Anderson, Jonathan. 2006. *Rebalance This.* UBS Investment Research, Asian Focus (December 12).

Anderson, Jonathan. 2008a. *How Long Can Energy Subsidies Last?* UBS Investment Research, China Focus (April 28).

Anderson, Jonathan. 2008b. *Chart of the Day: The Energy Subsidy Debate.* UBS Investment Research, Emerging Market Comment (August 12).

Anderson, Jonathan. 2009. *Chart of the Day: Still No Subsidy Worries.* UBS Investment Research, Emerging Market Comment (June 8).

Anderson, Jonathan. 2011a. *The Most Important Sector in the Universe.* UBS Investment Research, Global Investment Strategy (March 16).

Anderson, Jonathan. 2011b. *It's Still about Food—And Watch for the Turn.* UBS Investment Research, Emerging Market Comment (April 20).

Bank of China. 1999. Provisional Regulations on Consumer Credit (December 7). In *Almanac of China's Finance and Banking 1999*, China Banking Society, 348–52. Beijing: China Financial Publishing House.

Barnett, Steven, and Ray Brooks. 2011. Does Government Spending on Health and Education Raise Consumption? In *Rebalancing Growth in Asia: Economic Dimensions for China*, ed. Vivek Arora and Roberto Cardarelli, 129–38. Washington: International Monetary Fund.

Bergsten, C. Fred, Charles Freeman, Nicholas R. Lardy, and Derek Mitchell. 2008. *China's Rise: Challenges and Opportunities.* Washington: Peterson Institute for International Economics and Center for Strategic and International Studies.

Blanchard, Olivier, and Gian Maria Milesi-Ferretti. 2009. *Global Imbalances in Midstream.* IMF Staff Position Note (December). Washington: International Monetary Fund. Available at www.imf.org (accessed on January 6, 2010).

Brandt, Loren, Chang-tai Hsieh, and Xiaodong Zhu. 2010. Growth and Structural Transformation in China. In *China's Great Economic Transformation*, ed. Loren Brandt and Thomas G. Rawski. Cambridge: Cambridge University Press.

Bremer, Ian. 2010. *The End of the Free Market: Who Wins the War Between States and Corporations?* New York: Penguin Group.

Bullock, Richard, Jitendra Sondhi, and Paul Amos. 2009. *Tracks from the Past, Transport for the Future: China's Railway Industry 1990–2008 and Its Future Plans and Possibilities.* Beijing: World Bank China Country Office.

Cai Fang and Wang Meiyan. 2010. Four Topics on Wage Changes in the Chinese Economy. Paper presented at the 34th Pacific Trade and Development Conference, Beijing University, December 9.

Calderon, Cesar, Enrique Moral-Benito, and Luis Serven. 2009. Is Infrastructure Capital Productive? A Dynamic Heterogeneous Approach. Unpublished manuscript. Available at http://siteresources.worldbank.org/DEC/Resources/84797-1257266550602/CalderonC.pdf (accessed on September 15, 2011).

Chan, Kam Wing. 2010. A China Paradox: Migrant Labor Shortage amidst Rural Labor Supply Abundance. *Eurasian Geography and Economics* 51, no. 4: 513–30.

Chamon, Marcos, and Eswar Prasad. 2008. *Why Are Savings Rates of Urban Households in China Rising?* IMF Working Paper 08/145 (June). Washington: International Monetary Fund.

China Banking Regulatory Commission. 2010. *2009 Annual Report.* Available at www.cbrc.gov.cn (accessed on June 8, 2010).

China Banking Regulatory Commission. 2011. *2010 Annual Report.* Available at www.cbrc.gov.cn (accessed on May 5, 2011).

China Banking Society. 1997. *Almanac of China's Finance and Banking 1997.* Beijing: China Financial Publishing House.

China Banking Society. 1998. *Almanac of China's Finance and Banking 1998.* Beijing: China Financial Publishing House.

China Banking Society. 1999. *Almanac of China's Finance and Banking 1999.* Beijing: China Financial Publishing House.

China Banking Society. 2005. *Almanac of China's Finance and Banking 2005.* Beijing: China Financial Publishing House.

China Banking Society. 2008. *Almanac of China's Finance and Banking 2008.* Beijing: China Financial Publishing House.

China Investment Corporation. 2011. *Annual Report 2010.* Available at www.China-Inv.cn (accessed on September 15, 2011).

China Petroleum & Chemical Corporation. 2010. *2009 Annual Report and Accounts.* Available at http://english.sinopec.com (accessed on May 3, 2011).

Cline, William R. 2010. Decomposing the Reduction in China's Current Account Surplus from 2007 to 2009–2010. Unpublished manuscript (April). Peterson Institute for International Economics, Washington.

Cline, William R., and John Williamson. 2008. Estimates of the Equilibrium Exchange Rate of the RMB: Is There a Consensus and If Not, Why Not? In *Debating China's Exchange Rate Policy,* ed. Morris Goldstein and Nicholas R. Lardy. Washington: Peterson Institute for International Economics.

Cline, William R., and John Williamson. 2011. *Estimates of Fundamental Equilibrium Exchange Rates, May 2011.* Policy Brief 11-5 (May). Washington: Peterson Institute for International Economics.

Cooper, Richard N. 2005. *Living with Global Imbalances: A Contrarian View.* Policy Briefs in International Economics 05-3 (November). Washington: Peterson Institute for International Economics.

Council of Economic Advisors. 2010. *Economic Report of the President.* Washington: Government Printing Office.

Council for Economic Planning and Development. 1997. *Taiwan Statistical Data Book 1997*. Taipei.

European Chamber. 2009. *Overcapacity in China: Causes, Impact, and Recommendations* (November 26). Available at www.europeanchamber.com.cn (accessed on September 15, 2011).

Frazier, Mark W. 2010. *Socialist Insecurity: Pensions and the Politics of Uneven Development in China.* Ithaca, NY: Cornell University Press.

Freeman, Will. 2010. *The Big Engine That Can: China's High-Speed Rail Project.* GaveKalDragonomics, China Insight Economics, May 28.

Gagnon, Joseph. 2011. *Current Account Imbalances Coming Back.* Working Paper 11-1 (January). Washington: Peterson Institute for International Economics.

Garnaut, Ross. 2006. The Turning Point in China's Economic Development. In *The Turning Point in China's Economic Development*, ed. Ross Garnaut and Ligang Song. Sydney: ANU E Press.

Garnaut, Ross. 2010. The Turning Period in China's Economic Development: A Conceptual Framework and New Empirical Evidence. In *China: The Next Twenty Years of Reform and Development*, ed. Ross Garnaut, Jane Golley, and Ligang Song. Sydney: ANU E Press.

Goldstein, Morris, and Nicholas R. Lardy. 2009. *The Future of China's Exchange Rate Policy*. Washington: Peterson Institute for International Economics.

Green, Stephen. 2005. *CNY Reform: Change Could Be Imminent.* Standard Chartered on the Ground (May 11).

Green, Stephen. 2009a. *China—A Very, Very Rainy Day.* Standard Chartered On the Ground (February 17).

Green, Stephen. 2009b. *China—The Imbalance That Dares Not Speak Its Name*, Part 1. Standard Chartered On the Ground (December 9).

Green, Stephen. 2009c. China—*The Imbalance That Dares Not Speak Its Name*, Part 2. Standard Chartered On the Ground, December 14.

Green, Stephen. 2010. *China—Bubbly Land,* Part 2. Standard Chartered On the Ground (February 12).

Green, Stephen. 2011. *China—Our Big Real Estate Survey*, Part 3. Standard Chartered Global Research Special Report, July 4.

Guo, Kai and Papa N'Diaye. 2011. Employment Effects of Growth Rebalancing in China. In *Rebalancing Growth in Asia: Economic Dimensions for China*, ed. Vivek Arora and Roberto Cardarelli, 99–112. Washington: International Monetary Fund.

He, Jianwu, and Louis Kuijs. 2007. *Rebalancing China's Economy—Modeling a Policy Package.* World Bank Research Paper No. 7 (September). Beijing: World Bank. Available at www.worldbank.org.cn.

Huang Yasheng. 2011. Rethinking the Beijing Consensus. *Asia Policy* 11 (January): 1–26.

Huang Yiping and Xun Wang. 2010. Financial Repression and Economic Growth in China. Unpublished manuscript (May). Beijing: Beijing University China Center for Economic Research.

Huang Yiping and Tao Kunyu. 2010. *Causes and Remedies of China's External Imbalances.* Working Paper Series E201002. Beijing: Beijing University China Center for Economic Research.

IEA (International Energy Agency). 2010. *World Energy Outlook 2009.* Paris. Available at www.oecd-ilibrary.org (accessed on April 26, 2011).

IEA (International Energy Agency). 2011. *Oil Market Outlook* (March 15). Available at www.oilmarketreport.org (accessed on April 20, 2011).

ILO (International Labor Organization). 2008. *Global Wage Report 2008/09.* Geneva.

ILO (International Labor Organization). 2010. *Global Wage Report 2010/11.* Geneva.

IMF (International Monetary Fund). 1997. *People's Republic of China—Selected Issues.* IMF Staff Country Report 97/72 (September). Washington.

IMF (International Monetary Fund). 2006. *Global Financial Stability Report* (September). Washington.

IMF (International Monetary Fund). 2008. *World Economic Outlook* (October). Washington.

IMF (International Monetary Fund). 2010a. *Regional Economic Outlook: Asia and Pacific* (October). Washington.

IMF (International Monetary Fund). 2010b. *People's Republic of China: 2010 Article IV Consultation—Staff Report* (July). Washington. Available at www.imf.org (accessed on July 22, 2010).

IMF (International Monetary Fund). 2011a. *World Economic Outlook Update* (January 25). Washington. Available at www.imf.org (accessed on February 1, 2011).

IMF (International Monetary Fund). 2011b. *World Economic Outlook (WEO) Tensions from the Two-Speed Recovery: Unemployment, Commodities, and Capital Flows* (April). Washington. Available at www.imf.org (accessed on April 18, 2011).

IMF (International Monetary Fund). 2011c. *People's Republic of China: 2010 Article IV Consultation—Staff Report* (July). Washington. Available at www.imf.org (accessed on July 21, 2011).

IMF (International Monetary Fund). 2011d. *World Economic Outlook* (April). Available at www.imf.org (accessed on April 25, 2011 and June 28, 2011).

Jackson, Richard, Keisuke Nakashima, and Neil Howe. 2009. *China's Long March to Retirement Reform: The Graying of the Middle Kingdom Revisited*. Washington: Center for Strategic and International Studies.

Jin Hong. 2009. The Overview of GDP Estimates and Related Issues in China. Paper presented at the international workshop From Data to Accounts: Measuring Production in National Accounting, June 8–10, Beijing. Available at www.unstats.un.org (accessed on January 27, 2011).

Johnson, Robert, and Guillermo Noguera. 2011. Accounting for Intermediates: Production Sharing and Trade in Value Added. Unpublished paper (May).

Jun Ma, and David Folkerts-Landau. 2004. *RMB Reform: Technical Preparations Underway*. Deutsche Bank, Global Markets Research, November 17.

Kennedy, Scott. 2005. *The Business of Lobbying in China*. Cambridge, MA: Harvard University Press.

Kroeber, Arthur. 2007. Consumption: A Chinese Puzzle. *China Insight* 33 (February 13): 1–9. Advisory Services Ltd.

Kroeber, Arthur. 2010. Exploding the Local-Government Debt Myth (June 18). GaveKalDragonomics, China Insight Economics.

Lardy, Nicholas R. 1978. *Agriculture in China's Modern Economic Development*. Cambridge: Cambridge University Press.

Lardy, Nicholas R. 1992. *Foreign Trade and Economic Reform in China*. Cambridge: Cambridge University Press.

Lardy, Nicholas R. 1998. *China's Unfinished Economic Revolution*. Washington: Brookings Institution.

Lardy, Nicholas R. 2002. *Integrating China into the Global Economy*. Washington: Brookings Institution.

Lardy, Nicholas R. 2006. *China: Toward a Consumption-Driven Growth Path*. Policy Briefs in International Economics 06-6 (October). Washington: Peterson Institute for International Economics.

Lardy, Nicholas R. 2008. *Financial Repression in China*. Policy Briefs in International Economics 08-8 (September). Washington: Peterson Institute for International Economics.

Lardy, Nicholas R., and Patrick Douglass. 2011. *Capital Account Liberalization and the Role of the RMB*. Working Paper 11-6 (February). Washington: Peterson Institute for International Economics.

Li Deshui. 2005. *Key Achievements of the First National Economic Census with New Changes of China's GDP Aggregates and Its Structure* (December 20). Available at www.stats.gov.cn (accessed on February 3, 2011).

Liu Liping. 2008. The Estimation of Rents of Dwellings in China. *China Economic Review* 19, no. 3: 77–81.

Liu Mingkang. 2010. Chinese Bankers Carry Hopes for Future Balanced Development. Speech to the Asian Financial Forum, Hong Kong, January 20. Available at www.cbrc.gov.cn (accessed on September 15, 2011).

Liu Xiangfeng. 2007. SME Development in China: A Policy Perspective on SME Industrial Clustering. In *SMEs in Asia and Globalization*, ERIA Research Project Report 2007, no. 5. Jakarta: Economic Research Institute for ASEAN and East Asia. Available at www.eria.org (accessed on September 15, 2011).

Ljungwall, Christer, Yi Xiong, and Zou Yutong. 2009. *Central Bank Financial Strength and the Cost of Sterilization in China*. China Economic Research Center Working Paper 8 (May). Stockholm: Stockholm School of Economics. Available at http://swopec.hhs.se (accessed on June 28, 2011).

Luo Changyuan and Zhang Jun. 2009. Distribution of National Income in a Transition Economy. *Social Sciences in China* 30, no. 4: 154–78.

Ma Guonan. 2006. *Who Pays China's Bank Restructuring Bill?* CEPII Working Paper no. 2006-4. Paris: Centre D'etudes Prospective et D'Informations Internationales.

Ma Guonan and Wang Yi. 2010. *China's High Saving Rate: Myth and Reality*. BIS Working Paper 312 (June). Basel, Switzerland: Bank for International Settlements.

Ma Jiantang. 2009. *Tasks of the Second National Economic Census Basically Met with Significant Achievements* (December 25). National Bureau of Statistics of China. Available at www.stats.gov.cn (accessed on September 15, 2011).

McKinsey & Company. 2009. Competing for Asia's Consumers. *McKinsey Quarterly* 4.

McKinsey Global Institute. 2009. *If You've Got It, Spend It: Unleashing the Chinese Consumer* (August). Available at www.mckinsey.com.

McKinsey Global Institute. 2010. *Debt and Deleveraging: The Global Credit Bubble and Its Economic Consequences* (January). Available at www.mckinsey.com/mgi/reports (accessed on January 20, 2010).

Merrouche, Ouarda, and Erlend Nier. 2010. *What Caused the Global Financial Crisis? Evidence on the Drivers of Financial Imbalances 1999–2007*. IMF Working Paper 10/265 (December). Washington: International Monetary Fund. Available at www.imf.org (accessed on January 8, 2011).

Ministry of Civil Affairs. 2008. Statistical Communiqué on Program Development in 2007 (May 26). Available at http://cws.mca.gov.cn (accessed on August 16, 2011).

Ministry of Civil Affairs. 2009. Statistical Communiqué on Program Development in 2008 (February 4). Available at http://cws.mca.gov.cn (accessed on August 15, 2011).

Ministry of Civil Affairs. 2010. Statistical Communiqué on Program Development in 2009 (March 5). Available at http://files.cws.mca.gov.cn (accessed on March 12, 2010).

Ministry of Civil Affairs. 2011. Statistical Communiqué on the Development of Social Services in 2010 (February 9). Available at http://cws.mca.gov.cn (accessed on February 27, 2011).

Ministry of Human Resources and Social Security. 2007. Notice Concerning Publishing an Outline of Publicity Work for the Development of Urban Residents' Basic Health Insurance (July 24). Available at www.mohrss.gov.cn (accessed on September 15, 2011).

Ministry of Finance. 2009. *Report on the Implementation of the Central and Local Budgets for 2008 and on the Draft Central and Local Budgets for 2009* (March 5). Available at www.npc.gov.cn (accessed on September 15, 2011).

Ministry of Finance. 2010. *Report on the Implementation of the Central and Local Budgets for 2009 and the Draft Central and Local Budgets for 2010*. (March 5). Available at npc.gov.cn (accessed on March 19, 2010).

Ministry of Finance. 2011. *Report on the Implementation of the Central and Local Budgets for 2010 and on the Draft Central and Local Budgets for 2011* (March 5). Available at www.npc.gov.cn (accessed on March 18, 2011).

Mussa, Michael. 2011. Global Growth Prospects as of April 4, 2011: Continued Growth Despite the Turmoil. Paper presented at the 19th semiannual meeting on Global Growth Prospects, April 4, Peterson Institute for International Economics, Washington. Available at piie.com (accessed on June 14, 2011).

Nabar, M. Forthcoming. *Financial Development and Household Saving in China*. IMF Working Paper. Washington: International Monetary Fund.

National Audit Office of the People's Republic of China. 2011. *Report Concerning the Audit Work on Implementation of the 2010 Central Government Budget and Other Fiscal Revenues and Expenditures* (June 27). Available at www.audit.gov.cn (accessed on July 19, 2011).

National Bureau of Statistics of China. 1987. *China Statistical Yearbook 1987*. Beijing: China Statistics Press.

National Bureau of Statistics of China. 1997. *China Statistical Yearbook 1997*. Beijing: China Statistics Press.

National Bureau of Statistics of China. 2000. *China Statistical Yearbook 2000*. Beijing: China Statistics Press.

National Bureau of Statistics of China. 2003. Reform in the System of Calculating and Promulgating China's GDP Statistics (November 26). Available at www.stats.gov.cn (accessed on February 3, 2011).

National Bureau of Statistics of China. 2005. *China Statistical Yearbook 2005*. Beijing: Statistics Press.

National Bureau of Statistics of China. 2006a. *Report on China's Revised Historical Gross Domestic Product Data* (January 9). Available at www.stats.gov.cn (accessed on September 15, 2011).

National Bureau of Statistics of China. 2006b. *China Statistical Yearbook 2006*. Beijing: China Statistics Press.

National Bureau of Statistics of China. 2008a. *China Statistical Yearbook 2008*. Beijing: China Statistics Press.

National Bureau of Statistics of China. 2009a. *China Statistical Abstract 2009*. Beijing: China Statistics Press.

National Bureau of Statistics of China. 2009b. *China Statistical Yearbook 2009*. Beijing: China Statistics Press.

National Bureau of Statistics of China. 2009c. *Report on Revised 2008 GDP Data* (December 25). Available at www.stats.gov.cn (accessed on December 28, 2009).

National Bureau of Statistics of China. 2009d. *Chinese Large-Scale Industrial Enterprise Yearbook 2009*. Beijing: China Statistics Press.

National Bureau of Statistics of China. 2010a. National Economy: Recovery and Posing in the Good Direction in 2009 (January 21). Available at www.stats.gov.cn (accessed on September 15, 201).

National Bureau of Statistics of China. 2010b. *Report on Important Statistics for December and Full-Year 2009* (January 21). Available at www.stats.gov.cn (accessed on September 15, 2011).

National Bureau of Statistics of China. 2010c. *Report on National Economic and Social Development in the People's Republic of China in 2009* (February 25). Available at www.stats.gov.cn (accessed on September 15, 2011).

National Bureau of Statistics of China. 2010d. Announcement Concerning Revised Data on 2009 Gross Domestic Product (GDP) (July 2). Available at www.stats.gov.cn (accessed on September 15, 2011).

National Bureau of Statistics of China. 2010e. *China Statistical Abstract 2010*. Beijing: China Statistics Press.

National Bureau of Statistics of China. 2010f. *China Statistical Yearbook 2010*. Beijing: China Statistics Press.

National Bureau of Statistics of China. 2011a. Communiqué no. 1 (January 11). Available at www.stats.gov.cn (accessed on February 2, 2011).

National Bureau of Statistics of China. 2011b. The Overall Good Situation of China's Economy in 2010 (January 20). Available at www.stats.gov.cn (accessed on January 20, 2011).

National Bureau of Statistics of China. 2011c. *Report on China's National Economic and Social Development in 2010* (February 28). Available at www.stats.gov.cn (accessed on February 28, 2011).

National Bureau of Statistics of China. 2011d. China's Economy Maintained Stable, Comparatively Rapid Growth in the First Half (July 13). Available at www.stats.gov.cn (accessed on July 18, 2011).

National Bureau of Statistics of China. 2011e. An Announcement on Preliminary Verified GDP Data in 2010. (September 9). Available at www.stats.gov.cn (accessed on September 9, 2011).

National Development and Reform Commission. 2011. *Report on the Implementation of the 2010 Plan for National Economic and Social Development and on the 2011 Draft Plan for National Economic and Social Development* (March 5). Available at www.npc.gov.cn (accessed on March 18, 2011).

National Social Security Fund Council. 2011a. *2010 Annual Fund Report*. Available at www.ssf.gov.cn (accessed on June 10, 2011).

National Social Security Fund Council. 2011b. Table of Fiscal Appropriations to Funds of the National Social Security Fund. Available at www.ssf.gov.cn (accessed on June 27, 2011).

Naughton, Barry. 2007. *The Chinese Economy: Transitions and Growth*. Cambridge, MA: Massachusetts Institute of Technology.

Naughton, Barry. 2009. Loans, Firms, and Steel: Is the State Advancing at the Expense of the Private Sector? *China Leadership Monitor* 30: 1–10.

Naughton, Barry. 2010. China's Distinctive System: Can It Be a Model for Others? *Journal of Contemporary China* 19 (June): 437-60.

Naughton, Barry. 2011. Chinese Economic Policy Today: The New State Activism. *Eurasian Geography and Economics* 52, no. 3: 313–29.

Ni Jinlan, Guangxin Wang, and Xianguo Yao. 2011. Impact of Minimum Wages on Employment: Evidence from China. *Chinese Economy* 44, no. 1: 18–38.

Obstfeld, Maurice, and Kenneth Rogoff. 2010. Global Imbalances and the Financial Crisis: Products of Common Causes. In *Asia and the Global Financial Crisis*, ed. Reuven Glick and Mark M. Spiegel. San Francisco: Federal Reserve Bank of San Francisco.

OECD (Organization for Economic Cooperation and Development). 2010. *China*. OECD Economic Surveys (February). Paris.

Park, Albert, Cai Fang, and Du Yang. 2010. Can China Meet Her Employment Challenges? In *Growing Pains: Tensions and Opportunities in China's Transformation*, ed. Jean Oi, Scott Rozelle, and Xuegang Zhou. Stanford, CA: Stanford Asia-Pacific Research Center.

People's Bank of China. 2005a. *Annual Report 2004*. Beijing.

People's Bank of China. 2005b. Public Announcement of the People's Bank of China on Reforming the RMB Exchange Rate Regime (July 21). Beijing. Available at www.chinadaily.com.cn (accessed on September 15, 2011).

People's Bank of China. 2008. Balance in China's Financial Circulation in 2007 (January 11). Available at www.pbc.gov.cn (accessed on September 15, 2011).

People's Bank of China. 2009. The Rational Expansion of Money and Credit: Stable Development of the Financial System (January 13). Available at www.pbc.gov.cn (accessed on September 15, 2011).

People's Bank of China. 2010a. *Data Report on 2009 Financial Statistics* (January 15). Available at www.pbc.gov.cn (accessed on January 15, 2010).

People's Bank of China. 2010b. *Statistical Report on the Direction of Lending by Financial Institutions in 2009* (January 20). Available at www.pbc.gov.cn (accessed on January 26, 2011).

People's Bank of China. 2011a. *Data Report on 2010 Financial Statistics* (January 11). Available at www.pbc.gov.cn (accessed on January 13, 2011).

People's Bank of China. 2011b. *Statistical Report on the Direction of Lending by Financial Institutions in 2010* (January 26). Available at www.pbc.gov.cn (accessed on January 26, 2011).

People's Bank of China Business Management Office. 2010. A Summary of a Survey Investigation of the Demand to Purchase Housing by Urban Residents in Beijing Municipality in the Fourth Quarter of 2010 (December 30). Available at www.beijing.gov.cn (accessed on April 11, 2011).

People's Bank of China Monetary Policy Analysis Small Group. 2009a. *Report on the Implementation of Monetary Policy, Fourth Quarter 2008* (February 23). Available at www.pbc.gov.cn (accessed on September 15, 2011).

People's Bank of China Monetary Policy Analysis Small Group. 2009b. *Report on the Implementation of Monetary Policy, Third Quarter 2009* (November 11). Available at www.pbc.gov.cn (accessed on September 15, 2011).

People's Bank of China Monetary Policy Analysis Small Group. 2010a. *Report on the Implementation of Monetary Policy, Fourth Quarter 2009* (February 11). Available at www.pbc.gov.cn (accessed on September 15, 2011).

People's Bank of China Monetary Policy Analysis Small Group. 2010b. *Report on the Implementation of Monetary Policy, Second Quarter 2010* (August 5). Available at www.pbc.gov.cn (accessed on September 15, 2011).

People's Bank of China Monetary Policy Analysis Small Group. 2010c. *Report on the Implementation of Monetary Policy, Third Quarter 2010* (November 2). Available at www.pbc.gov.cn (accessed on November 2, 2010).

People's Bank of China Monetary Policy Analysis Small Group. 2011a. *Report on Implementation of Monetary Policy, Fourth Quarter 2010* (January 30). Available at www.pbc.gov.cn (accessed on January 30, 2011).

People's Bank of China Monetary Policy Analysis Small Group. 2011b. *Report on Implementation of Monetary Policy, First Quarter 2011* (May 3). Available at www.pbc.gov.cn (accessed on May 3, 2011).

People's Bank of China Monetary Policy Analysis Small Group. 2011c. *Report on Implementation of Monetary Policy, Second Quarter 2011* (August 10). Available at www.pbc.gov.cn (accessed on August 12, 2011).

People's Bank of China Statistical Investigation Office. 2010. An Analysis of Macroeconomic Trends in the Fourth Quarter of 2009 (January 29). Available at www.pbc.gov.cn (accessed on September 15, 2011).

People's Bank of China and China Banking Regulatory Commission. 2007. Notice Strengthening the Management of Commercial Mortgage Credit (September 27). Available at www.gov.cn/gzdt (accessed on October 21, 2008).

Pettis, Michael. 2009. *Sharing the Pain: The Global Struggle Over Savings.* Carnegie Policy Brief 84 (November). Washington: Carnegie Endowment for International Peace.

Pettis, Michael. 2010. China Has Been Misread by Bulls and Bears Alike. *Financial Times,* February 26, 11.

Pettis, Michael. 2011. *The Contentious Debate over China's Economic Transition.* Policy Outlook (March 25). Washington: Carnegie Endowment for International Peace.

Porter, Nathan, and TengTeng Xu. 2009. *What Drives China's Interbank Market?* IMF Working Paper 09/189. Washington: International Monetary Fund.

Pradhan, Jaya Prakash, Keshab Das, and Mahua Paul. 2011. Export-Orientation of Foreign Manufacturing Affiliates in India: Factors, Tendencies and Implications. *Eurasian Journal of Business and Economics* 4, no. 7: 99–127.

Reinhart, Carmen M., and Kenneth S. Rogoff. 2009. *This Time Is Different: Eight Centuries of Financial Folly.* Princeton, NJ: Princeton University Press.

Shen, Ce, and John B. Williamson. 2010. China's New Rural Pension Scheme: Can It Be Improved? *International Journal of Sociology and Social Policy* 30, nos. 5–6: 239–50.

Stanway, David. 2009. Fuel Prices: New, Improved—and Higher. *China Economic Quarterly* (March): 10–12.

State Administration of Foreign Exchange. 2011. Table of China's 2010 International Investment Position (May 30). Available at www.safe.gov.cn (accessed on May 31, 2011).

State Administration of Foreign Exchange International Balance of Payments Analysis Small Group. 2008. *Report on China's 2007 International Balance of Payments* (June 5). Available at www.safe.gov.cn (accessed on September 15, 2011).

State Administration of Foreign Exchange International Balance of Payments Analysis Small Group. 2011. *Report on China's 2010 International Balance of Payments* (April 1). Available at www.safe.gov.cn (accessed on April 1, 2011).

State Council. 1997. Notice on the Establishment of the National Urban Resident Minimum Living Standard Guarantee System (November). Available at www.mca.gov.cn (accessed on September 20, 2011).

State Council. 1999. Urban Resident Minimum Living Standard Guarantee Rules (September 28). Available at www.zhengwu.beijing.gov.cn (accessed on September 20, 2011).

State Council. 2001. Notice on Further Strengthening Urban Resident Minimum Living Standards (November 12). Available at www.gov.cn (accessed on September 20, 2011).

State Council. 2007. Notice on the Establishment of the Rural Resident Minimum Living Standard Guarantee System in the Whole Country (October 14) Available at www.gov.cn (accessed on September 20, 2011).

State Council. 2010. Decision Concerning the Acceleration of the Growth and Development of Strategic and Newly Emerging Industries (October 18.) Available at www.gov.cn (accessed on August 10, 2011).

State Council Leading Small Group Office on the First National Economic Census and the National Bureau of Statistics of China. 2005. *Report on the Important Data of the First National Economic Census* (released in three parts on December 6, December 14, and December 16). Available at www.stats.gov.cn (accessed on September 15, 2011).

State Council Leading Small Group Office on the Second National Economic Census and the National Bureau of Statistics of China. 2009. *Report on the Important Data from the Second National Economic Census* (December 25). Available at www.stats.gov.cn (accessed on September 15, 2011).

State Grid Corporation of China. 2009. *2008 Corporate Social Responsibility Report of State Grid Corporation of China.* Beijing.

State Grid Corporation of China. 2010. *2009 Corporate Social Responsibility Report of State Grid Corporation of China.* Beijing.

Taylor, John B. 2009. *Getting Off Track: How Government Actions and Interventions Caused, Prolonged, and Worsened the Financial Crisis.* Stanford, CA: Hoover Institution Press.

Ulrich, Jing. 2011. *China's Balanced Growth Strategy.* JP Morgan Hands-On China Series (June 13).

Walter, Carl, and Fraser J. T. Howie. 2011. *Red Capitalism: The Fragile Financial Foundation of China's Extraordinary Rise.* Singapore: John Wiley and Sons (Asia) Pte. Ltd.

Wang Tao. 2011a. *Measuring Property Bubble in China*. UBS Investment Research, Macro Keys (March 22).

Wang Tao. 2011b. *Bubble or No Bubble? The Great Chinese Property Debate*. UBS Investment Research, China Focus (March 25).

Wen Jiabao. 2007. The Conditions for China to be able to Continue to Guarantee Stable and Rapid Economic Development (March 16). Available at www.gov.cn (accessed on September 13, 2011).

Wen Jiabao. 2009. *Report on Work of the Government* (March 5). Available at www.npc.gov.cn (accessed on September 15, 2011).

Wen Jiabao. 2010. *Report on Work of the Government* (March 5). Available at www.npc.gov.cn (accessed on September 15, 2011).

Wen Jiabao. 2011. *Report on Work of the Government* (March 5). Available at www.npc.gov.cn (accessed on March 18, 2011).

Wolfe, Adam, and Jorund Aarsnes. 2011. *China's Banking Sector: The Big Payback* (March 23). Roubini Global Economics. Available at www.roubini.com (accessed on March 31, 2011).

World Bank. 2005. *SOE Dividends: How Much and to Whom?* Policy Note (October 17). Washington: World Bank.

World Bank. 2007. *Water Supply Pricing in China: Economic Efficiency, Environment, and Social Affordability*. Policy Note (December). Washington: World Bank.

World Bank. 2008. *Mid-Term Evaluation of China's 11th Five-Year Plan*. Washington.

World Bank. 2009. *Effective Discipline with Adequate Autonomy: The Direction for Further Reform of China's SOE Dividend Policy*. Policy Note (November 27). Washington: World Bank. Available at www.worldbank.org (accessed on May 3, 2011).

Wright, Tim. 2007. State Capacity in Contemporary China: Closing the Pits and Reducing Coal Production. *Journal of Contemporary China* 16, no. 51 (May): 173–94.

WTO (World Trade Organization). 2011. *World Trade in 2010*. Geneva. Available at www.wto.org (accessed on August 4, 2011).

Xu Lin. 2010. Taming "Local Government Inc." *China Reform,* no. 316 (January 15). Available at http://englishcaing.com.cn (accessed on September 1, 2011).

Xu Xianchun. 2002. Study on Some Problems in Estimating China's Gross Domestic Product. *Review of Income and Wealth* 48, no. 2: 205–15.

Zhang, Janet. 2011. The Export Juggernaut Rolls On … and On. *China Economic Quarterly* 15, no. 1: 6-7.

Index

property sector
  monetary tightening measures, 6–7
  mortgages (*See* mortgage loans)
  price inflation, 17–18
  residential (*See* housing sector)
  role of state-owned companies in,
      145–46
  sales tax on transactions, 7, 10
property tax, 18, 32, 90, 92

qualified domestic institutional investor
      (QDII) program, 90

rail development, 28–32
real estate. *See* housing sector; property
      sector
rebalancing, 67–128
  commitment to, 152–53
  endogenous, 115–23
  exchange rate policy, 94–106
  expenditure approach to, 112–13
  financial reform, 78–94
  fiscal policy, 68–78, 127
  global, 129–36
  implications for US, 153–54
  interest rate liberalization and, 113–15,
      127, 137–38
  international implications of, 3
  "policy light" approach, 122–28
  politics of, 137–43
  price reform, 106–15, 127, 137–38
renminbi
  capital account convertibility, 152
  exchange rate (*See* exchange rate)
rental yields, 91
required reserve ratio
  current account surplus and, 143
  raising of, 6, 14–15, 82–83, 98
  reduction of, 9
resource allocation
  exchange rate and, 57
  rebalancing policy and, 143
  stimulus program and, 33–34
retirement programs
  government expenditures on,
      76–78, 77t
  individual contributions to, 70–71
  insurance schemes, 64–65, 74–75
  rebalancing policy and, 113
  stimulus program and, 23
risk pricing, 84
Rizhao Steel Company, 36
rural areas, social safety net in, 73–75
rural-to-urban migration, 31, 120

sales tax, on property transactions, 7, 10
savings
  household, 80–82, 81*f*, 85–86, 91, 113
  national rate, 45, 62, 134–35
savings-investment imbalance, 44, 61–65,
      115, 140
self-employed individuals
  borrowing by, 35*f*, 35–36, 124–25, 125*f*
  defined, 34*n*
  income of, 58, 117, 162–63
services
  exports of (*See* exports)
  labor force employed in, 140–41
  output growth, 128
  share in GDP, 52–55, 53*f*, 61, 155–57
Shandong Steel, 36
Shanghai Stock Exchange, 90, 92
shidu kuansong (appropriately loose) monetary
      policy, 15
Sinopec, 109
small and medium-sized firms
      (SMEs), 34*n*
social safety net
  government expenditures on, 68, 69,
      73–74, 73*t*
  individual contributions to, 70–71
  rebalancing policy and, 112–14, 127
  surplus funds, 64
special interest groups, 140, 146, 148–51
State Administration of Foreign Exchange
      (SAFE), 100, 142, 146
State Capital Management Budget, 72, 150
State Council, 145, 150–51
  stimulus program, 5
State Grid Corporation, 30, 110, 111
State-Owned Assets Supervision and
      Administration Commission (SASAC),
      71–73, 150–51
state-owned companies
  asset growth, 39
  defined, 34*n*
  dividend policy, 71–73, 127, 150–51
  employment in, 113
  exports, 39
  performance of, 37–39, 38*f*
  private firm takeovers by, 36–37
  restructuring of, 113
  role in property sector, 145–46
  stimulus program and, 12–13, 33–41
State Price Commission, 106
statistical issues, 155–63
steel industry, 21–22, 36–37, 93
sterilization actions, 97–98, 142–43
stimulus program, 1–2, 5–6, 10–11

Other Publications from the Peterson Institute for International Economics

WORKING PAPERS

* = out of print

Free Trade Areas and U.S. Trade Policy*
Jeffrey J. Schott, ed.
May 1989   ISBN 0-88132-094-3
Dollar Politics: Exchange Rate Policymaking
in the United States*   I. M. Destler and
C. Randall Henning
September 1989   ISBN 0-88132-079-X
Latin American Adjustment: How Much Has
Happened?*   John Williamson, ed.
April 1990   ISBN 0-88132-125-7
The Future of World Trade in Textiles and
Apparel*   William R. Cline
1987, 2d ed. June 1999   ISBN 0-88132-110-9
Completing the Uruguay Round: A Results-
Oriented Approach to the GATT Trade
Negotiations*   Jeffrey J. Schott, ed.
September 1990   ISBN 0-88132-130-3
Economic Sanctions Reconsidered (2 volumes)
Economic Sanctions Reconsidered:
Supplemental Case Histories
Gary Clyde Hufbauer, Jeffrey J. Schott, and
Kimberly Ann Elliott
1985, 2d ed. Dec. 1990   ISBN cloth 0-88132-115-X
                            ISBN paper 0-88132-105-2
Economic Sanctions Reconsidered: History
and Current Policy   Gary Clyde Hufbauer,
Jeffrey J. Schott, and Kimberly Ann Elliott
December 1990   ISBN cloth 0-88132-140-0
                            ISBN paper 0-88132-136-2
Pacific Basin Developing Countries: Prospects
for the Future*   Marcus Noland
January 1991   ISBN cloth 0-88132-141-9
                            ISBN paper 0-88132-081-1
Currency Convertibility in Eastern Europe*
John Williamson, ed.
October 1991   ISBN 0-88132-128-1
International Adjustment and Financing: The
Lessons of 1985-1991*   C. Fred Bergsten, ed.
January 1992   ISBN 0-88132-112-5
North American Free Trade: Issues and
Recommendations*   Gary Clyde Hufbauer and
Jeffrey J. Schott
April 1992   ISBN 0-88132-120-6
Narrowing the U.S. Current Account Deficit*
Alan J. Lenz
June 1992   ISBN 0-88132-103-6
The Economics of Global Warming
William R. Cline
June 1992   ISBN 0-88132-132-X
US Taxation of International Income:
Blueprint for Reform   Gary Clyde Hufbauer,
assisted by Joanna M. van Rooij
October 1992   ISBN 0-88132-134-6
Who's Bashing Whom? Trade Conflict in High-
Technology Industries   Laura D'Andrea Tyson
November 1992   ISBN 0-88132-106-0
Korea in the World Economy*   Il SaKong
January 1993   ISBN 0-88132-183-4
Pacific Dynamism and the International
Economic System*   C. Fred Bergsten and
Marcus Noland, eds.
May 1993   ISBN 0-88132-196-6

Economic Consequences of Soviet
Disintegration*   John Williamson, ed.
May 1993   ISBN 0-88132-190-7
Reconcilable Differences? United States-Japan
Economic Conflict*   C. Fred Bergsten and
Marcus Noland
June 1993   ISBN 0-88132-129-X
Does Foreign Exchange Intervention Work?
Kathryn M. Dominguez and Jeffrey A. Frankel
September 1993   ISBN 0-88132-104-4
Sizing Up U.S. Export Disincentives*
J. David Richardson
September 1993   ISBN 0-88132-107-9
NAFTA: An Assessment
Gary Clyde Hufbauer and Jeffrey J. Schott, *rev. ed.*
October 1993   ISBN 0-88132-199-0
Adjusting to Volatile Energy Prices
Philip K. Verleger, Jr.
November 1993   ISBN 0-88132-069-2
The Political Economy of Policy Reform
John Williamson, ed.
January 1994   ISBN 0-88132-195-8
Measuring the Costs of Protection in the
United States   Gary Clyde Hufbauer and
Kimberly Ann Elliott
January 1994   ISBN 0-88132-108-7
The Dynamics of Korean Economic
Development*   Cho Soon
March 1994   ISBN 0-88132-162-1
Reviving the European Union*
C. Randall Henning, Eduard Hochreiter, and
Gary Clyde Hufbauer, eds.
April 1994   ISBN 0-88132-208-3
China in the World Economy
Nicholas R. Lardy
April 1994   ISBN 0-88132-200-8
Greening the GATT: Trade, Environment,
and the Future   Daniel C. Esty
July 1994   ISBN 0-88132-205-9
Western Hemisphere Economic Integration*
Gary Clyde Hufbauer and Jeffrey J. Schott
July 1994   ISBN 0-88132-159-1
Currencies and Politics in the United States,
Germany, and Japan   C. Randall Henning
September 1994   ISBN 0-88132-127-3
Estimating Equilibrium Exchange Rates
John Williamson, ed.
September 1994   ISBN 0-88132-076-5
Managing the World Economy: Fifty Years
after Bretton Woods   Peter B. Kenen, ed.
September 1994   ISBN 0-88132-212-1
Reciprocity and Retaliation in U.S. Trade
Policy   Thomas O. Bayard and
Kimberly Ann Elliott
September 1994   ISBN 0-88132-084-6
The Uruguay Round: An Assessment*
Jeffrey J. Schott, assisted by Johanna Buurman
November 1994   ISBN 0-88132-206-7
Measuring the Costs of Protection in Japan*
Yoko Sazanami, Shujiro Urata, and Hiroki Kawai
January 1995   ISBN 0-88132-211-3

Foreign Direct Investment in the United States,
3d ed. Edward M. Graham and
Paul R. Krugman
January 1995 ISBN 0-88132-204-0
The Political Economy of Korea-United States
Cooperation* C. Fred Bergsten and
Il SaKong, eds.
February 1995 ISBN 0-88132-213-X
International Debt Reexamined*
William R. Cline
February 1995 ISBN 0-88132-083-8
American Trade Politics, 3d ed. I. M. Destler
April 1995 ISBN 0-88132-215-6
Managing Official Export Credits: The Quest
for a Global Regime* John E. Ray
July 1995 ISBN 0-88132-207-5
Asia Pacific Fusion: Japan's Role in APEC*
Yoichi Funabashi
October 1995 ISBN 0-88132-224-5
Korea-United States Cooperation in the New
World Order* C. Fred Bergsten and
Il SaKong, eds.
February 1996 ISBN 0-88132-226-1
Why Exports Really Matter!*
ISBN 0-88132-221-0
Why Exports Matter More!* ISBN 0-88132-229-6
J. David Richardson and Karin Rindal
July 1995; February 1996
Global Corporations and National
Governments Edward M. Graham
May 1996 ISBN 0-88132-111-7
Global Economic Leadership and the Group of
Seven C. Fred Bergsten and
C. Randall Henning
May 1996 ISBN 0-88132-218-0
The Trading System after the Uruguay Round*
John Whalley and Colleen Hamilton
July 1996 ISBN 0-88132-131-1
Private Capital Flows to Emerging Markets
after the Mexican Crisis* Guillermo A. Calvo,
Morris Goldstein, and Eduard Hochreiter
September 1996 ISBN 0-88132-232-6
The Crawling Band as an Exchange Rate
Regime: Lessons from Chile, Colombia, and
Israel John Williamson
September 1996 ISBN 0-88132-231-8
Flying High: Liberalizing Civil Aviation in the
Asia Pacific* Gary Clyde Hufbauer and
Christopher Findlay
November 1996 ISBN 0-88132-227-X
Measuring the Costs of Visible Protection
in Korea* Namdoo Kim
November 1996 ISBN 0-88132-236-9
The World Trading System: Challenges Ahead
Jeffrey J. Schott
December 1996 ISBN 0-88132-235-0
Has Globalization Gone Too Far? Dani Rodrik
March 1997 ISBN paper 0-88132-241-5
Korea-United States Economic Relationship*
C. Fred Bergsten and Il SaKong, eds.
March 1997 ISBN 0-88132-240-7
Summitry in the Americas: A Progress Report
Richard E. Feinberg
April 1997 ISBN 0-88132-242-3

Corruption and the Global Economy
Kimberly Ann Elliott
June 1997 ISBN 0-88132-233-4
Regional Trading Blocs in the World Economic
System Jeffrey A. Frankel
October 1997 ISBN 0-88132-202-4
Sustaining the Asia Pacific Miracle:
Environmental Protection and Economic
Integration Andre Dua and Daniel C. Esty
October 1997 ISBN 0-88132-250-4
Trade and Income Distribution
William R. Cline
November 1997 ISBN 0-88132-216-4
Global Competition Policy
Edward M. Graham and J. David Richardson
December 1997 ISBN 0-88132-166-4
Unfinished Business: Telecommunications
after the Uruguay Round
Gary Clyde Hufbauer and Erika Wada
December 1997 ISBN 0-88132-257-1
Financial Services Liberalization in the WTO
Wendy Dobson and Pierre Jacquet
June 1998 ISBN 0-88132-254-7
Restoring Japan's Economic Growth
Adam S. Posen
September 1998 ISBN 0-88132-262-8
Measuring the Costs of Protection in China
Zhang Shuguang, Zhang Yansheng, and Wan
Zhongxin
November 1998 ISBN 0-88132-247-4
Foreign Direct Investment and Development:
The New Policy Agenda for Developing
Countries and Economies in Transition
Theodore H. Moran
December 1998 ISBN 0-88132-258-X
Behind the Open Door: Foreign Enterprises
in the Chinese Marketplace Daniel H. Rosen
January 1999 ISBN 0-88132-263-6
Toward A New International Financial
Architecture: A Practical Post-Asia Agenda
Barry Eichengreen
February 1999 ISBN 0-88132-270-9
Is the U.S. Trade Deficit Sustainable?
Catherine L. Mann
September 1999 ISBN 0-88132-265-2
Safeguarding Prosperity in a Global Financial
System: The Future International Financial
Architecture, Independent Task Force Report
Sponsored by the Council on Foreign Relations
Morris Goldstein, Project Director
October 1999 ISBN 0-88132-287-3
Avoiding the Apocalypse: The Future of the
Two Koreas Marcus Noland
June 2000 ISBN 0-88132-278-4
Assessing Financial Vulnerability: An Early
Warning System for Emerging Markets
Morris Goldstein, Graciela Kaminsky, and
Carmen Reinhart
June 2000 ISBN 0-88132-237-7
Global Electronic Commerce: A Policy Primer
Catherine L. Mann, Sue E. Eckert, and Sarah
Cleeland Knight
July 2000 ISBN 0-88132-274-1

The WTO after Seattle   Jeffrey J. Schott, ed.
July 2000   ISBN 0-88132-290-3
Intellectual Property Rights in the Global
Economy   Keith E. Maskus
August 2000   ISBN 0-88132-282-2
The Political Economy of the Asian Financial
Crisis   Stephan Haggard
August 2000   ISBN 0-88132-283-0
Transforming Foreign Aid: United States
Assistance in the 21st Century   Carol Lancaster
August 2000   ISBN 0-88132-291-1
Fighting the Wrong Enemy: Antiglobal
Activists and Multinational Enterprises
Edward M. Graham
September 2000   ISBN 0-88132-272-5
Globalization and the Perceptions of American
Workers   Kenneth Scheve and
Matthew J. Slaughter
March 2001   ISBN 0-88132-295-4
World Capital Markets: Challenge to the G-10
Wendy Dobson and Gary Clyde Hufbauer,
assisted by Hyun Koo Cho
May 2001   ISBN 0-88132-301-2
Prospects for Free Trade in the Americas
Jeffrey J. Schott
August 2001   ISBN 0-88132-275-X
Toward a North American Community:
Lessons from the Old World for the New
Robert A. Pastor
August 2001   ISBN 0-88132-328-4
Measuring the Costs of Protection in Europe:
European Commercial Policy in the 2000s
Patrick A. Messerlin
September 2001   ISBN 0-88132-273-3
Job Loss from Imports: Measuring the Costs
Lori G. Kletzer
September 2001   ISBN 0-88132-296-2
No More Bashing: Building a New Japan–
United States Economic Relationship
C. Fred Bergsten, Takatoshi Ito, and Marcus
Noland
October 2001   ISBN 0-88132-286-5
Why Global Commitment Really Matters!
Howard Lewis III and J. David Richardson
October 2001   ISBN 0-88132-298-9
Leadership Selection in the Major Multilaterals
Miles Kahler
November 2001   ISBN 0-88132-335-7
The International Financial Architecture:
What's New? What's Missing?   Peter B. Kenen
November 2001   ISBN 0-88132-297-0
Delivering on Debt Relief: From IMF Gold to a
New Aid Architecture   John Williamson and
Nancy Birdsall, with Brian Deese
April 2002   ISBN 0-88132-331-4
Imagine There's No Country: Poverty,
Inequality, and Growth in the Era of
Globalization   Surjit S. Bhalla
September 2002   ISBN 0-88132-348-9
Reforming Korea's Industrial Conglomerates
Edward M. Graham
January 2003   ISBN 0-88132-337-3

Industrial Policy in an Era of Globalization:
Lessons from Asia   Marcus Noland and
Howard Pack
March 2003   ISBN 0-88132-350-0
Reintegrating India with the World Economy
T. N. Srinivasan and Suresh D. Tendulkar
March 2003   ISBN 0-88132-280-6
After the Washington Consensus: Restarting
Growth and Reform in Latin America
Pedro-Pablo Kuczynski and John Williamson, eds.
March 2003   ISBN 0-88132-347-0
The Decline of US Labor Unions and the Role
of Trade   Robert E. Baldwin
June 2003   ISBN 0-88132-341-1
Can Labor Standards Improve under
Globalization?   Kimberly Ann Elliott and
Richard B. Freeman
June 2003   ISBN 0-88132-332-2
Crimes and Punishments? Retaliation under
the WTO   Robert Z. Lawrence
October 2003   ISBN 0-88132-359-4
Inflation Targeting in the World Economy
Edwin M. Truman
October 2003   ISBN 0-88132-345-4
Foreign Direct Investment and Tax
Competition   John H. Mutti
November 2003   ISBN 0-88132-352-7
Has Globalization Gone Far Enough? The
Costs of Fragmented Markets
Scott C. Bradford and Robert Z. Lawrence
February 2004   ISBN 0-88132-349-7
Food Regulation and Trade: Toward a Safe and
Open Global System   Tim Josling,
Donna Roberts, and David Orden
March 2004   ISBN 0-88132-346-2
Controlling Currency Mismatches in Emerging
Markets   Morris Goldstein and Philip Turner
April 2004   ISBN 0-88132-360-8
Free Trade Agreements: US Strategies and
Priorities   Jeffrey J. Schott, ed.
April 2004   ISBN 0-88132-361-6
Trade Policy and Global Poverty
William R. Cline
June 2004   ISBN 0-88132-365-9
Bailouts or Bail-ins? Responding to Financial
Crises in Emerging Economies
Nouriel Roubini and Brad Setser
August 2004   ISBN 0-88132-371-3
Transforming the European Economy
Martin Neil Baily and Jacob Funk Kirkegaard
September 2004   ISBN 0-88132-343-8
Chasing Dirty Money: The Fight Against
Money Laundering   Peter Reuter and
Edwin M. Truman
November 2004   ISBN 0-88132-370-5
The United States and the World Economy:
Foreign Economic Policy for the Next Decade
C. Fred Bergsten
January 2005   ISBN 0-88132-380-2
Does Foreign Direct Investment Promote
Development?   Theodore H. Moran,
Edward M. Graham, and Magnus Blomström,
eds.
April 2005   ISBN 0-88132-381-0

DISTRIBUTORS OUTSIDE THE UNITED STATES

**Australia, New Zealand,
and Papua New Guinea**
D. A. Information Services
648 Whitehorse Road
Mitcham, Victoria 3132, Australia
Tel: 61-3-9210-7777
Fax: 61-3-9210-7788
Email: service@dadirect.com.au
www.dadirect.com.au

India, Bangladesh, Nepal, and Sri Lanka
Viva Books Private Limited
Mr. Vinod Vasishtha
4737/23 Ansari Road
Daryaganj, New Delhi 110002
India
Tel: 91-11-4224-2200
Fax: 91-11-4224-2240
Email: viva@vivagroupindia.net
www.vivagroupindia.com

**Mexico, Central America, South America,
and Puerto Rico**
US PubRep, Inc.
311 Dean Drive
Rockville, MD 20851
Tel: 301-838-9276
Fax: 301-838-9278
Email: c.falk@ieee.org

Asia (*Brunei, Burma, Cambodia, China,
Hong Kong, Indonesia, Korea, Laos, Malaysia,
Philippines, Singapore, Taiwan, Thailand,
and Vietnam*)
East-West Export Books (EWEB)
University of Hawaii Press
2840 Kolowalu Street
Honolulu, Hawaii 96822-1888
Tel: 808-956-8830
Fax: 808-988-6052
Email: eweb@hawaii.edu

Canada
Renouf Bookstore
5369 Canotek Road, Unit 1
Ottawa, Ontario KlJ 9J3, Canada
Tel: 613-745-2665
Fax: 613-745-7660
www.renoufbooks.com

Japan
United Publishers Services Ltd.
1-32-5, Higashi-shinagawa
Shinagawa-ku, Tokyo 140-0002
Japan
Tel: 81-3-5479-7251
Fax: 81-3-5479-7307
Email: purchasing@ups.co.jp
*For trade accounts only. Individuals will find
Institute books in leading Tokyo bookstores.*

Middle East
MERIC
2 Bahgat Ali Street, El Masry Towers
Tower D, Apt. 24
Zamalek, Cairo
Egypt
Tel. 20-2-7633824
Fax: 20-2-7369355
Email: mahmoud_fouda@mericonline.com
www.mericonline.com

United Kingdom, Europe
(*including Russia and Turkey*)**, Africa,
and Israel**
The Eurospan Group
c/o Turpin Distribution
Pegasus Drive
Stratton Business Park
Biggleswade, Bedfordshire
SG18 8TQ
United Kingdom
Tel: 44 (0) 1767-604972
Fax: 44 (0) 1767-601640
Email: eurospan@turpin-distribution.com
www.eurospangroup.com/bookstore

**Visit our website at:
www.piie.com
E-mail orders to:
petersonmail@presswarehouse.com**